*f*P

Also by Phillip C. McGraw, Ph.D.

Life Strategies

Life Strategies Workbook

Relationship Rescue

Relationship Rescue Workbook

SELF MATTERS

Creating Your Life from the Inside Out

PHILLIP C. MCGRAW, PH.D.

FREE PRESS

New York London Toronto Sydney Singapore

*f*P
FREE PRESS
A Division of Simon & Schuster, Inc.
1230 Avenue of the Americas
New York NY 10020

First Free Press trade paperback edition 2003

FREE PRESS and colophon are trademarks
of Simon & Schuster, Inc.

For information regarding special discounts for bulk purchases,
please contact Simon & Schuster Special Sales:
1-800-456-6798 or business@simonandschuster.com

Designed by Karolina Harris

Manufactured in the United States of America

10 9 8 7 6 5 4 3 2 1

Library of Congess Cataloging-in-Publication Data for the Simon &
Schuster Source edition is available.

ISBN 0-7432-2423-X
ISBN 0-7432-2725-5 (Pbk)

To my wife,
Robin,
without whom I would not be living my best life;
and to my sons Jay and Jordan,
two amazing young men who humble me by being who they are;
and to my mother,
"Grandma Jerry,"
for making me feel special from day one,
and for showing me the true meaning of grace and courage
    under fire.

This book is also dedicated in memoriam to my father,
Joseph,
who never gave up and overcame tremendous odds to finally
    connect with his authentic self at the age of seventy-two.

ACKNOWLEDGMENTS

THE writing of this book has been a wonderfully transformative yet sometimes difficult experience for me personally. It has been an undertaking that I could not have completed without the help and support of a number of important and in some instances "pivotal people" in my life.

Thanks first to Robin, my wife and life partner of almost thirty years. Robin, you have been an inspirational and guiding force in my creating my own life from the inside out. It is your belief in and support of me that gave me the courage to step out and find my way back to my authentic self; back to being who I truly am instead of who others might want me to be. Without your spirit of adventure, I would to this very day be stuck in a life I did not want.

Thanks also to my boys, Jay and Jordan, for believing in and encouraging their dad. Both Jay and Jordan were at my side each day that I worked on this book. No messages of guilt, no long faces about the long hours, just support. That mattered greatly. Thanks boys for keeping me focused on what truly matters. In those times that I have found myself asking, "What's the point to all this scramble of life?" I have only to look at the hope and energy in your eyes and the answer is clear. I pray that as an adult I meet the standard of who you already are as young men.

I especially thank Oprah, my dear friend and a tremendously positive "pivotal person" in my life. It was a specific conversation with Oprah, riding along a desolate Texas road in the dead of winter, that inspired me to commit to one day demystifying the concept of self and creating a real world map for people to use in getting back to authenticity. Oprah, thanks for continuing to "raise the bar" for yourself and for me and for working to make a difference, and thanks for pulling me back into the work I love. Thanks Oprah for being in my balcony and allowing me to be in yours.

Thanks to Jonathan Leach for the writing and organizational skills brought to bear on this book. I have yet to write a single page in this or my other books that Jonathan has not scrubbed, rubbed, massaged, and made exponentially better. You are, in my view, the best there is and you make me a better writer and, in the process, a better person. Thanks Jonathan for the late nights and long weekends. (To Jonathan's wife, Linda, "Sorry, but you can have him back now, at least for a while.")

Thanks to Dr. Frank Lawlis for all of your input on content and writing as well. Frank was my major professor in graduate school, supervised my dissertation, and generally kept me on track. He helped when it would have been easier not to and has been a lifelong friend. We often debate whether he taught me everything I know or just everything he knows! Either way, he is in my opinion the leading authority in psychology today and his insight and analysis in this book was invaluable. As one of the few psychologists to ever hold diplomat status in both clinical and counseling psychology, he brought an expertise to this work that gave me great confidence that my views were on target.

Thanks to Gary Dobbs, my partner, best friend, and godfather to my children, for your continuing support in everything I undertake in this life. You are invariably in my corner personally, professionally, and spiritually. Gary has long been on the shortest of "short lists" of "pivotal people" in my life and makes a huge difference each and every day.

Thanks to Jan Miller and all of her staff at Dupree Miller. Jan is *the* literary agent in the world today and has committed her energy and already unrivaled career to getting my message into the "hands of every person on the globe that can read!" (Jan never shoots low!) You are an amazing and tireless cheerleader whom it is impossible to be around without getting hugely "pumped!" Thanks Jan for being the consummate agent and gilt-edge professional that never gets tired, but, more important, thanks for being a great friend and supporter.

Thanks to Dave Khan, my publicist/PR guy/assistant/friend/ tennis partner/never-say-no/make-it-happen guy. Dave lives and breathes our efforts to impact people's lives. Your gentle spirit and willingness to "take the plunge" so completely, contributed mightily to creating the space, time, and energy essential to completing this project. Thanks Dave for running interference while I wrote like a hermit.

Thanks to Scott Madsen, who wakes up every morning saying "What can I do to help you do what you do?" Again, a friend and supporter that created the space, time, confidence, and energy that enabled me to be focused on this project.

I also thank Carolyn Reidy, president of Simon & Schuster, for passionately committing to the creation of this work.

Last but not least thanks to Dominick Anfuso, my in-house editor at Simon & Schuster Source, for being so intimately involved with this book. Dominick, your input was invaluable and made *Self Matters* a much better book. Thanks Dominick, you are appreciated.

CONTENTS

SELF
MATTERS

*Creating Your Life
from the Inside Out*

"The life which is unexamined is not worth living."
— PLATO

1 WHAT IF . . . ?

> *"Somehow we learn who we really are and then live with that decision."*
>
> —ELEANOR ROOSEVELT

THE sun beat down relentlessly on the young man standing in the barren parking lot. There was not a breath of air, and the black asphalt was sticky and melting as it gave way to the afternoon heat. It radiated up into his face like a blast furnace. He wouldn't be here, using a pay phone, except that he was out of town and this was one call that absolutely had to go through an operator.

Over the years he had placed collect calls back home many times, but this one was entirely different. This time, he instructed the operator to be sure to emphasize that the call was from "doctor," rather than "mister." How strange it sounded to hear her say "doctor" in front of his name when his father answered at the other end. It was "Dr. Son" calling "Dr. Dad," an achievement that had been so very long and hard in coming. Eleven years, to be exact. Three hundred hours of college credit, tens of thousands of pages read and studied, and hundreds and hundreds of all-nighters in preparation for nearly as many tests and exams. There had been miles and miles of long walks from the remote parking lots at the hospital, where students, interns, and residents were "dog meat." More recently, it had been month after month of enduring the inescapable, acrid smell of Thorazine-laced urine on the psychiatric wards of the VA hospital—some might say warehouse—where he had spent long days and longer nights "treating" (storing) the inpatients on those cold and desolate wards.

No less painfully, there had been the days, weeks, and months of dealing with a variety of insecure, "emotionally interesting" professors, many of them white-coated Napoleons who were all too eager to wield the power of their petty fiefdoms. Their torments had culminated in that unforgettable final year, when he had walked the halls at school and put in his time at the hospital, armed with a signed letter of resignation on his clipboard, daring just one more anal-retentive, power-hungry mentor-turned-tormentor to say so much as "boo" to him.

In spite of it all, and as surprised as anyone who knew him, here he stood. He remembered one of his favorite profs telling him he would never make it because he had an "attitude" and refused to "kiss ass." He was told, "You have too many options in your life to put up with this fiasco of dysfunction, you aren't near desperate enough to tolerate the abuse!" Yet here he was. One by one, the department heads had signed off on his final requirements, shaken his hand, and congratulated him on earning the highest degree in his profession. Doctor—wow! He knew how proud his dad was going to be. This phone call would be a huge step closer to a father's dream come true: father and son, both doctors, practicing together, side by side!

Throughout the long ordeal, he had been powerfully influenced by his knowledge of his father's vision and dream. Theirs was a family of meager and simple beginnings. In fact, the young doctor and his father were the only ones from either side of the extended family ever to go to college, let alone earn doctoral degrees. Surely, then, this phone call was to be a proud moment indeed. The long journey was over. Victory was at hand, and parents and family were bursting with pride.

It was all cued up just right. Ready and waiting for him was a thriving practice, all set to explode with the energy and inspiration he would bring. That meant no more scrounging for money for him and his young wife. No more driving cars that were beyond old. No more living in apartments so small you had to go outside to turn around. Most importantly, the young doctor truly did care about helping people, and here was his chance to do just that. So there couldn't be anything wrong with any of this. Right?

Yet standing in that parking lot, mouthing the words of expected excitement—even as he heard his father's voice breaking with unmistakable pride—he looked over at his wife waiting in the car. There sat the only person in the entire world who knew him well enough to know that something was wrong. How could everything be so right, yet feel so wrong? He looked into her eyes. Without speaking a word, he knew that she knew.

But he would play the good soldier. He would shrug off the negative feelings and forge ahead. Soon he would be scrambling so fast that life would crowd out the nagging thoughts, and he would focus instead on meeting the expectations held by so many who loved him. He told himself it was probably just anxiety anyway, nothing a little hard work won't take care of. So with a healthy dose of dutiful self-righteousness, a work-your-butt-off commitment, and a naïveté that can only come from being young and stupid, he prepared to go to work. There were those doubts, and there was that vague uneasiness about the road he had started down. That nagging sense that something just wasn't quite right continued. But hey, he was going to make a lot of people really proud.

At the same time, he made a heartfelt promise to himself: **I don't care how much money I get to making—If I ever find myself doing this just for the money, if I am ever just going through the motions, I am out of here. I will turn on my heels and walk smooth away. I will never sell out and live without passion and fire just because it is secure, expected, or easy! I'm no one-trick pony. If I can succeed at this, I could succeed at a lot of things just as well, no problem.**

Ten years later . . .

Ten years and thousands of patients later, the not-so-young, not-so-stupid, and not-nearly-so-naïve doctor and his wife step off of a client's private jet at a busy airport in the heart of a teeming, fast-paced city. It is a crisp and beautiful Sunday afternoon in October. His practice has exploded to perhaps the largest in the country. He has mastered his profession. Successful? Yes, certainly by any standard he knows of. A secure lifestyle? Without a doubt. Houses and cars? Only the best. Two great children, a wonderful marriage, and proud parents: he has it all.

So why doesn't it feel any more right than it did ten years ago, standing at the pay phone in that hot, deserted parking lot? His self-righteous declaration of ten years ago haunts him more and more. He has often wished he had never said it. There are those dreadful times when "the truth" runs faster than he can. It is particularly bad when he is really tired, or in those rare moments when he has allowed himself to become very still. He has hated those times, because it is then that his private reality mocks him: **If I ever find myself doing this just for the money . . . if I am ever just going through the motions, I am out of here. I will never sell out. I will never live without passion and fire just because it is secure, expected, or easy. . . .**

The promise haunts him, because he knows that money and lifestyle have in fact "bought him," just as he swore they would not. Far from being vitally involved in his own life, he feels trapped by it. There is a part of him that remembers what it was like to have passion, hope, optimism, and energy. It is a part that has refused to succumb to and accept the roles assigned by an insensitive and sometimes hurtful world. It is a part of his concept of self that just wants to get in the game, the game *he* wants to play: a game that means something to him, whether it means anything to anyone else or not. It is a private, usually denied, part of himself that does not want to be controlled by what is expected. It is a part of him that knows what is genuine, yet it is a part that usually lives in silence.

The simple truth is that he is not living a life that he wants, or that he chose. He is living a life that pleases a lot of people, most of them well intended, but not him. He is doing what he does, simply because it is what his father did. He is even living in a place he did not consciously choose. In fact, it is the last place on earth he would have ever chosen. He has a life many would love, but his heart is not in it. It is not natural for him, so he has to do what he does by brute force: Everything is a chore. There is no passion; there is no excitement. He ignores his real dreams, but doing so is hard and getting harder. Being someone and something he is not is the hardest thing he has ever done.

Clearly, this is not some monumental tragedy. I mean, come on: "Poor baby has to work in a cushy office all day!" It is not the kind of cause célèbre that makes the evening news. Could he "get happy"? After all, his marriage and family are great. Could he be satisfied with that and just keep on keeping on? Yes. But it gets harder with every day that passes, days that have turned into weeks, months, and years. He sometimes hears a voice, his own voice, crying for relief, but he does not react. Sometimes it is just easier not to think about it. After all, does *feeling* right, does *having passion* really matter? Is he being just a ridiculous romantic to think that being "true to self" might be something more than just some high-handed philosophy? Shouldn't he be thankful for his many blessings, blessings that everyone else sure seems to hold in high regard?

He rationalizes that he really would make a change, give it all up and pursue something he truly has a passion for—but he has "responsibilities." He has a wife and kids, for God's sake: How could he ask them to give up their friends, schools, and lives, just so he can chase some dream? He wonders if that is really what holds him back, or if he is just afraid. Maybe he really is just a one-trick pony. Maybe he isn't talented at all. Maybe he just got lucky and could never succeed at something different. He doesn't seem to know that confident part of himself as well as he used to. It's there, but the connection grows weak, the image that once was sharp and clear is becoming dim and fuzzy.

At the precise moment when he is wrestling with those very

thoughts, his wife says, "Where were you just now? You have to tell me what you're thinking! Tell me where you go when you are lost in that hundred-yard stare." It's as though she is reading his mind. She says: "More and more each day, I feel like I'm losing a part of you. When it's just the two of us, or when we are alone with our boys, it's like the real you, the way you used to be before all of *this* we call our life. But as soon as the world creeps in, you glaze over. The phone rings, or something else breaks the spell, and you become totally different—like a robotic machine."

For some reason, on this beautiful afternoon, driving across town with the top down and the cool autumn air breezing through the car, he decides once and for all to stop denying himself. He decides to give his feelings a voice and tell the truth: "Bottom line—I'm going jack-ass batty in here. I hate to tell you this, but I think a huge part of my life absolutely sucks! I hate myself for getting in so deep that I feel like I can't get out. I hate my career. I hate where we are living. I hate what I am doing. I've hated it all since before the day I started it. I stood in that parking lot calling my dad on the phone ten years ago, knowing full well I didn't want to move to that godforsaken town and launch into that godforsaken career. I screwed up big time and now I'm stuck, trapped in a life I hate. I sold myself out and gave in to what everyone else wanted for me, not what I wanted. I have zero passion for what I am doing. I'm just going through the motions, and it is getting harder and harder every day. I should be excited about my life, but I am not, not even close. I'm cheating you and the boys because I'm not being me. I have one shot at this, one shot, and I'm choking, I'm blowing it. I'm now almost forty years old. I've wasted ten years of my life and I can't get them back no matter what I do. To even say that makes me sick to my stomach. I don't want to rock the boat, but I hate this deal, and if it were up to me I would shut this whole deal down, move away, and do something I want to do in a place where I want to do it. I'm sorry, but that's the truth. I feel like a fraud. I'm sorry to dump all of this on you, but you're asking and so I'm telling you. I'm running out of life energy here. I'm tired of being tired. I'm tired of not waking up excited in the morning. I'm tired of not being proud of what I do or who I am. It's no one's fault but my own, I've done it to myself because I didn't have the guts to stand up for myself. How dumb is that?"

I know every detail of this story, including what was said in that car, because I was in that car. The story, the "confession," is my own. I was the young man who stood in that parking lot in 1979, and it was me who drove out of Love Field in Dallas, Texas, with my wife, Robin, in 1989.

For those ten years, I lived a life of incongruency. The content of my life, the choices I had made, was incongruent with who I was and what I wanted. I was doing things I didn't have my heart in and was not doing the things I did have a passion for. On the one hand, I occupied a comfort zone where my life felt "safe," because it was as steady and predictable as the ticking of a clock. The problem was that everything I was doing was chosen to please other people by meeting their expectations while totally ignoring my own. I was miserable. If you had asked me, "Is this the kind of life you want?" "Is this the career you want?" "Are you fulfilling your purpose for being on this earth?" I would have had to answer, "No, not by a long shot." I knew I wasn't living the life I was meant to live. I knew there was something wrong with my life, but for those ten years, I avoided dealing with it because it just seemed easier to go along than to upset everyone. Instead of addressing the dull ache that I carried everywhere, instead of trying to root out what was bothering me, I chose to "keep on keeping on." Incredibly dumb, but it's the truth.

Like an enemy I knew as intimately as any friend, I came to know the nagging, constant emptiness of the incongruent life. I ignored my self and lived for people, purposes, and goals that weren't my own. I betrayed who I was and instead accepted a fictional substitute that was defined from the outside in. I betrayed myself, and mine was a life and an experience that was a fraud and a fiction.

So much of what I did—while totally okay *if* it had been what I had a passion for—was as unnatural for me as it would be for a dog trying to fly. There's nothing wrong with trying to fly, unless you happen to be a beagle instead of an eagle. I loved my family, but every other aspect of my life was, for me, a painful and forced ordeal because it didn't come from the heart. It wasn't something that sprang from who I really was. And in addition to the presence of negatives that came from being and doing that which was foreign to my authentic self, there was the glaring absence of positives. I wasn't having any fun or excitement. I wasn't doing what was meaningful for me. I wasn't doing what I was good at and therefore was not pursuing my mission in life, my purpose for being here. I never finished a day and said, "Wow! Great job today, be proud!" I needed that feeling, a feeling I missed when I looked in the mirror. I needed to feel like I belonged and was called to a purpose, but I didn't, because I wasn't. I was excited about nothing, zip, zero. It was not good.

Ultimately, I was able to totally reengineer those parts of my life that were not "me," and build on those that felt right because they *were* right. Once I stopped living that incongruent life and started to hear my own voice, my own needs, my experience of life changed monumentally. I didn't get those ten years back but they are a fading memory, daily being replaced with a life that is authentically me. (I'm going to tell you a whole lot about how I did it very soon.)

I will never completely forget the pain and emptiness of living the way I did for those ten years and I don't want to. Having spent ten years in that desolate territory, I know it's a place where I will never go again. I would starve or work for food and shelter doing what I love, before I would betray my self again at any price. If you have ever done anything that was really dumb for a long time, and then finally quit and made a change, you know how it feels. You look back and say, "Oh my God, how could I have been so stupid?! I wasted so much time!" I know the feeling because I've even had the revelation after doing trivial things like when I finally got eyeglasses; and when I finally built a fence so that I could quit chasing my dog. So you can imagine how I felt when I changed my entire life after *ten years!* Huge relief, huge! I got out, and if you are in that place, I want to get you out, too. Don't panic: I'm not getting ready to blow up your marriage or family. Living an incongruent life doesn't necessarily involve geography, occupation, time commitments, or even the people with whom you are sharing your life. The "fix" I'm talking about comes from the inside out. What it does always deal with is *how* you do what you do. It always deals with you being true to yourself from the inside out. I still do a lot of what I once did; I just do it very, very differently and the priorities are mine, not someone else's. It is always about being there for you, about being your own best friend.

Question: Is it possible that, just like me, you have a great chance for a tremendously more satisfying and exciting life, but you are selling yourself short and missing out because you don't know it, or, if you do know it, you are just stuck in your life and aren't doing anything about it? Is it possible that you are, in fact, an excitingly unique individual with the need to do and be *all* of who you are, yet you are denying that powerful individuality and remain bogged down and buried in a world of "responsibility traps" and "don't make waves" conformity?

Well, I'll confess that I'm setting you up, because those are "loaded" questions, and I'm betting the answer to both is, in whole or part, a big fat *yes!* If I am right, your self-concept is in trouble and you're cheating not only yourself but your children, your spouse, and everyone else in your life, just like I was. Read on and we'll see if I'm right. If I am right, don't despair because, I promise, I'm about to save you those ten years that I wasted. Together we are about to light your life up like you can't believe.

Warning: This is an extremely direct, plain-talking, tell-you-the-unvarnished-truth, common-sense book about how to take control of your entire life. The control I'm talking about is a control that comes from reconnecting with what I call your *authentic self*. In order to understand what I mean by your authentic self, you need only think back to the times in your life when you have been your best. I'm talking about the absolute happiest time in your life: the most fulfilled and especially the most real you have ever been. Think back to the you at the heart of those moments. In those moments, your life flowed with an energy and an excitement. At the same time, you may have felt a quiet calm within. You may have been at work, but work was play. You probably felt as if you were exactly where you were supposed to be, doing just what you were meant to do, and with exactly the right people. You had an unshakable understanding of your own worth. You trusted yourself. You were having fun, and you didn't care what others thought. There was no room in your life for fear or anxiety or self-doubt. Every part of your life was in harmony with the other parts. You were living fully in the present moment, yet you had a sense of optimism, an expectation that tomorrow was going to be just as interesting and gratifying as today. Life seemed to be filled with vivid colors. Your own life was the most interesting one you knew, and you couldn't wait to see what would happen next. Perhaps most important was the fact that you accepted yourself for who and what you were. The result was a kind of bulletproofing from the judgments of others. Because you felt so good about yourself, because you felt self-determined and in control, you couldn't care less what others thought about you. It was you that mattered, not in a selfish way, but in a confident way. Without judgment you were proud of yourself and walked with a sense of pride and self-assurance. You weren't sure what the future would bring, but you were sure that you could handle it. Self-acceptance was the foundation of the happiest time in your life and it was the engine that powered the train.

Connecting with this authentic self again means finding your way back to the no-kidding, real you that existed before the world started crowding you out. This is a control that comes from the inside out. That means that this is a book about you—no one else, just you. It is a how-to book that is designed to get you excited about and filling your life with what is genuinely important to you, instead of a lot of mindless, inherited, assigned, go-through-the-motions activity.

I'm talking about controlling virtually every aspect of your experience in this world. That means putting your life together in a way that you feel the way you want to feel, do the things you want, and more importantly, *need* to do. It means putting your life together in a way that you can respect yourself for who you are and what you do. It means you can look in the mirror and know that what is important to you is not being buried in favor of a "go along to get along" mentality. It means you are living in a way that those things you always dreamed of are still alive. It means putting your life together in a way that you don't sit around asking yourself: "What's the point? Why am I doing all of this?" "Life is a bitch and then you die" is not my idea of a good philosophy or life strategy. If you want to be totally, consciously in charge of *you* and everything you think, do, and feel, and use that control to create value for you, and therefore for everyone around you, you've come to the right place, but there is work to be done.

You see, I have a theory: I believe that you, me, all of us, have in the past and/or are currently "screwing up" in this game we call life. Too many people in this day and time have gotten so busy "getting by," so busy being busy, that they have let the colors fade from their lives. They have settled too cheap, way too cheap. Think about it: Your life, behind closed doors, can totally suck. It can be a major train wreck, yet you will get up in the morning and instead of working on your mind and your heart for even five minutes, you will obsess around for two hours, focusing totally on your appearance instead of your substance. You do it all throughout your life. You would do well to stop and think about just how much of your life energy is absorbed by the superficial rather than what you know in your heart really matters. A good example is found in our approach to "tying the knot." I see tons of couples getting married every year and I'll bet 90-plus percent of them spent months, or even years, planning their *wedding* and almost no time planning their *marriage!* How crazy is it to spend more time on the caterer and the flowers for a one-hour event and precious little if any time on kids, money, and life plan. (I'm not just saying that because I'm a *man* and don't get how important a wedding is to a woman! I have three sisters, all married. I get it. I'm just saying, plan the marriage, too!) The same is true with your life. Your life is created from the inside out, so you *must* get right with you on the inside—and that takes time and focus on you; not your social mask, but you.

This stuff about self, about who you are on the inside, matters, it really matters. Why? Because a life without color is a life without excitement and passion. It is a gray existence where you put one foot in front of the other and go through the motions without any emotions. You spend all of your energy meeting expectations and doing jobs and chores. You stop really living and instead start existing: You get up, feed the kids, worry about money, go to work, come home, do the laundry, cook dinner, worry about the kids, mow the yard, worry some more about money, watch TV, eat some more, worry some more, go to bed; then you get up and do it all over again, and again, and again, and again, three hundred and sixty-five days a year. Make no mistake about it: When chores, routine existence, and just playing it safe become the only purpose in life, there is no purpose, and one must be found. You *need* to know your "highest and best use" in this world, and then to pursue it. How tragic would it have been if Einstein had spent his life as a merchant or a sailor; if Elvis had remained a truck driver; if Mother Teresa had been an accountant or a waitress? When mindless, unchallenging, routine existence and safety are blindly accepted and become unthinking goals, there can be no authenticity, because you and everyone else has a mission, a purpose in life that cannot be denied if you are to live fully. If you have no purpose, you have no passion. If you have no passion, you have sold your self out. I know that, because I know that within each of us there are passions that, if acknowledged and released, will energize and excite the experience of life.

In a passionless life, superficiality becomes the substitute for the things that ought to matter. False goals like money, approval from others, and the accumulation of "stuff" will come to dominate your life and its energy. You are then trapped in a descending circle of aimless existence. If you are committed to nothing, if you believe in nothing, including yourself, you can be led to and suckered into anything. You are uniquely equipped for a mission in this world, and to fail to recognize and commit to finding that mission and then achieving it is to wither in mind, body, and spirit. You cannot play the game of life trying not to lose, trying to play it safe. You must live to win; however, you may personally define "winning." To do otherwise is to deny who you are.

Now you may be convinced that your life never had any color or passion to begin with. But if it did, can you remember it? Reflect on that, then ask yourself, How much have I let those colors fade? It may have been hard to notice because it happened a little bit at a time; just a bit here and there. Either way, have you gone from a life that was in full living color to one that is nothing more than shades of gray? Ask yourself how long it has been since you were really excited about some meaningful aspect of your life. I'm not talking about getting a new car or a piece of jewelry or a great fishing pole; I'm talking about the passion and excitement of knowing you are fulfilling your purpose and are doing it well. I'm talking about the feeling of confidence that comes from self-trust; the calm assurance that you experience when you know that you have the courage to be who you really are and to be there for yourself when it really counts. It's the kind of courage that will help you stand up for yourself with an abusive mate, when choosing the career *you* want, or in deciding whether or not to have children. Passion, excitement, and confidence are important medicines that you need every day. And they can come in a form as simple as claiming your right to some joy and fun in life now—not as some fleeting memory from your past, but now.

Here's a "gotcha": Are you one of those people who sit around and talk about how "crazy and fun" you *used* to be? Do you reminisce about times gone by, often saying, "Remember when we used to . . . ? "? Do you just accept the fact that the most fun or fulfillment you will ever have is in your past, because now you have responsibilities and bills and kids and whatever else you can think of to rationalize neglecting yourself and what matters to you? Well, let me tell you, if that's how you think, that's just crazy! I went to a college reunion-type deal not long ago and got together with a bunch of my former teammates. Some of them have really gone on to create and live wonderful lives with great wives, families, and careers. Others have been absolutely "stuck" in their memories of the glory days of when we played football. These guys were basking in the fading glow: "Hey Phil, remember the fourth quarter when we blitzed that OU quarterback without a single defensive back left in the secondary? Man, were we crazy gamblers or what?" I respond: "Yeah boy, that was really something, wasn't it." What I'm really thinking is: Hell no, I don't remember that, I've done about nine million things since that one play thirty years ago, and apparently you haven't. And by the way, this glory you're basking in, hotshot, is a bunch of hooey. The truth is we were terrible! In fact, now that I recall the fourth quarter of that game you've been boring your kids with stories about, we were behind about sixty to nothing! God, get over it. You sound like my dad; by the time he got through telling it, he used to walk three miles to school every day through a foot of snow and it was up hill *both* ways!

The only reason you would want to continue focusing on some fantasized past is if the present you have created is not as good. I don't know about you, but I don't want to be twenty again. Some of the times were good but a whole lot of them weren't. Another thing my dad used to say when he would reminisce about being in the navy or playing college ball was: "I wouldn't take a million dollars for the experience and I wouldn't give you a dime to do it again." That's how I feel about an awful lot of where I've been, although there is some of it I would sell you back "for a dime"!

If the best part of your life is in the past, something is way out of whack. Here's how the deal is supposed to work: As we get older, we are supposed to be *more* competent, not less. Life is supposed to get *better*, because we are supposed to be *better at it*. Attempting to rationalize or justify ignoring yourself and what you truly want and need is BS. I want to put you center stage for a while and talk about getting your self-concept to a place where you won't sell out your wants, dreams, needs, and visions.

Now you may be thinking, Dang, you're being hard on me, and you don't even know me. Give me a break here! How can you think you know all of this about me and my life when you haven't even met me?

Well, I don't think you really want me to "give you a break," and I sure hope you don't tune me out because I'm being so direct and telling you things that aren't fun to hear about. Anybody can tell you what you want to hear, and frankly, it would be a lot easier for me to do just that. But then this book would be just like a hundred others, and you didn't pick this book up so I would blow smoke at you. You bought this book because you care about your life and want to do as good a job as you can at taking care of you and everybody who means something to you.

I do think I know a lot about what may be going on in your life. I think so for two reasons. One, I lived it in my own life, and two, because I deal directly with thousands and thousands of people just like you and me every year, and I see it in their lives, their faces, and their eyes! They're too busy, too caught up in roles, too entrenched to consider themselves. You're probably thinking, Oh great! I thought I was doing fine until I bought this damn book—now you're telling me I only thought I was happy. Thanks a lot!

Sorry, but as your parents always said, "You'll thank me for this someday!" The only difference is, this time it's true.

Just hear me out, and if when you finish you conclude that you are in fact happy and doing just fine, then great. At least then you will know it with the confidence of having audited your life, mind, and spirit. But again, I'm betting you're going to be shocked at what you find and ultimately be thankful that you got a wake-up call. And boy, oh boy, do I intend to give you a wake-up call, because I *don't* want you to sleep through your life like I did for ten years.

YOU AND THE WORLD

I think a lot of this losing ourselves has happened because our world has sped up to the point of being absolutely, out-of-control insane. It has sped up to the point of so overstimulating us with input from the outside that we can't or don't even hear any voices or messages coming from the inside. We have lost ourselves in the rush of the world.

Five hundred TV channels, the Internet, rental videos, two or three jobs all are conspiring to steal ourselves from us. Kids without a minute of unprogrammed time are racing from school to dance, soccer, drama, debate, one activity after another. We are on a merry-go-round spinning too fast for us to hold onto, and too fast for us to jump off of. In response, we "hunker down" and just try to get through it. If somehow you happened to have some quiet, unstructured, undemanded-upon time, you don't use it to focus on or deal with you. Instead, you get nervous; you panic and start looking for something to do or someone to tell you what to do. You're so busy doing stuff you didn't choose and probably wouldn't choose that you don't even think about what you do want, need, and care about anymore.

Here's some quick, "litmus test" logic for determining whether you are passively accepting or even choosing behaviors that ignore who you really are, or have been choosing behaviors and life circumstances that naturally flow from your true, authentic self.

If you are constantly tired, stressed, emotionally flat, or even depressed, worried, and unhappy, you are ignoring the authentic you and living a "go-through-the-motions" existence. If your life includes things you profess to hate, yet you continue to do them anyway, that, too, indicates self-betrayal. For example, are you always complaining about being overweight, yet you continue to be? Do you fail to exercise, go back to school, change jobs, confront your dead marriage, get a date, get a hobby, or deal with the pain of abuse or neglect that has scarred you from childhood? If so, you can't possibly be living in concert with who you were originally designed to be. If your life is dominated by constant anxiety and worry, but you don't do a damn thing to change it, that, too, is a bad sign. (My dad used to say that "worrying is like rocking in a chair: it's something to do, but you don't get anywhere.")

If your mind has gotten dull and you just aren't as sharp as you used to be, you aren't getting old or dumb; it's just that your authentic self is getting buried. It's fighting for air. If your emotions are marked by cynicism, apathy, hopelessness, and a lack of optimism, it is because you have abandoned yourself and what matters to you. If you are choosing what you do, what you think about, and put at the top of your priority list based on what you think others expect instead of what matters to you, then you have the "fictional infection." Your authentic self has been infected with a lot of nongenuine living that has ignored who you are and has created a fictional self instead.

Ignoring who you truly, authentically are can literally be killing you. Yes, I said "literally." If you are ignoring who you really are, your entire "system" is so distressed that it will wear out, and you will be old beyond your years. Forcing yourself to be someone you are not, or stuffing down who you really are, is incredibly taxing. It will tax you so much that it will shorten your life by years and years. I wonder how many obituaries in the newspaper should actually read something like:

"Jackson, Robert. Mr. Robert Jackson died yesterday of complications from doing a lifetime of crap that he didn't really want to do. His condition was further complicated because he also failed to do much, if any, of what he did want to do. Experts report that he died from cramming someone else's idea of life into his body, his brain, and his life. Attempts by Mr. Jackson to fill the voids with work, cars, excessive eating, alcohol, three wives, two thousand rounds of golf, and meeting everyone else's expectancies but his own, were dismally unsuccessful. Unfortunately, this all took so much out of Mr. Jackson that he was just worn flat out and died about twenty years too soon. Miserable in his last years, he passed unpeacefully yesterday at his

home. He was surrounded by colleagues from the job he hated, and
family members who were all just as miserable as he was."

Okay, that was kind of smart-ass, but I'm not kidding here. Medical experts tell us we can lose as many as fourteen years from our
life expectancy by living the kind of prolonged stress I'm describing.
This is why I am telling you, you are playing with fire here.

So if I am right, how did all of this happen? Obviously, nobody
slipped you a stupid pill, and you aren't some moron who should be
in an institution. You just got caught up in this runaway train we call
life. You just got used to not being excited. Across time, it got easier
to tell yourself no than it was to tell someone else no. You very likely
got some programming that taught you that it was selfish to focus on
you. That programming, of course, came from a bunch of *other people* who would a whole lot rather you focus on them and what they
want, instead of you and what you want. Duh!

Now if, on the other hand, you *are* excited about something in
your life every day, feel really good about who you are and what you
are doing, you are very likely living consistently with your authentic
self. If you are often peaceful and fulfilled and feel like you are in
touch with and focused on your mission and purpose for being in
this world, then you are living in concert with who you really are.

Let me tell you what I would wish for you to be thinking and saying now, during, and after you read this book:

"Hey, wait a minute here. Screw the expectancies; screw living for
everyone else. They (whoever 'they' are) don't pay my rent, they don't
come home with me at night and bathe my kids and cook my dinner!
Why, then, am I living for what I think some ill-defined bunch of people expect of me? They don't get a vote anymore. I will no longer give
my power away. I want it back, and I'm going to use it to be me.

"I want to make *me* happy by being true to myself doing what I care about. If I love music, I want to have music in my life. If I want a career, then I want to find a way to have it. If I'm tired of being fat, I want to prioritize that change into my lifestyle. If I'm not being treated with dignity and respect, that's not okay, not now, not ever. I would rather be alone than sick with someone else. If I miss God being in my life because my husband is not spiritual, then he will need to adjust, not me. I'm tired of being scared all the time. Scared about kids, money, job, boss, parents, and acceptance. I want some upside here. I want to feel alive. I want to feel valued by others and myself. I want to get up in the morning, instead of dreading it. I want to have tremendous clarity about why I am in this world and what I am supposed to do while I am here. I want to realize this is not a dress rehearsal; it is my life, my one shot. I want my kids to know and have all of me instead of some half-assed counterfeit. I want them to really see all of the real me, my interest, my sense of humor, my values. I believe that children learn what they live, and I want to teach them *by example* to be proud, instead of showing them how to compromise. I want to live with peace, fulfillment, joy, and excitement. I want to be able to finish a day and say that the day 'felt really good.' I want to be able to say that I am proud of me and proud of what I did today. I want to be able to say, 'I like who I am and what I'm all about.' I want to feel calm and peaceful. I want to feel satisfied. I want to be able to say, 'I feel good.' I want to feel like I belong and I deserve what I want just because—just because! I want to like me for being there for me and putting what's important to me on my priority list."

Are you in total shock right now? You're probably thinking I've gone walleyed, steer-headed, over-the-top "selfish-crazy."

Wrong! That's just your politically correct, "tell 'em what they want to hear" thinking taking over. How can it be selfish to take care of yourself when you know that it's absolutely true that you cannot give away what you do not have? So, if you're being self-righteously selfless, you may be a great, well-intentioned martyr, but regardless of your intentions you will cheat everyone in your life—your kids, spouse, friends, coworkers, your church—you cheat the whole world out of you. Even the Bible tells us to "love your neighbor *as* yourself." You have to take care of yourself before you *can* take care of anyone else.

How long has it been, if ever, that you really, no kidding, guilt free, took care of you? Ask yourself how long it's been since you could say, "I am doing what I'm doing today because it's what I want to do today, instead of doing what I'm doing today simply because it's what I was doing yesterday?"

Well, I don't want you to mindlessly go from one day to the next anymore. I want you to make a deep, uncompromised, committed decision to bringing your world in line with the person that you truly, authentically are. I don't want you living consistent with some fictional self that doesn't have a damn thing to do with you or what's important to you. I want you to start asking yourself what is important to you: What do you want? What do you need to be part of your life? Look at the following list and see if you can spot things on there that you wish were a part of your life, or were at least a bigger part of your life, yet they just aren't:

Music
Art
Work
Kids
Spiritual life
Honesty
Free time
Pride in work
Pride in appearance
Living with dignity
Health
Being in nature
A career that uses your strengths
Permission to say, do, and be who you are

Volunteer work
Hobby
Different lifestyle
Passion
Excitement
Independence
Meaningful relationship
Different body type
Feeling like a giver

I could go on and on. I just offer these to get you percolating and thinking about things that you might want in your life. If those things are not there, and I'm betting that many of them aren't, I'm going to show you exactly, precisely why and how they have been robbed from you, and exactly, precisely how to restore them to your life.

The good news is that the only person we need to fix all of this is you. You don't need your parents, your spouse, your boss, or anyone else, just you. My theory is this is all about you, because you have either passively allowed or actively been jerking yourself around by putting you and what's important to you at the bottom of the priority list. Whether you know it or not, you may very well have sold out. Typically, when we do that, when we sell out, the things we abandon first are the things that matter only to ourselves. Why? Because that way we don't disappoint anyone else and God forbid we do that. Remember, when you put yourself at the bottom of the priority list you are cheating not just yourself, but also everyone around you.

What I'm telling you here is that you don't just have a right to find your way back to the authentic and true you; you have a responsibility to do it. We're talking about your entire life here. We're talking about the one shot you get in this world. If you are just so fundamentally self-righteous that you can't justify doing this for yourself, then do it for your kids, do it for your family, and everyone else you love. Otherwise, you aren't getting you, they aren't getting you, and that's not okay.

When you're through with this book, I want you to be able to say, "I get it, and I am now there for me and everybody in this world that I care about." I want to introduce you to a key, foundational reality that is the sum and substance of where we are starring in your particular life and that is Your Personal Truth.

YOUR PERSONAL STARTING PLACE

In order for you ever to effectively figure out and map out how to get to where you want to go, you have to first know exactly where you are starting. Where you are now, everything you are, everything you do, begins with and is based on what I call your personal truth. By personal truth, I mean *whatever it is that you, at the absolute, uncensored core of your being, have come to believe about you.* This personal truth is critical, because if you believe it, if it is real to you, then it is for you the precise reality that you will live every day. We all have and live our own personal truth, whether we want to or not. If you are honest in truly acknowledging what you really think and feel about your self in your most candid moments, you know that what I'm saying is true. You know it because you have seen your personal truth come to light when you wished it would not. You may tell me and the rest of the world Story A and hope we buy it, but you're telling yourself what you believe to be the "real deal," at least as you see it, and we both know that version isn't even almost Story A! What you're telling yourself is the story you live; that's the one that jumps up and trips you when the pressure is on. You're always wondering if today is the day that the masquerade will come crashing down, and you will be "found out." No matter how hard you try, you can never escape your personal truth; it always gets you in the end, which is why it is so critical that you clean it up and get rid of all the doubt and distortion. You don't have to look far to find negative examples of personal truths that jump up and bite those who try to hide them: the schoolyard bully who folds like a cheap tent in the wind when someone finally calls his bluff because his personal truth is that of a coward; the bragging, yet insecure athlete who chokes at that critical moment in the competition; the "confident" beauty queen who is in truth lonely and scared and eventually takes her own life.

Yours may be a positive, accurate truth or it may be a "train wreck" of misbeliefs grounded in a history of fear, pain, and confusion. Most likely it is a combination of all those things. My job, our job, is to get real about those parts of what you believe about yourself that aren't working for you. You cannot hide from nor exceed the boundaries imposed by what you believe you "know" about yourself on the inside. You cannot play the game of life with confidence and assurance if your personal truth is riddled with fear and apprehension. Your "personal best" will never be better than the one your personal truth dictates for you. If it is distorted and fictional, be assured that it *will* show itself at the worst and most inopportune times, because that self-critical voice is relentlessly whispering in your ear. This personal truth business is a big deal, a huge deal. If you don't get yours straight, it will ruin even the best-laid plans to revitalize your life and everything in it. As we move forward, don't dare cheat yourself with some deluded thinking because you don't have the guts to tell yourself "out loud" what it is that you really believe on the inside. Unless and until you confront your personal truth you will never, ever have a chance to be the person you can be. You, like every other living person, get mixed and faulty messages from the world and from all of your experiences in it. The result is a distortion of your personal truth. Failing to confront that ill-conceived personal truth is a crucial betrayal of you, by you. Let's look at why I say your personal truth is so very important.

Now I'll just confess that about half of the time, I don't even know what the "experts" who talk and write about our lives mean when they throw around words like "self-realization," "inner self," "actualized self," being "centered," and whatever other buzzwords they manufacture to sound smart. A lot of it is beyond me, I'm afraid, way too fancy and convoluted for this ol' country boy. But to my simple way of thinking, who you are in this world, who you become, all boils down to this personal truth, this set of beliefs you have about you. It is so critical because it sets up and defines what I call your self-concept. If your beliefs about you are an authentic reflection of who you truly are, then you will live with a self-concept that empowers you and equips you to be absolutely the most effective and genuine person possible. If not, if there is distortion instead of accuracy, then you will have a limited and fictional self-concept that betrays who you truly are, and one that will cripple you in all of your pursuits. Not good!

We will talk in more detail about the authentic self and the fictional self in the next chapter. In the meantime, just understand that you have only one "self," but it is one that, like a chameleon, takes on the emotional colors of the history and environment in which it has existed. Your self-concept moves up and down a continuum anchored on one end by an authentic self-image (who you were created to be), and on the other by a fictional and distorted self-image (who the world has told you to be). Where you are on that continuum depends on what your external experiences in life have been, and what personal truth you have created from observing and interpreting yourself across the years.

This personal truth, and the self-concept that flows from it, is the "DNA" of your personality. Know this DNA, and you know your starting place in the journey to reconnect with your life.

As we move forward, I intend to show you how, whatever your DNA *is,* this came to be. I will then lead you to "deconstruct" those elements that are just plain wrong and have not served you well. I will also lead you through the steps necessary to reconstruct your authentic self-concept in a way to insure your success.

The process will work this way. I intend to demystify all this business about self-concept and how you think, feel, and believe about *you.* I intend to show you, in plain-talk terms, how that personal truth has and will determine the quality of virtually every aspect of your life, and how to change it by ridding it of distortion. This is a knowable process and one that we can break down into manageable steps. Those steps will involve events that happened externally, as well as events that happen and already have happened internally.

As we progress through the coming chapters, we are going to review your most relevant history by identifying the key life experiences that have written on the "slate of *you*" and define your personal truth and concept of self. We don't have to dissect every event in your entire life. To do so would be to just get bogged down in a bunch of details and minutiae that don't matter. Instead, we are going to deal with an amazingly few external and internal events that have determined the outcome of your entire existence. When you see how few events have so powerfully dictated who and what you have become, you are going to be absolutely shocked! But it is what it is, and at least that makes our job manageable. By answering some very pointed questions, reflecting on the various factors that contribute to your self-concept, and generally conducting a thorough and brutally honest audit of your own life, you will begin to feel a power and a peace that you may not have known for years, if at all. Whatever your current circumstances may be, this is work that you can do. All that it requires is a willing spirit and the desire to see it through. And it is work that you must do. If now is not the time to reconnect with your authentic self, when will there be a better time? This is hard work; I confess that to you up front. At this particular moment in time, you may doubt that you are worth the effort or that it is even possible to really "get right" with you and unlock your true passion, strengths, gifts, and talents. Trust me when I tell you that it is possible and you are worth it. I also want you to realize that whether all of this takes a week, a month, or a year, that precious and limited time is going to pass whether you are doing something about your life or not. I promise you that at this precise moment next year, your life will be better or worse than it is right now. It will not be the same; the choice to improve it or let it decay is wholly and undeniably yours. I will show you the way. Whether you need a little "polishing up" or feel totally and hopelessly lost, I am coming for you. I need your help and at a minimum your open mind and willing spirit. Let's get busy.

2 DEFINING THE

AUTHENTIC SELF

*"The only thing in the world you can
change is yourself and that makes all the
difference in the world."*

—CHER

NOW, I hate to start off sounding critical, the first rattle out of the box, but if we are going to make a difference in your life, I have to tell you the truth as I see it. As the old saying goes, "You can BS your friends, and I'll BS mine, but let's not BS each other!" What you're about to read is my view of how *most* people live. When I say "live," I mean their personal, private experience of life, not the image they project. No one will know if I'm right about you but you. I'm not asking that you substitute my judgment for your own, but I am asking that you weigh what I have to say carefully. I'm also asking that you be totally honest with yourself, even if it is scary to admit certain things about yourself and your life. Remember: You cannot change what you do not acknowledge.

Here's how I see it. If your life is like that of most people in this world, and in fact like mine used to be, you may be, whether you know it or not, smooth out of control. It may not look that way to other people, but so much for appearances. We don't care about what others want for you right now; our focus has to be totally on what *you* want. There will be plenty of time to balance it all later.

Like the duck that looks so smooth and graceful as it glides across the glassy pond, you're doing okay—at a surface level. But think about what that same duck is doing below the waterline: It's kicking and reaching, in a chaotic contrast to its seemingly effortless surface appearance. Such is life.

Just for the sake of argument, fantasize with me for a moment. I wonder what you might choose for your self if, all of a sudden, you could just rewrite the script of your life from as early as you might want, right up until now. If you hadn't been pulled into the suck hole of life, with all of its messages, traps of "responsibilities and expectancies"; if you hadn't inherited the status quo; if you weren't born into a certain family and station in life and weren't buried so deep that you seemed to have no choices, what would you choose? What would you choose if you weren't financially strapped, for example, living paycheck to paycheck, or didn't have so many people depending on you? If you weren't chronically overweight and tired, how would you live differently? If instead of being trapped, you had the opportunity to shape your life around who you really are and what really defines you and matters to you, what would your life be like? How and what would you change? What if you questioned what difference it really makes which car you drive, where you live, how much money you earn, or why it matters whether some person likes or doesn't like you?

Given a second chance, would you change things or would you decide that the "familiar" was safer, and you'd just stick with what you had? Would you grab the second chance or would you choke at the last minute, afraid to venture into something new? Would you settle for what you have because you fear that there is nothing else out there for you? You are about to find out that these are not just "hypothetical" questions. You are about to discover that you have a whole lot more choice about what happens in your life than you could ever imagine. You are about to learn how to unravel your past in such a way that it no longer can control you and your future. This is a journey that begins with you refusing to accept and even make excuses for you and your life. If you don't have what you want and need, you must be willing to say so, and say so with conviction.

When you ask someone, "Who are you?" you'll hear a lot of them answer, "Well, I'm a mom." "I'm a doctor." "I'm a plumber." "I'm a wife." "I'm an accountant." "I am the mayor." "I live in Beverly Hills." You even hear your children do it: "I'm a cheerleader; football player; honor student; troublemaker." Both children and adults don't answer about who they are; they answer about what they do, what their social station is, or how they see their function in life. They define themselves by their jobs or their roles. They answer with "what" they do, because they *can't* answer with "who" they are. They can't tell you who they are, because they don't know. Yes, you exist at many levels, and the behavioral plane is one of them. What you do is certainly a factor in who you are. But there is a whole other level of existence, distinct from what you do, that is the real, true, genuine sum and substance of who you are. For lack of a better word, that real, true, genuine identity is what I have been referring to as your authentic self. I would predict that you would have a hard time describing your authentic self to someone else because you probably haven't seen or in any way been in contact with that part of yourself in a long, long time, if ever.

So: Let's get real. Who are you? Why are you doing what it is that you do? Is what you are doing with your life something that reflects and utilizes who you really are? Given a choice, would you choose differently? Do you even know what you would choose if you had an option? Are you in touch with this authentic self? Do you "get" what "it" is, or is this just a bunch of psychological talk? Wouldn't it be tragic if a very different, vibrant you was buried under a pile of worldly to-do lists, and you were mindlessly accepting the world's expectancies? There is an authentic self within you. Maybe you are living a life that reflects that authentic self, and maybe you aren't. Maybe it is buried. Interesting question, don't you think? What if . . . ?

So, what is this authentic self I keep talking about? The authentic self is the *you* that can be found at your absolute core. It is the part of you that is not defined by your job, or your function, or your role. It is the composite of all your unique gifts, skills, abilities, interests, talents, insights, and wisdom. It is all of your strengths and values that are uniquely yours and need expression, versus what you have been programmed to believe that you are "supposed" to be and do. It is the you that flourished, unself-consciously, in those times in your life when you felt happiest and most fulfilled. It is the you that existed before and remains when life's pain, experiences, and expectancies are stripped away. It is the you that existed before you were scarred by your parents' divorce or wounded when that cute boy in school made fun of your braces or your dress. It is the you that existed before your spouse demeaned you in argument after argument, while you just took it for fear of being left. It is the you that existed before you were in fact left abandoned by your spouse or even your children. It is the you that wants to require you to be more than you are, that doesn't even know what it is to settle or sell out.

Do you know, in vivid detail, who that authentic you is?

If the answer is no, vital life energy is being wasted and you are living a compromised existence that cheats you out of a chance to be truly happy and at peace.

Did you at one time listen carefully to that voice? Do you suspect that somehow, somewhere along the way, you have lost contact with it?

If so, you must once again find that voice and heed its message, rather than having an ear only for the voice of the world and all those within it who seek to control you.

Is your behavioral life, your public persona, at odds with the values, beliefs, desires, passions, and visions that define your authentic self?

If so, you have given up control and are living a life defined from the outside in, rather than from the inside out.

Not living faithfully to your authentic self creates a void, an ever-present feeling that you are incomplete. You find yourself wondering whether you should be doing something different with your life. There's a restlessness, a yearning emptiness that won't go away. It's as if there is a hole in your soul. You may try to fill that hole in any number of ways: by smoking or drinking; by incessant working; by overinvesting yourself in a mate or children. Maybe you sit down and eat a chocolate cake with a half gallon of ice cream. Maybe you have an affair. You have kids. You get divorced. You get married. You get a new job. You cast about to find something, anything to fill that hole in your heart.

At times you may feel very, very lonely. Strangely, even when you're in the midst of people, there is an ache of separation. You talk to others, but never feel totally listened to. You may feel misunderstood, even when you are brave enough to risk sharing your feelings. You may often fear another's touch, because you can't discern that person's meaning or intention, no matter how close they may seem, including your own family members. Painfully, you may have learned that friends and family alike have the capacity to leave you or ignore what is important to your authentic self, opting instead to have you be and do what is convenient for them. And if your struggle to fill the void has gone on long enough, you may have developed an underlying pessimism. You may have become passive in your quest for change and fulfillment. Bottom line: There is seldom a time in your life when all is at peace and in balance.

We need to be candid about what is at stake. Living in this world with assigned roles, rather than an authentic self, drains you of the critical life energy you need for the constructive pursuit of things that you truly value. By contrast, once you start living your life with an authentic sense of self, then all of that diverted energy, all of that otherwise wasted life energy starts speeding you down the highway of your life. You gain speed, efficiency, and smoothness. You become so much more successful in your life by being who you want and need to be.

To understand the energy it takes just to suppress your authentic self, think back to happy childhood memories of going swimming in the summer. If you were lucky enough to have a beach ball, it was always great fun to try to hold the ball underwater. (In fact, if you were like me, you got hours of pleasure from this intellectually stimulating pursuit.) Remember how that beach ball used to constantly fight to break through the surface of the water, then pop up into the sunshine? Remember how much effort and energy it took to hold it under you as it squeaked and wriggled from side to side, trying to avoid your suppressing hands and claim its natural buoyancy? Think about how tired you became as the seconds wore on. Isn't this exactly what happens when you deny your *authentic self* its natural expression? Just imagine the exhaustion you have accumulated, fighting that same fight every minute of every hour of every day of your life.

Now let's think for a minute about how much energy it takes to live that fictional life I have been talking about. I'm talking about a life that has you ignoring your true gifts and talents, and has you instead performing in those assigned or inherited roles that are just not who you are. Imagine pushing a huge boulder up a long, steep hill. Feel the weight and bulk of that boulder, fighting you all the way as you struggle and sweat to get the job done. Now picture yourself at the top of the hill, giving that boulder one last shove. It slips easily away from you and tumbles down the other side. Compare the two different tasks. At the end of a long, exhausting day, you might get one boulder up the hill, whereas you could roll a thousand boulders down that same hill in the same amount of time and still feel like you were just getting started. That's because rolling them downhill would be consistent with the principle of gravity, an example of the natural order of the universe.

The same principle holds true in your life. You have certain core traits, qualities, gifts, talents, needs, and desires. You have a core purpose for being in this world. By suppressing who you were meant and need to be, you are doing something entirely unnatural. If you're living for the fictional self, then you are unnecessarily trying to hold a beach ball under water with one hand while trying to push a boulder uphill with the other. You are draining precious life energy in a battle against nature, energy that you could otherwise be spending on what you are really all about.

This book is about letting go of that beach ball. It is about stopping the mindless and draining performance of all the roles you would never choose but have been assigned. To do any less would be to cheat you mentally, emotionally, spiritually, and physically.

As I said in the "obituary" in Chapter 1, the consequences for your health are undeniable. It is a well-known medical fact that whether or not an individual gets sick is determined much more by the vulnerability of his or her immune system than by exposure to the disease itself. It is also well documented that stress, both emotional and physical, greatly depletes the immune system. Study after study shows that the incidence of flu and colds increases with the immediacy of stress. College students' visits to the infirmary increase greatly as exam time approaches. The huge majority of widowers die within two years of their spouses' deaths, regardless of age. In the face of stress and self-disorder, our immune systems simply break down.

There could be no greater stress than that generated by denying the authentic self. Because your life energy is being diverted and therefore depleted, you are compromised mentally, emotionally, spiritually, and physically. What about the long-term, cumulative effects of all this? I wasn't just being dramatic when I said denying who you really are can kill you. In his book *Real Age,* Dr. Michael Roizen points out that for every year that you live with high stress, you shorten your life expectancy by three years. According to his research, if you don't have an outlet for your true passion, it costs you another six years. If someone is draining your energy due to constant turmoil and conflict, you lose another eight years. In fact, if you add up the number of years that might be lost because of stress and living in the fictional self, it would be thirty-two years! Think about that! Thirty-two years is more than a third of your expected life span, all because you choose to continue living in your fictional cage, rather than discovering and living your life in congruence with your authentic self.

Knowing human nature as I do, I understand that remote consequences, such as health problems that will not affect you for another thirty years, are sometimes not powerful motivators. The idea of a shortened life span can seem irrelevant in early and midlife. Let me assure you: Those consequences can and will be very real at some point in your life.

Suppose, for example, I came to you on your deathbed and said, "Here are fourteen years longer for you to live, fourteen years for you to enjoy watching your grandchildren grow, fourteen years to experience life in any way you wish—do you want those extra years?" How would you respond?

It takes so much energy to be what you are not. It takes so little to be what you truly are. If at the end of your life, your answer would be, "Yes, I want those fourteen years back," then let it be yes now.

You will quickly discover that when you are on the right track with yourself, there is an enormous energy that uplifts you. You feel inspired and healed. Put simply, you will know how it feels to be *empowered*. Empowerment is the ability to distill the life force to a single focus. Empowerment makes it possible for two parents to lift the corner of a two-ton car to rescue a child that is trapped. It is what gives the warrior a tremendous advantage over his foe. It is what enables an outnumbered band of soldiers to defeat an army several times its size.

Once you commit to reconnecting with your authentic self, you will view even those tiresome "dailies"—the formerly irritating events of your life—in a new light. No longer will the five minutes that you were challenged at the supermarket by a rude cashier bother you, threaten you, or ruin your afternoon. You will know that there is nothing that can rock you, nothing that can put you off balance, because you have the balance inside yourself. You will have the tools to challenge the fictional self, to determine what is good and what is bad, what is painful and what brings joy, what is you and what is not you.

It is very important that I establish a clear target in your mind as to what an authentically dominated life is. One way to bring home the experience I am looking for is by example, through people who live and radiate an authentically directed life. I encountered just such a person in my childhood. This was a very unusual person, with a very unusual occupation, and he made an indelible impression on me. His name was Gene Knight. Gene became a marker for me in the passion and authenticity categories.

At some time or another, all of us have encountered people who seemed to be larger than life somehow, people whose experience of life was filled with color and excitement. In short, they were excited about life and were having a ball. For these people, there seems to be no boundary between working and playing. Watching them at work, it's as if they're at play and you just happened to have come by. Their lives are anything but gray. And it is through them that we catch a glimpse of what the authentic life is like.

Gene Knight was one of those people for me. I'll tell you right up front, I did not grow up in a sophisticated, blue blood-type family or environment. Gene Knight, one of my icons for authenticity, was a bootlegger! I could have made up some more respectable occupation for him, but hey, it is what it is.

In the mid to late 1950s, we lived in a really small town in Oklahoma, where a lot of counties were "dry." Gene was a part of the primitive network that supplied that for which there was plenty of demand in those counties: case after case of Jim Beam and every other kind of whiskey you could imagine. Looking back, it's clear to me now that Gene's real dream was to be a barnstormer, but he was about thirty years too late for that. So instead of barnstorming, people paid him to fly cases of whiskey all over Oklahoma. He could have just as happily have been a bush pilot in Africa, or flown medical supplies into the Amazon jungle. The point is that Gene Knight was a born pilot. When he climbed into the cockpit, there could be no doubt that Gene was doing what he absolutely, unequivocally, passionately loved.

I was probably eight or nine years old when I first met Gene. I remember my dad loading me up to go meet the plane. We would drive well out of our little town, turning off one dirt road and then another, until we were out in the middle of a huge cotton patch where there was a clapboard shed, presumably used to store farm equipment. The location was supposedly chosen so that you could see a car coming for miles in any direction. This, I was told, was to make it easier to avoid a run-in with the law, although I can hardly remember a time that Sheriff Tucker wasn't helping us unload! I remember my first trip to the "shed." It was a numbingly cold afternoon, growing colder as the sun began to set. Inside the shed, I wormed my way through a small group of men that huddled around a small wood-burning stove. I had barely had time to rub my hands and hold them out over the stove when one of the men said, "That'll be Gene," and sure enough, there was a sound like a mosquito's, far away but growing louder, and we all shuffled outside.

After the really old airplane had bounced and clattered to a stop, out stepped Gene Knight. It may sound hokey, but this was a guy who could have passed for Errol Flynn. He had coal-black hair, wore a leather flying jacket, and stood about six foot four. He hopped down from the plane, grinning ear to ear. As he shook hands, slapped backs, and exchanged stories with all of the men, there was an air about him, an air of absolutely infectious joy. As the men dashed about to offload the cases of whiskey, Gene was just grinning away, as if to say, "Isn't this the greatest? Could it get any better than this?" He would talk about his plane like it was the Concorde, showing first one and then another some new gadget, or the scratch marks where he had clipped a treetop on a recent run. He headed into the shed, where he warmed his hands over the stove and chatted a little with my dad. Soon all the men came back in, not so much to get warm as to get a piece of the freedom that Gene seemed to carry with him. Standing there rubbing his hands and tapping his feet, he seemed to me like some kind of racehorse, barely able to contain his excitement before the next race.

Not surprisingly, those Saturday afternoons became a favorite ritual. I could not wait to get out to that cotton patch with my dad. Gene would talk about flying and his eyes would just beam. He loved his "job," loved his life, and loved the people he encountered along the way. Eventually, the day came when Gene took me up for a ride. Let me tell you, Buck Rogers had nothing on me! As soon as we were airborne, I told myself, I'm gonna be a pilot, and just as soon as I came of age, I got my license. I have been flying my entire life, a direct result of Gene Knight's influence.

Now more than forty years later, with the perspective of hindsight, I recognize that Gene never made much money. His plane was old and slow and dilapidated. I know that he, just like my dad and all the other men out there, had bills to pay and promises to keep. But the unforgettable truth about Gene was that he lived to fulfill his passion. He didn't live to pay his bills. He was born to fly, and he knew it. He loved what he was doing, and he liked himself, but he had no need to strut around. He was a humble man, but a contagiously happy one. The life he lived was his currency; his "income" came in the form of taking that plane aloft and setting it down in the midst of a cotton patch, miles from the nearest airport, to do his task and see his friends. Every time he hopped down from that airplane, I'm convinced he couldn't wait to hop back in again, regardless of the destination. I knew Gene for thirty-five years, and I can tell you that he kept flying, right up until the year he passed away. He died a happy and fulfilled man.

. . .

Now it is time to talk specifically about you. Don't you think it's time to give yourself a turn—in fact, don't you know it's past time? I suspect that you take care of everyone and everything else in your life first and almost always get to you and your needs last, if at all. Yet the fact that you are reading this tells me you must feel a need. At some level, you are ready to do something different with your life, and I want to seize on that readiness. You know I'm right. What you may not know is how deadly serious I am about you getting real about you, and how dramatically your life can change when you reclaim an incredible power that you may not even know that you have lost. You are better than you are living. You are capable of more than you have and are experiencing. You can make your life hum if you will link up your true self and your world. To do that, you have to get intimately in touch with you.

That's why you need some guided self-diagnosis. Answering questions about yourself—the right questions—can help you take a step back from the situation, to get honest with yourself, and to start thinking about your options. If you're saying, "I'm okay," but you're saying that because you've compromised, then you need to know that. Accordingly, your progress through this book will be interactive: with virtually every concept that is introduced, I'll ask you to call "time out" in order to apply that concept to your own life experience.

Let's make a deal before we even start. As we move forward, you absolutely must deal with nothing but hard, objective *fact*. As you address the question of you, I'm challenging you, starting now, to stop dealing in opinions or assumptions, and start dealing in facts.

That means no untested assumptions. I guess what I'm telling you is that you cannot just automatically trust that you have been, or are currently being, objective about you. Just because you have believed something for a long time or have convinced yourself that you just "are" a certain way doesn't even almost make it true. You have to be willing to challenge virtually every single thing you have ever believed about yourself. For example, if you have for a long time felt that you were inferior or a second-class citizen, where is the proof? If you had to argue your second-classed-ness in a court of law, could you do it? Is it fact, or is it just some opinion you have carried for a long time? Let's agree to use the "Joe Friday approach," from the old show *Dragnet:* "Just the facts, ma'am, just the facts."

Now that may sound easy, but you need to recognize that when it comes to dealing with yourself, all of your momentum may be the other way: it may have been years since you dealt only in facts. Remember, a lie unchallenged becomes the truth. You've either been told, or told yourself, some of this crap for so long you just automatically believe it. That would never happen if you required yourself to deal with only the facts. For example, nobody could ever convince you that you're a thief, because *factually,* you know better. You know, as a matter of indisputable, objective fact, that you do not steal stuff, period, end of discussion. You can simply and unequivocally reject that accusation because you have the data, and whatever someone else might "think" doesn't change it one whit. As a result, it's a piece of information that never gets a foothold in your self-concept. Being "I'm a thief" will never become a part of your personal truth.

But suppose someone confronts you about some aspect of yourself that is not so objective and easily measured, such as your value, your worth, your desirability, or your sensitivity. Those things are not nearly so cut and dried. I can't show you a quart of your worth, or a pound of your value. Whether it is you or someone else who is "opining" that you, for example, are worthless, you have to know the facts or you're dead meat. If you don't have the absolute bottom-bottom-line scoop on the real deal, you'll go for the con job like Jesse went for the train!

Yet through some bizarre logic that will never cease to amaze me, I watch people get suckered time after time. Some jerk (a.k.a. boyfriend, mother-in-law, boss, skinny friend, etc.) will level some vague and unfounded criticism, and because we haven't done the work to amass the facts, we buy into it and stick it right dead center in our self-concept. We even do it to ourselves with our own opinions! In examining your self-concept, then, you need to be really clear about what's fact and what's not. Opinions are only opinions, and opinions can be changed. *What I want to help you do is stop dealing with opinions about yourself, and instead get in touch with the facts about yourself.*

Once you know the facts, you'll engage the world in an entirely different way. You'll stop saying to yourself, I have to earn my right to be here by being clever, rich, funny, pretty, anything. Instead, you'll communicate to the world, I have the right to be here, because I *know from the inside out* that I have qualities that are worthy of your acceptance. I know that about myself. It may take you some time to see that or not, but I know who I am, and I know that if you know me, then we are good to go.

I'm making such a big deal out of this because I know that in any life, too much distortion (baseless opinion) creeps into self-perceptions and thinking. Often times it happens without your even knowing it. It's as if your authentic self were an image projected on a wall. In the beginning, the image was crisp and focused. The colors were brilliant, its edges were razor sharp; there could be no doubt about what that picture was. If you had been asked, "Who are you?" you would have pointed at the image and said with confidence, "That's who I am."

Then the world started bumping the projector. Upsets and challenges and difficulties jostled and shook it so that the image blurred. Your own responses to those events contributed to the shimmying and shaking. This commotion went on for years. Along the way, you stopped testing everything for accuracy, and certain things started getting to you. Now, when you look up at the wall, you see only a hodgepodge of fuzzy lines and motley colors. Your authentic self has fallen completely out of focus, facts blurred by the opinions of you and others who may not have had your best interest at heart.

This all means that you must now be willing to begin testing virtually every thought, feeling, or reaction you have about you. It is natural and normal to trust your thinking, but what if you are wrong? What if you are missing some very important aspects of *you?* If you accept your thoughts as facts, then you will no longer be looking for new information, because you assume that you have all the answers. You will deny key factual realities of self that you cannot afford to miss. You'll be getting your information from an image that is entirely out of focus and untrustworthy.

I'm challenging you to start being skeptical of familiar patterns, familiar information. Find out, instead, exactly what have been your "distorters," the things that have jostled your projector. Together, let's understand what has distorted you so that we can challenge those things. Search for new information about you, because I'm telling you that there are aspects of you, your authentic self, that are about to emerge from within that mess of world experiences and self-choices. It would be tragic for you to fail to recognize your very own self because you had your head so far up your darkest regions that you missed the unveiling!

Speaking of facts, if, on the other hand, you're committed to dealing in "just the facts," now is a good time to lay some essential ones out on the table. Here are a few that are universal. And these facts must become cornerstones of your journey to discover or rediscover your authentic self.

FACT: Every one of us, you included, has within us everything we will ever need to be, do, and have anything and everything we will ever want and need.

God is wise in so many things that we don't see. I strongly believe that He starts out each person with everything they'll ever need to successfully fulfill their role. We have the tools, we have the ingredients, we have all the things that we need to get out in the world and live as our authentic selves. And for each of us, that set of gifts is uniquely different. He gave you different gifts than He gave me. He has given you different gifts than He gave the next-door neighbor. Nevertheless, each of us, with all of our differences, has within us all of the resources that we need. Those resources are found within the authentic self. If you feel inept or ill equipped to deal with your life, and this is a hard fact to accept, then go with me on blind faith if necessary, because I promise that under all the garbage that you may have accumulated on your journey through this world, lie the gifts and skills that I know are there. If you feel disconnected from your pursuits, whether personal, professional, emotional, physical, or spiritual, it may well be not that there is something wrong or inadequate about you, but that you are chasing the wrong things.

In the field of industrial psychology, we often deal with the challenge of achieving the proper "man-task interface." The objective is to get the right person doing the right job. Two people of equal intelligence, for example, might have very different results when performing the same job. The reason lies in differing core traits that exist at the level of their authentic self. Even though they are of equal intelligence, one matches up to the specific requirements of the job, and the other simply does not.

If you are struggling in any aspect of your life—career, relationships, finances, family, or feelings and expectancies about self—it is entirely possible that the problem is not with you, but with your personal "man-task interface." You may in fact be pursuing people, goals, objectives, or experiences of self that are incongruent with your authentic core. As I said earlier, don't get caught by rigid thinking. You must be willing to challenge virtually every single aspect of your life, including the reality that you may be wanting and pursuing things that simply aren't right for you.

FACT: Your authentic self is there, it has always been there, and it is fully accessible to you. You are not the exception to this fact. There are no exceptions.

Your particular traits and characteristics, and your store of accurate, undistorted knowledge, are what define you and differentiate you from every other human being in the world. This distinction of you is true, however, if and only if you live a life in which everything that is uniquely you is allowed to come out. You must seize every *genuine* characteristic that is you and allow it to take center stage in your life. And it can be done. Rediscovering the authentic self is not esoteric, mystical work that can be done only by some philosopher on a mountaintop somewhere—it's a job that can and must be done by you. You can't *be* you if you don't *know* you. You may have access, but it is up to you to exercise it. Failing to do so renders you nothing more than the eighty-third "sheep" from the left in Row 487,000,946!

FACT: The self that now runs your life didn't just happen. It is the result of

1. Certain key events that you have experienced in your life, your external factors; and

2. A process of reaction and interpretation that happens within you, your internal factors.

Your life in this world consists of a series of interactions, some external, some internal. Through these external interactions, the world either affirms and builds on what you start with or it countermands, attacks, and erodes it. The internal factors and reactions are just as powerful as, if not more powerful than, the external ones as you interpret and react to what happens in your life. The end result, if you are a product of an unkind and insensitive journey in your life, is a fictional self. It is fictional because those negative experiences in your life and—perhaps more importantly—your reactions to and interpretations of those experiences, pull you away from who you once knew you were. The result is that you begin to ignore who and what you are and what you want and need. This self opts instead to shape you into a nonwave-making conformist: just take it, don't make trouble, just take it. That conforming definition of you may be convenient for the world, but it can leave you frustrated and lacking hope, passion, and energy. In order to disconnect from this fictional self and reconnect with your authentic self, you must understand how both sets of influences, external and internal, have contributed to the life you're living right now, and how those influences can be controlled by you to create what you really want and need.

For example, if you have been rejected (external event), and you're really hard on yourself, blaming yourself for not being good enough (internal event), you are altering your connection with your authentic self and connecting instead to some fiction that, in truth, probably has very little to do with you and a whole lot to do with the other person.

FACT: Your fictional self is the source of wrong identity and wrong information.

Not only does the fictional self send you false information about who you are and what you should be doing with your life, it actively *blocks* the information you need in order to maintain the connection with your authentic identity. Relying on information from the fictional self means you're putting your trust in a broken compass.

Think of it this way: When you come to a crossroads and you should go right, you go left instead. That is a double bad deal. Left is taking you where you don't need to go, but just as importantly, it is also keeping you from going in the right direction. If you travel ten miles left when you should have gone ten miles right, you've made a thirty-mile mistake: the ten miles you went in the wrong direction, the ten miles you have to go back to get to where you started from, and then the ten miles you have to go to get to where you were going. That's the kind of compound error that characterizes life in the fictional self. It explains why you've got to call "time out," now, and determine where you are. Is the direction you are headed with your life *in fact* the way you want to go?

FACT: Your life is not a dress rehearsal.

If it's true that there is more to you than you are living, you need to be asking yourself, Why aren't I living it?—and you need to be asking that right now. You need to be asking yourself *how* to take control right now. Maybe you're not requiring enough of yourself because you think you are in a trap. You think you have no choice. Maybe you're being held down by a lack of money or opportunity or by people in your life who would be threatened if you were more successful. Maybe you just don't know which way to push, or what to want or reach for.

Whatever your circumstance, you cannot let those "reasons" become "excuses." Easy or hard, I'm telling you that you have the responsibility to be all that you can be, for your family, for the world. It's your life and the clock is ticking. If you remain imprisoned in self-denial, then days, weeks, months, and years will continue to be wasted: time that could and would have been amazing and significant in your life.

Is today a perfect example? Think about it. Like so many other days, it is now over and lost forever. Whatever you did or didn't do, felt or didn't feel, suffered or reveled in, shared or didn't share, it's done. The difference is that, by reading this book, by opening your mind and heart to the possibility of a difference, you are making a difference with this very day. You have started a journey, a journey to dig through the clutter of life and the world, a journey back to you.

Let's start the journey with a couple of short tests, designed to give you a "first look" at how much of your life energy you're giving to your authentic self, and how much you're giving to a fictional self. To do these tests, you'll need something to write with, and enough privacy and quiet time to develop your most thoughtful, honest answers to these questions.

THE AUTHENTICITY SCALE

You'll see that each numbered item below offers two alternative choices. Think of each of these alternatives as "poles" or ends of a spectrum. Maybe the left-hand answer is more true for you; on the other hand, maybe the right-hand answer describes you better. Let's take item number 1 as an example. For number 1, read the description on the left-hand side. Does that accurately describe how you are motivated? Now travel directly across the page, to the alternative description on the right: Would it be more accurate to describe you as being motivated by internal factors? Once you decide which description—the left side or the right—describes you better, you then need to decide *how often* or how consistently that description you've selected is true for you. For example, let's say you tend to be motivated by a need to please people in authority, and that this characteristic is true for you **most of the time.** In the set of parentheses second from the left for item number 1, you're going to place an X, since the second column applies to behavior that is true most of the time. Now move down to item number 2. Consider each alternative; decide which one more accurately describes you; decide whether it is true of you **all** or **most** of the time; then put an X in the appropriate set of parentheses for item 2. Do this for all thirty-eight items.

The Fictional Self	True all of the time of the left (1)	True most of the time of the left (2)	True most of the time of the right (3)	True all of the time of the right (4)	The Authentic Self
1. I am motivated by a need to please authority and win approval from others.	( )	( )	( )	( )	I am motivated by internal factors, such as a sense of a mission in life and honest thinking about myself.
2. I follow orders for fear of disapproval.	( )	( )	( )	( )	I make choices based on self-best-interest.
3. I lack confidence to function without authority figures; I lack initiative.	( )	( )	( )	( )	I am confident to function effectively with self-decisions.
4. My self-esteem is based on what others think, I desperately want approval.	( )	( )	( )	( )	My self-esteem is defined internally with or without external approval.

The Fictional Self	True all of the time of the left (1)	True most of the time of the left (2)	True most of the time of the right (3)	True all of the time of the right (4)	The Authentic Self
5. I have difficulty in seeing connection between personal behavior and consequences without others' reactions.	( )	( )	( )	( )	I am able to see connection between personal behavior and consequences.
6. I have difficulty making choices based on personal priorities.	( )	( )	( )	( )	I am able to make choices based on self-priorities.
7. I have feelings of dependency and fear.	( )	( )	( )	( )	I have feelings of self-confidence and strength.
8. I avoid internal feelings.	( )	( )	( )	( )	I seek internal knowledge.
9. I am compliant to others.	( )	( )	( )	( )	I am cooperative with others.
10. I am oriented to avoid punishment.	( )	( )	( )	( )	I am oriented to self fulfillment.
11. I am generally uneasy about what people expect of me.	( )	( )	( )	( )	I am usually confident around other people.
12. I feel frightened most of the time.	( )	( )	( )	( )	I am happy with myself most of the time.
13. I feel lost in my life.	( )	( )	( )	( )	I have a purpose to my life.
14. I always feel as if I do not belong here.	( )	( )	( )	( )	I have a kinship with everyone.
15. I hate to make decisions.	( )	( )	( )	( )	I enjoy making decisions.
16. I hate myself most of the time.	( )	( )	( )	( )	I am amazed at myself.
17. I cannot forgive myself.	( )	( )	( )	( )	I have made mistakes, but I have learned from them.

continued on next page

The Fictional Self	True all of the time of the left (1)	True most of the time of the left (2)	True most of the time of the right (3)	True all of the time of the right (4)	The Authentic Self
18. I call myself names, like "stupid" and "dummy."	( )	( )	( )	( )	I appraise myself honestly and objectively.
19. I feel like a loser.	( )	( )	( )	( )	I am a winner.
20. I still hear my parents talk to me in my head.	( )	( )	( )	( )	I have let go of my parents' judgments.
21. I worry that I am going to screw up.	( )	( )	( )	( )	I cannot let pessimism into my life.
22. I always wonder if others are evaluating me.	( )	( )	( )	( )	I pay attention to my own values rather than others'.
23. I often wonder why despite my best efforts it seems so hard to get what you want in life.	( )	( )	( )	( )	I find it simple to obtain what I want in life because I can focus correctly.
24. When I am alone I find myself staring into space and feeling disconnection.	( )	( )	( )	( )	When I am alone I find I am good company and I enjoy my space.
25. When I cannot sleep I wonder how I am going to make it through the next day.	( )	( )	( )	( )	When I cannot sleep I allow my mind to be creative, knowing that tomorrow will be exciting and rewarding.
26. I find that hope and joy give way to tired "going through the motions of life."	( )	( )	( )	( )	I find hope and joy easy to experience.
27. I often find it hard to get off my butt and get into the game.	( )	( )	( )	( )	I find it easy to get started on a new project.

The Fictional Self	True all of the time of the left (1)	True most of the time of the left (2)	True most of the time of the right (3)	True all of the time of the right (4)	The Authentic Self
28. I often worry why other people are successful and I am not.	( )	( )	( )	( )	I find it easy to understand why other people are successful.
29. I am usually in the grips of depression and anxiety.	( )	( )	( )	( )	I am usually happy and hopeful.
30. I am often frustrated and want to just give up and scream.	( )	( )	( )	( )	I can handle frustration.
31. I often wonder why I am never the boss or respected as a leader.	( )	( )	( )	( )	I am often the boss and respected.
32. I struggle to comprehend why my marriage is hard and my children are not adjusting well.	( )	( )	( )	( )	My family life is secure and comforting.
33. I want to run away from the world, especially when the bills come.	( )	( )	( )	( )	I find life fun and bills just a small part of life.
34. I feel that I am living a masquerade life, not one of my own.	( )	( )	( )	( )	I am living my own life.
35. I am sick and tired of my life.	( )	( )	( )	( )	My life is wonderful and exciting.
36. I shake my head when I commit to starting a new job, a new diet, etc., because I will probably fail.	( )	( )	( )	( )	I look forward to new challenges, knowing that success is possible.
37. I have come to the conclusion that I am living a life that I did not design or want.	( )	( )	( )	( )	I am living my life, my purpose.

continued on next page

The Fictional Self	True all of the time of the left (1)	True most of the time of the left (2)	True most of the time of the right (3)	True all of the time of the right (4)	The Authentic Self
38. I am bitter about my life and how it has turned out.	( )	( )	( )	( )	I am not bitter but I am glad I designed my life, however it has worked out.

Scoring: For every **X** in the far left column, give yourself a 1; for every **X** in the second column, give yourself a 2; for every **X** in the third column, give yourself a 3; and for each **X** in the fourth column, give yourself a 4. Adding up the numbers for all thirty-eight items, your total will be in a range of 38 to 142.

Interpreting Your Score:

38–70   A score in this range suggests that you are seriously disconnected from your authentic self. You need to be asking how much of your experience of life is what you really want.

71–110   This range suggests that you are operating, most of the time, from a fictional self-concept that has become distorted and is therefore a fictional version of who you really are. It would not be surprising if you were usually confused about what you should be doing, at any time, or what would be the best use of your time. You may be bewildered about what the world expects of you, and you may feel really disconnected from your life. In many ways, a score in this range is the most problematic: The person who scores here may be aware of his or her fictional self and may understand that life does not have to be this way, but he or she may also fear the responsibility of change.

111–139   This score indicates that your self-concept is distorted into a fictional version, at least some of the time. You may be afraid to be totally yourself, because of the power the world has over you, but you are also aware of and may also want desperately to serve your authenticity. The problem is that when the challenges get too great the person with this authenticity score often fails himself or herself.

140–152   A person who scores in this range is fortunate enough to operate mostly in tune with his or her authenticity. This person has a clear idea of his or her authentic self and what he or she wants from life. In the midst of difficult situations, this person looks naturally into the self, so that goals remain clear and consistent with his or her authenticity.

TEST OF CONGRUENCY

This profile will help you get some idea of the degree to which your current life experience—how you are currently thinking, feeling, and living—compares to what your experience would be if you were living an ideal, fully authentic, and fulfilling life. For example, are you 90 percent congruent with your full potential, or has your self-concept been distorted into some fictional version of who you once were?

The test of congruency addresses that question in three steps. First, you will describe your full potential by rating yourself on certain dimensions *as you would be in an ideal situation and life experience*. Second, you'll rate yourself on the same dimensions, this time as those dimensions reflect *who and what you believe you really are*. Finally, you will determine the percentage of difference between the two. It is that difference—the gap between your authentic/ideal thinking, feeling, and living and the less desirable reality you call life—that will give you an early benchmark as to the health of your personal truth and self-concept.

Below are two identical sets of words that you are to use to describe yourself, first as you would be in an *ideal life,* and then as you are *now.* Like the Authenticity Scale, this exercise deserves your utmost candor and focus. Once you have completed both lists as instructed, you will be ready to make some highly revealing comparisons.

1. Circle all the words that you think describe the ideal person you want to be, the person you believe is the full potential of who you are and will ever be.

pretty attractive beautiful cute nice-looking appealing cool sweet spiritual wise nice friendly faithful leader strong supportive moral ethical principled good honest decent warm loving tender warmhearted demonstrable caring kind affectionate cordial hospitable welcoming amiable cheerful passionate fiery enthusiastic zealous arrogant egocentric altruistic sympathetic humane selfless philanthropic smart dependent free gentle thoughtful domineering submissive autonomous creative compassionate self-sufficient private liberated conventional objective elegant clever stylish intelligent quick charming tidy neat thoughtful attentive careful watchful alert reliable inspired inventive resourceful ingenious productive exciting energetic lively vigorous bouncy active joyful blissful pleased ecstatic cheery sane rational sensible reasonable normal complete capable genuine inspiring proud approachable peaceful honest giving nurturing accomplished whole perfect undivided achiever great confident compassionate content humble unassuming happy satisfied comfortable at ease relaxed able knowledgeable skilled proficient expert adept rich wealthy affluent prosperous full gorgeous valuable abundant fruitful powerful deep productive prolific understanding dynamic useful helpful constructive beneficial positive functional worthwhile

Now count the number of words you circled in step 1. This will be called the Total Potential Score.

Total words circled in step 1   =   Total Potential Score

2. Now circle the words below that describe how you actually are at present.

pretty   attractive   beautiful   cute   nice-looking   appealing   cool sweet   spiritual   wise   nice   friendly   faithful   leader   strong supportive   moral   ethical   principled   good   honest   decent warm   loving   tender   warmhearted   demonstrable   caring   kind affectionate   cordial   hospitable   welcoming   amiable   cheerful passionate   fiery   enthusiastic   zealous   arrogant   egocentric altruistic   sympathetic   humane   selfless   philanthropic   smart dependent   free   gentle   thoughtful   domineering   submissive autonomous   creative   compassionate   self-sufficient   private liberated   conventional   objective   elegant   clever   stylish   intelligent quick   charming   tidy   neat   thoughtful   attentive   careful watchful   alert   reliable   inspired   inventive   resourceful   ingenious productive   exciting   energetic   lively   vigorous   bouncy   active joyful   blissful   pleased   ecstatic   cheery   sane   rational   sensible reasonable   normal   complete   capable   genuine   inspiring   proud approachable   peaceful   honest   giving   nurturing   accomplished whole   perfect   undivided   achiever   great   confident   compassionate content   humble   unassuming   happy   satisfied   comfortable   at ease relaxed   able   knowledgeable   skilled   proficient   expert   adept   rich wealthy   affluent   prosperous   full   gorgeous   valuable   abundant

*fruitful powerful deep productive prolific understanding dynamic
useful helpful constructive beneficial positive functional worthwhile*

Now count the number of words you circled in step 2. This will be
called the Actual Self Score.

Total words circled in step 2   =   Actual Self Score

3. The Congruency Score is the percentage of words you circled in
step 2 (Actual Self Score) as compared to the total words scored in
step 1 (Total Potential Score).

$$\text{Congruency Score} = \text{Total Potential Score} \sqrt{\text{Actual Self Score}} \times 100$$

For example, if your Total Potential Score was 120 and your Actual
Self Score was 90, then your Congruency Score would be:

$$120 \sqrt{90} = .75 \times 100 = 75\%$$

If you are a little uncomfortable with division, check with the *table
for conversion of Potential Scores and Actual Self Scores* below for
an estimate of your Congruency Score. To use it, locate the range of
your Total Potential Score on the bottom and the range of your Actual Self Score on the side and the corresponding percentage that is
in the same column as the Total Potential Self Score and row of the
Actual Self Score is the Congruency Score. In our example, see how
75 percent is in the same column as 120 and the same row as 90.
(*Note:* These are *estimates* and may vary from the actual calculated
Congruency Score.)

Actual Self Score

81–90	60%	64%	69%	75%
71–80	53%	57%	62%	67%
61–70	47%	50%	54%	58%
51–60	40%	43%	46%	50%
41–50	33%	36%	38%	42%
31–40	27%	29%	30%	33%
21–30	20%	22%	23%	25%
11–20	13%	14%	15%	17%
0–10	7%	7%	8%	8%
	141–150	131-140	121–130	111–120

Congruency Score

Total Potential Score

Interpretation: If your score is 90 to 100 percent, you are operating in your **full potential** range most of the time, finding happiness and joy from within. You are fulfilling your mission as you see it and very likely have good mental health.

If your score is 75 to 90 percent, you are in the positive range of **living consistently with your authentic self.** You have escaped serious damage to your personal truth, and it is largely unaffected by any negative life experiences you may have encountered. You have good self-esteem that will help you be successful.

If your score is 50 to 75 percent, you are in the positive range and have realized **some good aspects** of who you truly are. However, there are important aspects of your authentic self that you are not fully in touch with. There are very powerful strengths that you are denying yourself and there are some goals you do not feel worthy to achieve. You very likely have some self-doubt and lack of self-confidence in truly appreciating your potential.

If your score is 35 to 50 percent, **you are limiting yourself** and using only a small part of who you really are. You need to make a concerted effort to get back to who you really are. You have been listening to the world telling you who you are, instead of being guided by an undistorted personal truth and concept of self. Much work is needed.

If your score is 1 to 35 percent, **you are living in your fictional self.** Your personal truth and self-concept have been seriously damaged and distorted. You are wasting precious life energy. Your power is infected with fictional concepts and your efforts are misdirected to goals that are not your own.

Think of your results from these tests as a "snapshot," a glance at where you're situated, right now, in terms of your authenticity. If your scores suggest that you are miles away from your authentic self, then we need to talk, and through these pages we will. First I have some bad news, and then I have some good news. The bad news is *you* are making the choices that have put you in this life circumstance; the good news is *you* are making the choices that will put you in a better life circumstance. As I have said many times, you create your own experience.

Now, there are some people, perhaps those who scored in the middle range of one or both of these tests, who'll be tempted to say, "You know, I'm pretty functional. I like myself pretty well, thank you very much. This stuff is for people who are crippled." The reality is that psychology often works best for those who "need it" the least. You might be muddling along and not even know it. Think about it: If all you have ever driven is a 1958 VW with no heater, then you don't know that there are Cadillacs and Mercedes-Benzes and Rolls-Royces out there that give you a different experience of the ride. We are talking here about your ride through life. You may tell yourself that life is good enough—but if it could get a whole lot better, wouldn't you want to know that now rather than find it out later? If right now you feel pretty good about yourself, that's great: It means you'll be starting this process a little farther down the road. On a scale of zero to one hundred, if you are starting at ten you've got a long way to go, and this book will take you there. If on the other hand you are starting at seventy, then we are building on strength. We'll be enhancing who and what you are.

Table for converting Total Potential scores and Actual Self scores into Approximate Congruency percentages.

Actual Self Score

	141–150	131–140	121–130	111–120	101–110	91–100	81–90	71–80	61–70	51–60	41–50	31–40	21–30	11–20	1–10
141–150	100%														
131–140	93%	100%													
121–130	87%	93%	100%												
111–120	80%	86%	92%	100%											
101–110	73%	79%	85%	92%	100%										
91–100	67%	71%	77%	83%	91%	100%									
81–90	60%	64%	69%	75%	82%	90%	100%								
71–80	53%	57%	62%	67%	73%	80%	90%	100%							
61–70	47%	50%	54%	58%	64%	70%	78%	88%	100%						
51–60	40%	43%	46%	50%	55%	60%	67%	75%	86%	100%					
41–50	33%	36%	38%	42%	46%	50%	56%	63%	71%	83%	100%				
31–40	27%	29%	30%	33%	37%	40%	45%	50%	57%	67%	80%	100%			
21–30	20%	22%	23%	25%	28%	30%	34%	38%	43%	50%	60%	75%	100%		
11–20	13%	14%	15%	17%	19%	20%	23%	25%	29%	33%	40%	50%	67%	100%	
1–10	7%	7%	8%	8%	9%	10%	12%	13%	14%	17%	20%	25%	33%	50%	100%

Ranges of Total Potential Scores

Now don't feel overwhelmed if your test results suggest that you wouldn't recognize your authentic self if it came up and tapped you on the shoulder. No matter how far removed from authenticity you feel—no matter how poorly you scored on either or both of these tests, you are not weird, weak, stupid, or crazy. BUT: *You are burning daylight if you're letting your life slip by when you know full well that things just aren't right.*

You will soon see that everything you have and have not become is no accident. It is no accident, because there are no accidents. Even though you may feel like you are trapped in your own life and circumstance, you are not. You aren't a prisoner of the past or a captive to a life that may feel like it is set in stone. You are going to learn that your quality of life didn't just happen; it is, instead, ultimately a product of choices you have made, both internally and externally. That means that whether you knew it or not, you have had, and will always have, a tremendous power to determine your life.

The problem has been that you may not have known that you were in fact making such defining choices, or that there were even choices to be made. Believe me when I tell you that there are always choices to be made and you have always made them. In fact, the truth is you cannot "not choose," even if you wanted to. You cannot not choose because "not choosing" is itself a choice. As we start to deconstruct your life in the following chapters, some things that may have seemed confusing and inaccessible are going to become very clear. You will quickly come to see that you can build on the strength of the good choices you have made, and overcome weaknesses by changing or rechoosing some of the poorer choices you have made. Of particular interest are those choices you have made with regard to how you treat and deal with you.

Bottom line: You, through the choices you have made, either to act or react, have programmed you from the inside out. What's more, you have done so with such a powerful dominance that you have absolutely dictated both the immediate results and the long-term outcomes in your life. The world can pound on you, but you have to choose to "buy it" before you can be impacted by it. We are going to challenge what you may have, at one time, bought into and accepted on blind faith. (Jeez, are you in for an awakening! When you realize some of the crap you have been buying into, you are going to be shocked; I know I was.) All of this process of acting, reacting, choosing, and trying not to choose sometimes happens in an almost invisible, imperceptible fashion, but it is happening nonetheless. Your mind is so busy processing every minute of every day to such a degree that if it were all conscious, it would be overwhelming.

Either way, mysterious or not, overwhelming or not, you are about to "break the code." We are going to slow things down and you are going to stop taking "wooden nickels" when it comes to what you have been accepting and settling for about you! There is a truth and clarity that is available to you, but it can only come from getting real about you and ultimately reconnecting with your authentic self, so that you can make yourself the star in your own life.

Now don't lock up on me here, thinking, I hear you, but I'm stuck! You have no idea how long and stubbornly I have been where I am and what I am. Yes, I do know. This whole deal takes courage. I'll bet that just like me, there have been times in your life when, once you finally woke up to something, that once you called BS on it, once the lightbulb came on, you were stunned that you had been suckered for so long. Well, boy, is that about to happen to you big time. But be honest in answering everything I ask you to think about and deal with, and I mean really honest. Just keep turning the pages, doing the work, and being honest; that's all I ask for now.

The change that has to happen in your personal truth—your self-concept—in order to maximize your life, comes totally from the inside out. That's a good thing, really. Think about it: You can't change the world, you can't change its agendas, and you can seldom change those in your immediate circle. What you can change is the manner in which you engage your world and everyone in it. When you move your position on you, when you reopen the "data window" on who you are, when you begin to reevaluate your concept of self and discover new options, new capabilities, and recognize new control, then you can begin to focus on your authentic self, which is real, instead of your fictional self, which is not. Again, the good news is that the only person you need to successfully get the authentic part of your self uncovered, back in focus, and back in control, is you.

I intend for this book to bring you face-to-face, eye-to-eye, with who you truly are. I intend for you to meet yourself—perhaps for the first time—and discover every unique gift, skill, and ability that has been bestowed upon you, however deeply buried it may be. I intend for us, through the process of this book, to unearth the true self that is uniquely you. I believe that process will energize and empower you in ways that you cannot even imagine.

Let this book serve as your map, your guide for cleaning up your personal truth and self-concept. Let it help you learn the story of you, so that, knowing yourself, you can begin *living by design*.

I want you to reclaim and rebuild your authentic self, the soul that is truly you. In order to do that, you'll need a blueprint. You'll need to have some understanding of the architecture of the self. Unfortunately, in recent years this architecture has been grossly oversimplified. We're all familiar with the image of the little red devil whispering in one ear while the pristine white angel whispers in the other. There are scores of contemporary references to "awakening the sleeping giant" or "letting the inner child come out and play." But things are just not that simple. I strongly believe that either you have been taught nothing at all about discovering and being who you really are or you have been given a bunch of euphemisms, buzzwords, and psychobabble. The rhetoric may be cute and clever, but it has little to do with the architecture of your life and of your being. That's a deficiency that this book will address.

MY FIRST TASK

Understand that this is not an all-or-nothing proposition. As I did, you may have parts of your life that you absolutely love and parts that you absolutely hate. There may be parts that you wish could be added to an otherwise great life. Living for your fictional self, whether it is a totally dominant force or just a partial one, is a dangerous state of being that diverts, absorbs, and robs your life energy. It is a life marked by a forced way of thinking, feeling, and acting. It is a way of life that, whether in whole or in part, is, in the end, highly toxic.

The problem is that the world needs you to behave in a certain way. It needs you to not make waves. It needs you to fit into a bigger plan, a plan that frankly doesn't even begin to consider you as an individual. If you're like most of us, you were raised to be a "good kid," and you were rewarded for pleasing those in authority. Not upsetting the status quo has become a priority for you, whether you recognize it or not. You have gone right along with the expectancies imposed by other people. You have actively participated in your own seduction by selling out for what you don't want. You've gotten used to living an assigned role, rather than living true to who you really are. You have participated in a devastating conspiracy, with you as the unwitting fall guy.

What I mean is that, while you inhabit an insensitive society that is more than happy for you to pass your days as a faceless, obedient statistic, you are not totally a victim. You make an essential contribution by accepting the roles that are assigned you, sometimes almost fortuitously, by those who make up your world: your parents, teachers, friends, spouse, employers, the media, marketers, neighbors, old flames who may have rejected you, and the whole of society. You may have originally resisted, but then ultimately sold out, giving them what they demanded, without consideration for what you truly want.

You may be asking yourself, If that's the case, then why have I not done this reformulation of self before? I always say that there are two primary differences between humans and animals: thumbs and reason. Now we know what you have been doing with your thumbs all this time. What have you been doing with your reason?

I am betting that you are distracted so much of the time by just trying to keep up with the pace of life that there is little, if any, time to work on you and what is really important to you, versus just "dancing for the world." The expectancies and demands that compete for your time and energy are increasing at a dizzying rate. Result? You have lost yourself—literally—in a blur of hyperactivity and diversion.

Then there is fear: the fear of change, of stepping out into the unknown. Fear is a crucial issue, and one that we will have to address together: your fears connected to your job, your marriage (or lack thereof), your health, the challenges facing your children, watching your body age, or a million other things that may be keeping you paralyzed, pessimistic, shut down, and insecure. Finding the positives about yourself can be difficult, even when you consciously focus on the task.

But make no mistake: At the core of every human being is a uniqueness, individuality, and distinctiveness that demands to be expressed. You are no exception. However deeply your individuality may currently be buried—no matter how lost or nonunique you may feel—you *are* in there. Through these pages I am coming, and I am coming for *you*. *Your* job is to jump into this project with a willingness to give to it your time, your unadulterated candor, and your utmost passion. You must commit to reconnecting with yourself, whether you are encouraged by others to do so or not. You must be willing to ask yourself the hard questions that I'm going to pose to you and give honest, no-nonsense answers to them, no matter how unbecoming those answers might be. Starting now, you must hold yourself to a new standard of self-examination.

My promise, in turn, is to show you the fallacies of the inauthentic life, the conspiracies in which you are a hapless participant, and a way to get back to your authenticity. Conspiracy happens in the dark. It happens in the deep recesses of who you are. Monsters and ghosts work in the dark, just as our fears mount without light. And the fictional life, the mythical life, is a monster. We are going to flip the switch and turn on the floodlights. We will watch the myths shrink away like cowards. You are going to get back your power so that you can serve yourself and, therefore, those you love.

YOUR FIRST TASK

Beginning right now, with only the second chapter of this book, I am asking you to call a huge "time-out" from this scramble you call life, and to focus on the one doing the scrambling: *you*. I am asking you, demanding of you that you focus fully and unapologetically on you. This will not be a journey of selfishness and self-absorption. You are not the hub of the universe, and all things do not revolve around you.

I hold to the rather old-fashioned belief that each of us is blessed with particular gifts given to us by God, and that it is our sacred obligation to identify, to cherish, and to exercise those gifts for the betterment of ourselves and of those in our lives. I believe that the more responsibility you exercise toward yourself, the more responsible you can become toward others. I believe that one of the greatest gifts you can offer the other people in your life is your authentic self, rather than your fictional self. From the authentic self flows a peace and clarity that can only benefit and enrich the lives of those you love.

The process of reconnecting with your authentic self will be an incredible experience. Living in daily authentic congruence will yield a joy and freedom of indescribable proportion. The process will be detailed to you in upcoming chapters. Expect that you will be immersed in a series of challenges that will require a commitment of both heart and soul. You will:

- Examine and demystify your past life experiences, so as to control rather than be controlled by them.
- Identify with refreshing clarity your purpose for being in this world.

- Identify with the same degree of clarity the composition of your authentic self, and the skills and abilities that define you at your absolute core.
- Create a "track to run on," where you, by your choices and actions, allow your authentic self to find expression.
- Give up your fear of the unknown and climb out of your comfort zone.

You must be very, very careful not to let others in your life dissuade you from your task. People truly do fear change, particularly when it involves their most personal lives and relationships. They may become especially frightened if what you are doing might involve requiring more from them. If the people closest to you get the idea that the "price of poker" is about to go up, that you are all of a sudden going to stop being the silent and obedient sheep and start expecting more from yourself and others, they may get threatened in a big way. You can be sensitive to that and help them to a degree, but you must let them own and be responsible for their own feelings. This is about you; it is not about them.

We are going to begin by demystifying your past and this concept of "self." Once we turn the floodlights on over your self-concept and put your past under the microscope, you are going to hear yourself saying, "Oh! Now I get it—now I see what has been driving my life. More importantly, I now see what I can do to let my authentic self take control!" If you're ready to begin this process of discovery, read on.

3 YOUR SELF-CONCEPT

"What lies behind us and what lies before us are tiny matters compared to what lies within us."

—RALPH WALDO EMERSON

FOR this book to be meaningful—in fact, life-changing—I must "operationally" define the self. I cannot afford to be vague about it or you can't use the information very well. "Operational definition" is a term of art used in the scientific literature and when you define something "operationally" you eliminate any chance for confusion. What it boils down to is breaking down even the most complex concept in terms of its steps: A, B, C, D, and so on. If you know every step or element of that which is to be defined, you are crystal clear about what is meant. Now, I'll confess that, as with a lot of my thinking, I *read* about this concept in school, but I *learned* about, I truly figured it out, in the real world (that means I did something really stupid, but did learn a lesson).

One summer right after high school, I got offered the job of tearing down an old house near my parents' home in Texas. I knew the old man who owned the lot and he wanted it cleared so he could build a new house there. The existing house was a dilapidated wreck. It had no windows or doors; the ceilings had long since caved in, and it was full of old furniture, auto parts, and fifty-five-gallon drums. When he offered me the job, the owner simply said, "Hey, tell you what. You're good at tearing stuff up. I'll pay you two hundred and fifty bucks to get rid of that old house. Just scrape her off the slab and haul her off." Well, I was, in fact, pretty good at destroying things and damn proud of it. My dad used to say that he could give me an anvil at noon and I would tear it up by dark! There's an art and a skill to being an irresponsible screwup and being totally worthless all summer and I was so good at being worthless that I think I was what worthless wants to be when it grows up!

In short, this sounded like it was right up my alley, and $250 was more money than I'd ever seen in one place, ever. So, done deal! I would "scrape her off." I recruited a buddy who had at least as much destructive flair as did I, and we showed up early the next morning, pumped and ready to go. Much to our dismay, we soon found out that the walls of this fifty-year-old house were a foot thick and made of solid plaster. I'll promise you that those walls were harder than any substance known to man before we started the space program. In fact, I think it was in those walls that we discovered titanium! And inside those walls were wood framing, doorjambs, window jambs, and incredibly heavy beams. Looking around this fortress, we realized that, at $250, that old boy had really put the britches on us. He was no doubt laughing all the way to the bank over that deal. I was about to wipe that smile right off his face; neither of us knew it yet, but I was.

Well, for two days we attacked that house with sledgehammers, crowbars, ropes, and chains. After two days, we were more battered and bruised than the house was. We were getting absolutely nowhere. Now, having always considered myself rather cerebral, I decided that we just needed to work smarter, not harder. So I immediately knocked small holes in the walls, looped chains around the corners of the house, then hooked them onto the pickup, with the theory that we would just pull the whole thing down in one fell swoop, load her up, and that would be that. Not only did that not work, we burned up two good tires trying. That poor old pickup truck was "crying" under the strain as we just smoked the two rear tires. Then the chain broke, and we shot forward like a rocket, careened through the neighbors' front hedge and wiped out a pillar on their porch. This did not help the pickup and we seemed to be tearing down the wrong house. Now, I was pretty upset about that damage until, about an hour later, as we were hauling a load of concrete chunks to the rock quarry, I backed too close to the edge, and the left rear tire slipped over the side. Let me tell you, all hell broke loose in the blink of an eye. All the rock in the back immediately slid to one side, flipped the pickup in the air, and rolled it six times down the ravine. Suddenly, I found I wasn't near as upset as I had been about the fender that had been dented on the front porch. So much for working smarter.

But not being one to give up, and wanting to be innovative, I had a great idea. "What if we burned that sucker to the ground?" I figured if we could torch everything inside the plaster walls, we'd be able just to shovel it out. Next, I figured we could take our already beat-up truck and ram the walls until they caved in. (I know, I know, but I was only seventeen; what can I tell you?)

In any event, we showed up early Sunday morning with three gallons of gasoline, and doused the entire inside of the house. With one match, that old house went up like you wouldn't believe. Standing there watching the fire do its thing, I remember thinking, This is going to work out okay—an instant later, the fire burst through the roof, caught all the surrounding trees on fire, and burned through the power line overhead. Concerned that flames were shooting close to a hundred feet in the air, some neighbors called the fire department, right before everybody's electricity and phones went out in about a six-block radius. Here came the fire department. They were battling the blaze when it got so hot inside the house that the fire ignited the sewer gas, which promptly exploded. The explosion blew the toilets loose in houses all over the neighborhood. Manhole covers were blown twenty feet in the air. Not good, not good at all.

Now, here's my point. When that guy that put the britches on us for $250 told us to "take her down," he did not *operationally de-*

fine what he meant. If he had been specific enough to operationally define what it was he wanted us to do, there would never have been a fire. He didn't grasp the creativity with which I could be stupid at the age of seventeen. If he had appreciated my full capacity, and had operationally defined getting rid of the house, he might have said:

1. Remove the roof with pry bars, tossing it to the ground where it can be loaded and hauled off.
2. Strip the framing from inside the house, stack it onto the truck, and haul it off.
3. Tear out the floors, braces, and beams, and haul them off, as well.

He could have gone on and on and on. Instead, with my seventeen-year-old reasoning, and since he wasn't clear, I just set the neighborhood on fire and blew up the sewers for six blocks.

What that incident taught me was that if you are unclear in defining what you're talking about, there's too much room for error and poor judgment. Not that you're as stupid as I once was, but I don't want to have that problem when we're talking about self-concept. I don't want you trying to "freelance" when it comes to understanding it. I want to tell you specifically what operations define self-concept, so that there's no mystery about what's going on.

By that I mean that I must identify not just what the self is, but how it comes to be what it is. I have to write with "verbs in my sentences" so that it's clear what you must *do* in order to make important changes. I must also answer some important questions:

- What are the actual, real-world, internal, and external actions you have done and are doing to create yourself as an entity in this world?
- What are the thought and feeling patterns that both influence and result from how you see and feel about yourself?

- What are the behaviors, actions, and reactions that have created the results you have gotten in your everyday life, results that have, once perceived by you, shaped who you have become?
- What are the choices that you have made that have led to those results that you now live with?
- How do you come to make new choices and new behaviors, to create new and more productive results?

Once you appreciate the meaning and importance of these questions, and begin to ask them about your own life, you will have begun the crucial task of understanding your own **self-concept.** That may sound like "psychologist talk," so let's stop right here and get comfortable with the term.

Everybody, including you, has a detailed self-concept. Self-concept is the bundle of beliefs, facts, opinions, and perceptions about yourself that you travel through life with, every moment of every day. Please understand that you have a self-concept right now. You are not going to "get one" just because you are reading this book. The problem is that you may not be consciously aware of half of the stuff that's in there. By that I mean that if I handed you a pen and paper right now and asked you to write down everything you believe about yourself, you wouldn't be able to come up with even half of what you believe about yourself.

That's a problem. It means you may have powerful beliefs about yourself that you can't challenge or change, *because you're not even aware that they exist.* It means there are an awful lot of things influencing you, and how you present yourself to the world, that you don't even know about. Your self-concept may be constantly changing or it may seem to have been set in stone a long time ago, but you do have a self-concept. It is there, and it determines your life. Everything you do and feel and, more importantly, *how* you do it or feel it, stems from this perception of self.

It should be obvious, then, why self-concept is so important. A person whose self-concept is flush with confidence will engage the world differently than a person whose self-concept is riddled with doubt. What you believe about you, what you treat as your own self-reality, is dramatically important in your plight in life. In fact, it is so crucially important that it is not an overstatement to say that there is a direct link from your concept of self to the ultimate outcome in your life. The dots connect this way:

You accumulate certain life experiences that you react to and interpret;

The result is a set of beliefs about yourself: judgments about competency, worth, lovability, acceptability, and strength and power;

Based on that self-evaluation, and the assignment to self of certain attributes, you adopt a consistent persona that you present to the world;

Based on that bundle of self-relevant and self-generated identifying characteristics and its presentation to the world, you make a statement to the world and everything that happens: Every success or failure, every result in terms of love, money, achievement, recognition, peace, and harmony, flows from that self-determined identity.

When I say you make a statement to the world, know this: I mean you send messages verbally, behaviorally, emotionally, physically, spiritually, and interactively. Only 7 percent of all communications are verbal, and for every thought you have there is a physiological correlate. Ask yourself what your other 93 percent is screaming if your self-concept (which you thought you hid so well) is compromised. Think about your demeanor and your attitude of approach to the world. What is it saying about you?

As I have said many times, when you choose the behavior, you choose the consequences, and your choice of demeanor is no different. You are a creator of the responses you get from the world. If you prefer the "shrink term" for this, you are a *stimulus* of those responses. That simply means that the manner and style with which you engage other people is going to determine how they respond to you. When you approach with anger, you tend to get anger in return. When your style of engagement says "loser," the world tends to treat you as such. When your conversation, posture, and bearing communicate "victim," you soon wear everybody out; sympathetic at first, they eventually become impatient and restless. That, however, is not the only way you can "run them off." The opposite approach can be just as obnoxious. When your message to the world is, "I'm in charge here—this is *my* sandbox and I don't care one whit about you or what you want," then once again the people in your life quickly decide that they don't want to play there anymore. Everybody has his or her own style of engagement. Very few people, however, have ever stopped to consider what their style is. Yet it is a topic of the utmost importance. Why? *Because as you begin to engage the world differently, then all of the responses and reactions you get change, as well.* Your style of engagement stimulates an entirely different quality of give-and-take with the world. Accordingly, your style of engagement is most definitely a topic for us to address. You must realize and accept a fundamental truth about relating to others: You are either contributing to or contaminating all of your relationships, sixty minutes an hour, twenty-four hours a day, seven days a week. There is no neutrality. As we move forward you must remain cognizant of the fact that you are doing one or the other *all* of the time.

What is truly amazing is that this fundamental and outcome-determinative element of our life experience so often develops and then occurs both passively and unconsciously. The shaping of your self-concept, and many of the choices you have made in life that contributed to that concept and then how it gets expressed, may very well have happened with little or no appreciation of the gravity of what was going on. You may have sent messages that said you would passively allow the world and all the people in it to assign you roles that you wouldn't have chosen in a million years—and so they did. With enough time and repetition, those roles, inherited because of the statement you made that invited their assignment, ultimately become so embedded in the fiber of your being and personality that they seemingly consume you.

We all recognize, for example, how acute the sting of rejection can be. Not getting picked for the team; not being asked to the dance; being turned down for a date; being turned down for a job you really wanted; having a marriage that ends with rejection and failure; getting fired. Those moments of rejection are naturally painful. What happens is that, for most people, that rejection is treated as "data." It's a piece of information that gets incorporated into your deepest understanding of who you are. No matter what the factual circumstances of the event were, or what the facts are now, the pain of the rejection overwhelms and distorts the facts. If this is true in your life, it means you may have developed a self-concept that is based almost entirely upon how you feel or imagine other people see you, and we're back to opinion again. It's true that beauty is in the eye of the beholder. Why in the world would you give your power away to some random "beholder"? So some boy or girl in school did not think you were cute and funny and worthy of dating, *so what*! As the old saying goes, "Nobody died and left them in charge." Yet you may have dragged that experience, or some other just like it, around with you for many, many years and not even been aware of how it was affecting you.

I will give you a clue as to my thinking: I think there's a high likelihood that there has been a whole lot less *conscious* self-determination in defining who you are and a whole lot more input that you have automatically adopted. It's as if you've got this vessel called "self" that people can come by and throw things in. Suppose I asked you to evaluate each item and decide whether to keep it or pitch it out. You might pick up each thing, look at it, and say something like, "Okay. This part of me is where I really worked hard and did well in school, and I'm proud of that. That stays. Okay, now this piece right here is where my dad, who never had a happy, peaceful day in his life, constantly criticized me and told me what a piece of scum I was—well, I'm throwing that out. I'm not going to keep that." But people don't do that. They don't say, "How did I get where I am?" Those things inside the self are just there. People don't evaluate how they got there; they're just there.

That passive approach is what I call the Popeye theory of life management: "I am what I am." It's an approach that asks no questions, seeks no answers, and leaves you stuck right where you are. It's an attitude that I flatly reject, and so should you. That is why I want to **demystify every bit of your self-concept.** My goal is to help you look inside the vessel. I want you to examine its contents, item by item. Together, let's find out what your self-concept is, and how it came to be what it is. If you care about your life, and if you'll commit to do the work required, this journey into you will be a fascinating revelation of being. That's a fancy way of saying, "You're not going to believe how little you know about who you are, and how much you're getting ready to learn about who you are!"

Ultimately, I want to empower you to walk out of your history. You hear people say things like, "You've got to 'rise above your raising,' " or "You can't be a prisoner of the past," or whatever. But those sayings are too general and abstract to be of much use. They demonstrate why I say the self is often discussed and seldom understood. It may be more helpful to think of the mechanics this way: *The past reaches into the present, and programs the future, by your recollections and your internal rhetoric about what you perceived to have happened in your life.* I recognize that that's a mouthful. But I don't want you just to "blow by" a truth that is so fundamental to your understanding of your own self-concept. In order to get the most from the chapters that lie ahead, you'll need to be familiar with the formula. "Stacking" the individual elements may help you to see them better, and to bring each one into proper focus:

The past reaches into the present
And programs the future

By your recollections
And your internal rhetoric
About what you perceived to have happened in your life.

Looking at this formula, you'll have some idea of the roadmap we'll be following. You'll see that if you're serious about rising above your raising—if that is going to be an action-filled step in your life, rather than just a trite expression—you'll need to get really honest with yourself about what that raising was. You will need to be candid and thorough about what your past contains. You'll want to account for the significant events, and your memories of them, that have entered your self-concept. Finally, as we progress through this book, you'll understand that one way your past seeps into the present is through your own internal rhetoric: that is, the dialogues in which **you tell yourself what you have been told, so persistently and destructively, by others in your life.** That means that before you can hope to step out of the prison of your past, you need to identify with great clarity what it is that you say to yourself, when, and why.

As all of this suggests, it is vitally important for you to know your history, and that's what we'll be working on. But keep your eye on the ultimate goal: Know your history, *so you can walk out of it.* The only reason that you need to evaluate where you've *been* is so you can make the appropriate decisions about who you are and where you're going. You won't hear me say, "Okay, you were abused as a child, so you aren't responsible for being so shy and reclusive. Go ahead and keep on being that way. At least you know why you are how you are; now you have insight." Not even close. I look at it and say, "You were abused as a child, which may explain *why* you have chosen to be shy and reclusive, but now that you realize that, you're going to have to do something about it." It's not an excuse; it's just a diagnosis. This of course presupposes that you will at least acknowledge that there is more out there for you, and that you want it.

• • •

In talking to people about the authentic self, I've often noticed a strange phenomenon. As soon as I start talking about how the authentic self gives you power, vision, and passion, some people just stare at the ground; they grin sheepishly and dig their toe in the carpet; they look around to see who in the world I'm talking to. It's as if they're saying, "Power? Vision? Passion? Did somebody famous just come in the room?" They can't imagine that I'm talking about them. They're saying to themselves, Hey, I'm not some movie star. I'm no world leader or hero, righting the wrongs of the world. I'm just living my life day to day, going to work or raising kids, trying to make my bills, control my weight, watch a little television, and worry about tomorrow.

It may be that you, just like the "toe-diggers" I've met, don't feel like a big deal, either. Maybe it sounds melodramatic to be describing your life with words like power, vision, and passion, because, after all, we're just talking about you, right? There may be a little voice inside that says, "Those things are for other people. That's just lofty talk you put in books. He can't be talking about me."

But if you're really honest with yourself, don't you admit that, at least occasionally, you do seem to know or at least think about the possibility that there's more to you than you are living? More ability, more joy, more peace? Okay, so you may not become a movie star or a world leader in the sense of having the prestige of the world stage, but you *can* become a star: the star of your own life. You can, you should, and you will.

Fairly exciting concept, don't you think? However grandiose it may sound, I believe that this world was designed with *you* in mind. I believe that you have a special place in the order of life, a particular role to fill. And yes, it is one filled with vision, passion, and power. So hang on and get ready to get way more consciously into your own life. Don't feel selfish or egotistical because you are saying, "I want more!" If you were fully in touch with your authentic self, you wouldn't be apologetically thinking, Hey, it's just me—no big deal. You would be thinking, Hey, this is *my life* we're talking about, and

I want my shot! I want to star in my own life. If you are not quite ready to say that yet, then trust me enough to let me say it for you.

In turn, you've got to acknowledge your responsibility here. Every silver lining has its dark cloud in the middle, and this one is no exception. It's a great deal to have the opportunity to enhance your life, but I'm not just saying that you have the right to do it; I'm saying that you have a *responsibility* to do it. You have a responsibility to maximize the opportunity. Choosing to live reactively and passively, instead of taking the initiative to discover and actively live true to your authentic self, cheats you, the world, and everyone in it. It particularly cheats those with whom you directly share your life. Failure to fully connect with and live out your best qualities means that your sons or daughters, your husband or wife, your family and friends, settle for some second-best, counterfeit you: your fictional self.

In essence, you have a duty because it is true that to whom much is given, much is expected. Whether or not you feel like it right now, I promise you that you have been given much. So guess what? From you, much is expected. Effectively living your unique and authentic self demands that you maximize all of your distinct attributes.

Bottom line: Maximum results demand maximum you! Your job is to find, plug into, and live consistently with your core, authentic self. The first step in that process is to become intimately acquainted with your self-concept.

To make your ride through your self-concept a little smoother, we need a working vocabulary, key terms to apply along the way without the need for further explanation. For starters, let's revisit the two big categories that were mentioned just briefly earlier: external factors and internal factors. It is in the development and interaction of these two categories that the self-concept is created.

As you've already seen, **external factors** are events, experiences, and consequences that shape your self-concept from the outside. They are myriad different occurrences that influence how you perceive yourself and how you engage with the world. You can be impacted either directly, by experiencing the direct consequences of your own actions and through your own involvements, or you learn vicariously, by observing the behavior and consequences of others. For example, as you watch what happens to family members and friends as they succeed or fail, their experiences in life also write on the slate that is you.

The father of a patient I treated years ago had tried all his life to "make the big play," to "have his ship come in": in other words, to have the big payoff. Unfortunately, all of his repeated attempts at the big payoff ended in financial disaster. His wife, my patient's mother, struggled for years with the frustrations of a husband who never experienced anything but failure. After watching all this, my patient taught herself never to create any kind of high expectations and never to believe in men. Her mother's experiences guided her own behavior well into adulthood. In other words, her mother's pain— pain that she lived vicariously—became an external factor in her life.

Some of the most powerful external factors are those I call *defining moments*. Your defining moments may include episodes of trauma or tragedy; maybe they are instances of victory or perseverance. The point is that, no matter who you are or how routine your life may have become, you will find that against this backdrop of routineness are certain moments in time that stand out in sharp relief and are crystal clear in your memory. It is those few moments, a surprisingly small number, that may well have shaped the entire rest of your life.

You have also made a number of *critical choices*. Again, most of the choices in your life today may be commonplace and unremarkable. You choose what to wear each day, where to have lunch, what TV shows to watch: These are the routine choices of everyday life. Yet reflecting on your personal history, you should also be able to identify a handful of critical choices, choices you've made that have shaped the remainder of your life. As with defining moments, those decisions can teach you much about who and how you have become who you are.

Along with your defining moments and critical choices, you have also encountered a small number of *pivotal people* who have shaped you both positively and negatively. Identifying who those people are, and what role they have played in forming your personal truth and self-concept, will be a key element of getting in control of your future life quality.

You will recall that your self-concept is impacted by another set of factors, as well: the **internal factors**, reactions that you create within you in response to the world. These are very specific processes that go on inside you and determine how you perceive your place in the pecking order of this life and your entitlement to quality. Internal factors encompass the things you tell yourself, the things you believe about yourself, all of the internal dialogue that shapes your self-concept. These internal factors comprise the content of your personal truth.

It is best that you think about internal factors as *behaviors*, behaviors that you perform internally. Now behaviors, by definition, must be observable. The behaviors we're talking about in this case are observable only by a public of one: you. They are behaviors, even though you never move a muscle, because you are actively making choices. Through these choices you can either behave your way down the tubes or you can behave your way to what you want and deserve. That is both the good news and the bad news. You may be choosing really dumb stuff that is not good for you—but you can also choose differently. It's under your control. This category of internal factors recognizes that there is no reality; only perception: What is true about you in your mind, you will live. If you believe that you are inferior, inadequate, worthless, incompetent, you will live down to that truth. If you believe that you are the opposite of all that, you will live up to that truth. It's like the old saying: If you think you can or you think you cannot, you are probably right! As I have said, we all have our own personal truth, and we live that truth.

As we prepare to lift things out of your vessel of self, examining each one, let me introduce these factors in a little bit more detail. Getting familiar with the names of these powerful factors now will smooth your journey through the coming chapters.

Locus of control asks, Where is the source of my power? Where is the source of responsibility for the events that happen in my life? How people perceive their own locus of control determines, to a great extent, how they interpret and respond to events. Generally speaking, people's locus of control is either *external* or *internal*. If your locus of control is external,

Whatever bad happens, you take no ownership of it,
Whatever good happens, you take no ownership of it.

Whereas a person with internal locus of control operates from a self-concept that says,

Anything bad that happens is my fault.
Anything good that happens, I deserve credit for.

Internal Dialogue

This is the conversation that you have with yourself about everything that's going on in your life. You have just read a sentence from this book; what you are thinking about it is your internal dialogue. If you were to put the book down, your internal dialogue might continue to be about this book, or it might shift to something entirely different, *but it would not stop*. In fact, that is one of the three fundamental characteristics about internal dialogue that you must understand, right now:

1. Your internal dialogue is **constant;**
2. Your internal dialogue happens **in real time:** It unfolds at the same speed with which you would say the actual words if you were speaking them out loud; and

3. Your internal dialogue provokes a **physiological change:** As a result of every thought you have, there is a physical reaction.

We will address each one of these characteristics and its consequences for your life in the pages that follow. Just be aware that all three of them have been, are now, and will be at work in determining and understanding who you are.

Labeling

Humans have a need to "organize" everything, including one another, into groups, subgroups, classes, teams, functions, and the like. We tend to categorize ourselves and others under certain headings or labels. I repeat: We attach labels, not just to other people, but to *ourselves.* Whether these labels are wrong or right, fair or unfair, they have a powerful influence on the perception of self. As you will see, you live to the labels that you apply to yourself.

Tapes

These are things that you have come to believe at such a deeply ingrained, overlearned level that they become automatic. Tapes are values, beliefs, and expectancies that constantly "play" in your head and program you to behave in a certain fashion. They often influence your behavior without your awareness because they can be so overlearned that they occur at lightning speed. As contrasted with a label ("I'm a loser"), a tape has a context: As you go into a job interview, you say to yourself, I never get the good job. When you're trying to get the cute girl or guy to go out with you, you're saying to yourself, I never win, because I'm never interesting. It should be clear, then, that the particular danger—and promise—of a tape is that *it has the power to set you up for a specific outcome.* Often that outcome can be defined by the beliefs, thoughts, and mental rules that bind you to these labels. I call these fixed beliefs/limiting beliefs.

Fixed Beliefs/Limiting Beliefs

Fixed beliefs are beliefs you have about yourself, other people, and the circumstances in your life that have been repeated so long that they have become entrenched; they are highly resistant to change. Limiting beliefs are beliefs that you have specifically about yourself that cause you to limit what you reach for, and therefore, what you achieve. The problem with such beliefs is that they cause us to close the data window. For example, having grown up in a hostile, abusive home, you might conclude, "I'm trash." Result? *Slam!* goes the data window to any conflicting information. The mechanism through which you receive new data goes into "confirm mode": with that radar we talked about earlier picking up a very small sample, a select few bits of information, namely, only things that confirm what you already believe—"I'm trash." You don't listen to contrary, positive information, *because it is simply impossible for you to believe.*

To help frame these concepts in "real world" terms, allow me to share with you an episode from my own family life. After my dad died some years ago, my wife, Robin, and I invited my mom to come live with us. Immediately after my father's untimely death, "Granma," as we all called her, was understandably reeling in the worst way. She was confused, afraid, and living alone in a cavernously empty house after fifty-three years of marriage. My wife and I were, just coincidentally, in the process of building a new home nearby. With a very few changes, we were able to create a private, yet integrated place for her in our home, which we willingly, excitedly did. Our two boys were dancing in the streets to have their Granma moving in. That way she could spoil them full-time! We helped her sell a lot of the things she and my dad had accumulated over the years, box up the rest, and move into a beautiful portion of our new home.

Everything was going to be set up just right for her. Robin and I were determined that, after a lifetime of hard work keeping house, picking up after her kids, tending the yard, and being devoted to her family in every way, Granma was going to get the royal treatment.

Every day, a housekeeper came in to make her bed. Breakfast, lunch, and dinner were ready and waiting, whenever she wanted, without her having to lift a finger. From her quarters, she could look outside and watch the sun rise over beautiful landscaping, flowerbeds, and a lawn that the yardman kept immaculate and lush. As her grandsons grew up, she would have a front-row seat. Her job was simply to enjoy it, and to tell us if she needed anything. She was excited and receptive, and she moved right in.

After about a year of this, it became clear to me that she wasn't enjoying it. The spark had faded from her eyes. She seemed to just shuffle from room to room, listless and withered. She was noticeably "old."

"Granma," I said to her one day, "you don't look okay. Is something bothering you?"

Tears welled up in her eyes. There was an awkward pause, as she seemed to struggle to find the words. Finally, she looked up at me and said, "How can I tell my son and daughter-in-law, who have been so kind, that I don't want to live in their warm and wonderful home?"

I encouraged her to speak her mind. She said, "I miss my house. I miss my life. There's no carpet to vacuum, no bed to make. I haven't got a yard to mow or a garden to take care of. There's no purpose for me. I have no reason for being here."

When she said "no reason for being here," it was clear to me what she meant: "I have no reason for being *in this world.*"

Well, we remedied that situation in a hurry. Once again, the family gathered, this time to help Granma relocate to her very own little "dollhouse" in a busy, hustling and bustling neighborhood close by. You can try going over there, but you may not get much of a visit: Granma will probably be too busy pushing a mower around her little yard at full throttle, smoke billowing out of the machine, or else you'll find her whacking away at some weed that dared to intrude among her rows and rows of flowers. That yard is now as luxuriant and beautiful as any green at Augusta National Golf Club, and the house is a little jewel: a perfectly arranged, perfectly comfortable dollhouse of a home. She's got more projects going on over there than any of the rest of us can keep track of. Neighbors are constantly stopping by for conversation and coffee, and kids like to play in her yard and on her sidewalk, because they know Granma always has a big smile and a kind word.

The activity around her house only hints at the changes in my mom. She is a completely different person. Please understand: She would be the first to tell you that she still misses my dad, and that she deeply appreciates the fact that my wife and I gave her a place to be while she came to grips with her life-altering loss. At the same time, she has carved out for herself a life that she loves. Twenty years seem to have fallen away from her: there's a light in her eyes, a spring in her step. I could swear her IQ jumped by half as her mind got active again, and she's definitely got her sense of humor back. The move to her own place has completely transformed her.

My mom's experience illustrates some of the terms that we've been talking about, terms you need to become familiar with before we start examining and reorganizing your self-concept.

The first thing to observe is that, in my mom's life, there was a *defining moment:* her husband died. That was an event that clearly was going to affect my mom's life in a variety of profound ways. Few things in life create as much upheaval and change as the loss of a spouse.

Secondly, once the defining moment had occurred, my mom's *internal factors* kicked in as she began interpreting what had happened in her life. Her conversation with herself, her internal dialogue, probably sounded something like this: Joe is gone. He was my partner, my support. I can't make it on my own. I was dependent on him for so long, I am afraid that I don't have what it takes. I'm seventy-two years old. I haven't had a job in thirty years. There's no way I can take care of myself.

Next, she made a *critical choice*. Having experienced the defining moment and begun the internal dialogue, she arrived at this decision: I will allow myself to be taken care of. People want me to do it; they expect me to do it; they love me, and they mean well. They probably know what's best for me at my age. I don't really want to give up my independence, my home, and my things I spent my life acquiring, but I have no choice. I'll miss my furniture, my pictures, my privacy, but I have no choice. I'll do it. That was a choice that would prove to make a world of difference to her self-concept. Once the die was cast, and she moved into our house, I'll bet that Granma's internal dialogue started up again with a vengeance and was going on all the time. Whenever she found herself restless or uneasy, the internal dialogue was right there to tell her, I don't have what it takes. There's no way I can take care of myself. Family knows best. I'd better act happy, or else I'm going to hurt a lot of people's feelings. I need to just go along to get along.

And what was her result? The outcome of this sequence—**defining moment, internal dialogue, critical choice**—was a prolonged gloom: month after month of confusion, unhappiness, and self-doubt. Without our—or her—being entirely aware of what was going on inside her, my mom was becoming more and more miserable. No one was keeping her captive, yet she felt like a prisoner in a gilded cage. She was living to a fictional self, created and imposed upon her, with the best of intentions, by loving relatives and by her own internal dialogue.

Now consider this. If you had asked her, at any time, during those first months in our home, "Granma, how are you doing?" I know with certainty that she would have forced a smile and answered, "Fine, thank you. I'm doing just fine." She would not have been lying. Lying would imply that she could distinguish, with clarity, her authentic self; it would mean that she recognized that she wasn't fine, but was saying otherwise. On the contrary, she simply assumed that she could trust the information she was getting from her fictional self: I'm old, I'm a widow, I need to be taken care of, I'm being taken care of by people who love me; therefore, I must be fine.

Such is the power of the fictional self. Life can be cruel and confusing, causing even the most balanced, focused, and well-intended person to lose his or her way. You may have at one time lived with passion and excitement, clearly recognizing your strengths, gifts, values, and other unique characteristics—only to have your experiences in life blur your vision.

Any number of things may have affected your perception of self. It wasn't necessarily the death of a loved one. Maybe your hope, optimism, and innocence died as a result of tragic and painful experiences in your childhood. Perhaps it happened later in life, when someone you loved and sought companionship from rejected you. Perhaps it occurred even later, when despite your hard work, a business or marriage failed. You may even have felt separated from God when tragedy inexplicably filled your life.

Unfortunately, life is not a success-only journey, and sometimes these unwanted results can shake our faith and make us doubt who we really are, or even **why we are.** In your own life, events may have slowly accumulated toward an unnoticed erosion of confidence and identity; by contrast, maybe your negative consequences struck like lightning. It may be that years of self-doubt have brought you to a crisis of self, a painful compromise of dreams and vision. On the other hand, maybe for you it's less defined. Perhaps there's just a quiet awareness that you can and want to do more, that you want to add to a life that in many respects is working well. Maybe a part of you says, Everything is just fine, while another part, subtly but insistently, asks, Fine, yes—but *compared to what?*

Either way, whether the need is dramatic or subtle, to settle for anything less than a full and passionate life is to **give in to the distortions of life.** It is to deny your authentic self. Again, let me emphasize: No matter how much you doubt it, your authentic self is there. Life may blur the vision; events may accumulate and bury everything that defines you; but it's there.

And whether or not you accept it yet, I hope you at least understand my earlier statement that you are an active contributor to the self-concept that you are now living. Certainly, as we have just discussed, there have been defining events in your life. Those external factors explain a great deal about who you are. But just as importantly, if not more so, you have reacted to and interpreted those experiences. You have responded with a variety of internal factors that you must now be willing to put under a microscope.

Here's the deal: knowledge is power. I want your experience of this book to be a leap into knowledge. I'm going to present you with what I hope are a lot of extremely thought-provoking questions, designed to bring you back into contact with your authentic self. By answering the questions honestly and thoughtfully, you will begin to exercise the real power that comes with the courage of honesty. You will learn that you cannot be who and what you are unless you have a lifestyle, both internally and externally, that is designed to support that definition of self. Once you **take control of** such things as your internal dialogue (**you're not going to believe the crap that you've been telling yourself**), and your other interpretive behaviors, you are going to love the power you have to create the experience you want.

All of this is likely to be a huge stretch, because it will mean letting go of some long-standing and powerful momentums in your life. Remember: You must be willing to challenge virtually every thought, attitude, behavior pattern, and life circumstance in which you find yourself.

To sum up: You have a self-concept and I want you to know how you got it. It didn't just happen. You entered this world with certain core qualities and characteristics, but almost immediately the world began to write on the slate that is you. You have been both an active and a passive participant in its creation. To some extent, your self-concept was forced on you by others, and to some extent you have just automatically accepted it, even elicited it. Either way, you became who you are living as today and I intend to show you how to take total control of you and this process of fashioning your "self," in the here and now. When we are finished, you will be able to fully and completely overwhelm your history and momentum.

Together, let's find out what your self-concept really contains.

Let's challenge every message you have ever been given about your-self and discard those messages that are toxic. And let the destina-tion that we're traveling toward be this: **From here forward, your external and internal factors will be affected by you, instead of the other way around.**

INTRODUCTION TO
EXTERNAL FACTORS

*"Faced with crisis, the man of character
falls back on himself."*

— CHARLES DE GAULLE

YOU now know that your concept of self is at the very core of your life experience. Apathy, pain, fear, frustration, anger, and the sense of being disconnected from your own life are the price you pay for losing touch with your authentic self. Obviously, you would not create such an existence on purpose. If your life isn't working the way you want it to, it's not because you planned it that way. You're not some moron who can't tell the difference between pain and pleasure. Given the clear choice, all of us, you included, would definitely choose a life that was consistent with the authentic side of your self. You would create a life that was fun, fulfilling, exciting, and meaningful. You would never get up some morning and decide to see how many chores and favors for others you could heap on yourself in one day (and your one day off at that!), just so you could be miserable and beyond exhausted, living some distorted and unfulfilling life where you "danced" for the world and ignored what mattered to you.

So how does it happen? How does anyone wind up stuck in a life that ignores what, given the choice, they would want to have? In order for you to maximize your life quality, you must understand exactly and precisely the process by which your authentic self gets modified, buried, and ignored. That process begins with the external factors that were briefly introduced in Chapter 1. We humans are social beings. I suppose that is both good and bad because others can sure come in handy when we are lonesome, but they can also be a huge cramp in your side. And when they stop being supportive and start becoming a pain, it can dramatically change who we are, depending on their power and relevance in our lives. Hear what I said: "They *change* who we are." Things that happen on the outside get to us on the inside. External events, once internalized, leave scars that can last a lifetime. Life can be cruel and when it is, your authentic self—which might have otherwise been doing just fine—is altered, and that's not good.

Your authentic self may have started out solid and pristine, like a new car sitting on the showroom floor. It was bright, shiny, and well constructed—not a scratch on it. If that sleek and perfect car were allowed to remain in the safety of the controlled environment of that showroom year after year, it would still be in pristine condition five, ten, even fifty years later. But once you drive that car out the door and it begins interacting with the world, it is subjected to the forces and demands of a life that takes a toll. It starts to show "battle scars," the wear and tear that comes from being out there.

After years of its being subject to door dings, a blazing sun, bone-jarring chuckholes, fender benders, and maybe even catastrophic collisions and wipeouts, it is hard to look at that car and even imagine that it was once the same shiny and solid automobile that sat on the showroom floor. But it was. And even a thirty-year-old, beat-up jalopy can be restored to its original condition. I'm not saying it's easy, but you sure do have something when you get through.

Now you may feel like a New York City taxicab with more door dings, dented fenders, and chipped paint than a demolition-derby winner, but you can find your way back. You may have hit a million potholes along the way; you may even have had a catastrophic collision with life. But knowledge is power, and we're going to break your life down so you know exactly when and where your authentic self took its hits.

Don't be overwhelmed by thinking about trying to sift back through and analyze your entire life, because it is not necessary. With the help of a few simple but penetrating exercises, we are going to focus on that select set of external experiences that will give us an absolute blueprint to your current concept of self.

As I alluded to earlier we are going to focus not on your entire life, but instead on three categories of events. Here's a shocker: Social scientists tell us that the entire origin of your self-concept, and therefore the determination of who you ultimately become in your life, can be traced to the events of a precious few days and the actions of an amazingly few key people involved in those happenings. I'm telling you that out of all the thousands of days you have lived, out of the thousands and thousands of choices and decisions you have made, and out of all the thousands of people you have encountered, the basis of your entire life and who you have become can be boiled down to:

Ten Defining Moments
Seven Critical Choices
Five Pivotal People

If you think about that for a minute, it's not as outrageous as it sounds. An airline pilot once described his job as hours and hours of total, monotonous boredom, punctuated by moments of stark terror! Isn't that life? Days and days of routineness and monotony, all of which has little impact on you or anyone or anything, punctuated by defining, critical, and pivotal happenings, some that take place in the blink of an eye. Scary thought, I know, but good or bad, that's the deal, and we have to get real about it to understand and take control of your self-concept.

Some of your ten defining moments, seven critical choices, and five pivotal people have provided positive input to your self-concept, lifting up and affirming your authentic self. Other defining moments, critical choices, and pivotal people have poisoned that authenticity and distorted how you see yourself. You will be amazed by the clarity you will gain when you identify these key factors, when you mentally and emotionally step back and take a view of life in which the routine, mundane minutiae simply drop away, and you instead highlight just the outcome-determinative occurrences and players from your life.

It will be like looking at one of those optical illusion "magic eye" pictures, consisting of thousands of dots of color with an image disguised and embedded somewhere within them. (I hate to admit it, but I have never been able to see the damn image until someone points it out to me!) Once you take away all the background minutiae, the camouflage wallpaper that conceals the target image, then that image of course becomes crystal clear. The ten defining moments, seven critical choices, and five pivotal people from your life are that image. When you focus on just those key external experiences, the origin of your self-concept will be revealed to you with shocking clarity.

In thinking about your most important external experiences, I want you to be especially sensitive to and on the lookout for a particular kind of life experience and associated consequence that may have had a hugely powerful impact on your life and your self-concept. I am talking about what I call **psychic disfigurement**. Psychic disfigurement explains how something that happened to you in the fifth grade, for example, can affect you when you are forty-two years old. If there is some possibility that it plays a part in your self-concept, now is the time to begin thinking about that possibility.

Psychic disfigurement can best be understood through the analogy of a burn to the skin. When people are traumatically burned, often the incident itself is over almost as soon as it began. There may be only milliseconds between the skin's first contact with the flame, acid, or other agent, and the time when both layers of skin, as well as the underlying tissue, are completely destroyed. Considered in one way, the injury is "over." The burning has stopped. Yet we know that the injury is far from over. For instance, a person who has been unfortunate enough to suffer a burn on his or her face, and who is noticeably scarred as a result, will tell you that it changes how they feel about their adequacy. They become far more uncertain about going out into the world. In other words, the same disfigurement they have suffered physically has also affected their psyche. If there is a visible scar on their face, they say, "I cannot and will not go out there and present myself."

Now suppose that a person has suffered some traumatic injury that leaves no physical scars. Perhaps a trusted relative molested them. Maybe they were verbally assaulted by a parent or betrayed by a person they had come to rely on as a friend. Perhaps, as a young child, they watched helplessly as some horrible tragedy unfolded before their eyes. Again, the incident itself may have ended in a flash. From the moment the injury began until it ended may have taken less time than it takes to snap your fingers. Yet what happens to that person's self-concept, their psyche? It is wounded, scarred, disfigured.

If a traumatic event of this kind has happened in your life, you may be living just as if your skin had been burned. Unlike a physical scar, psychic disfigurement is visible only to a public of one, and that is you. You may be responding to the invisible scar just as you would to a visible one: by avoiding the world, by shying away from competition and participation, by withdrawing into the shadows of reticence and self-consciousness. You may be living a life that is dispirited and passive.

The point is that psychic disfigurement may be just as crippling and debilitating to your self-concept as physical disfigurement would be. If your own self-concept is in disrepair, it may be time for you to consider whether a psychic disfigurement has occurred in your life. The upcoming chapters on external factors will help you to make that determination. Doing the exercises there will help you address that part of your history, and will help you to begin taking steps out of the shadows and back toward the authentic self.

Admittedly, there are other factors that influence your self-concept, particularly the internal factors that we will address in the next section of the book. You must know, however, that every chain has a first link. And in the chain of an evolving self-concept, that first link is almost assuredly an external/interactive one. Prepare to be enlightened by examining the first links in your life chain.

THE LIFE CHAIN

Since I'm about to ask you to write down the defining moments in your life, I might as well give you a head start. One of the most powerful, outcome-determinative circumstances that you will ever experience in your life has already happened, and you inherited it. You were not consulted, and you had no choice in the matter, yet it was a huge deal, I guarantee it. Before you rack your brain too hard trying to figure out what could be so important, just think about the fortuitous nature of where you were born, what family you were born into, and who you grew up around. In other words, without question, a defining moment of overwhelming significance for you was the moment of your birth. You didn't get a vote; it just happened. One day, there you were! All of the choosing was done for you. Even as you grew up, you probably didn't have any idea that life offered anything other than what you were living. You simply became part of a long chain, its links consisting of your parents, your grandparents, and your siblings. All you had, all you knew, all you had available to you was what your parents, siblings, extended family, and life station offered up to you.

Consider the momentum that this chain created; the messages and expectations that passed from one link to the next, through the generations. That chain sealed much of the fate that was to be yours. For example, if you grew up with a mother and father who believed that they, and therefore you and the rest of your family, were all second-class citizens who should keep their heads down, their mouths shut, and by all means not make waves, you probably learned to just be glad that you were permitted to even be in this world. Bottom line: You may well have initially adopted a self-concept that was largely determined by the "blind luck of the draw"! You did not have the slightest choice about the links in your life chain, at least not until you picked up this book. But you do have a choice in them now. That choice looks to the future, not the past.

Enough about the "victim" side of the story. It is also extremely important that you understand that you have very likely become an actual participant in this "life chain lockdown." You are an active player (contaminator) in this drama because, like all people, you *internalize* your experiences. You internalize information, data, and experience in such a way that your concept of self is either confirmed or altered. At first, the forces are impacting you only from the outside, but almost instantaneously you begin to think about and *interpret* what is happening out there. Once you assign it a meaning, once you integrate it into your thinking, you make its impact all the more powerful. Your "perceptual navigation system," with its guiding compass and screening radar, starts to steer you *exclusively* in the direction that is consistent with what you already think.

Obviously, your existing life chain is a huge programmer of what your radar will pick up. You scan information consistent with what your life chain has taught you about you and your possibilities, or the lack thereof. For example, if you get fired and interpret that as a personal failure, you will now internalize that perception and be more inclined to pick up other failure-type messages; you'll be less inclined to pick up success-type messages. Your radar goes into "confirm only" mode as it scans the landscape of your life, looking for information that will make you "right," even if it makes you unhappy. The limiting effect of what you are willing to reach for is a tragic outcome, and one that is highly resistant to change.

Researchers have demonstrated this experience-based, self-limiting tendency in every organism you can imagine. They have even documented it with a bunch of fleas! If you have ever owned an outside mutt that had fleas, you know the damn things can jump halfway across the room and that they will do so just as soon as you get soft and let the mangy thing in the house. Apparently, these researchers (who obviously had way too much time on their hands) put a bunch of fleas in a jar with a lid on it. Not surprisingly, the fleas jumped so high that they hit the lid, time after time. But even a flea gets tired of bumping its head. (These fleas were smart, obviously from some highbrow poodle.) The fleas "learned" that if they jumped to a certain height, they knocked themselves silly hitting that lid. So they started jumping about a half inch short of the lid. The environment shapes even fleas. But here's the point: Eventually, you can take the lid completely off that jar, but the fleas won't jump out. They'll keep on jumping a half inch short of where the lid was. Based on history, and in conformance with their environment, they steadfastly limit what they allow themselves to do.

Is it so hard, then, to understand how your "head-bumping" activity, how your life chain, has gotten you to pull back and limit yourself? You've learned your role, whatever it is. It's been put on you with great clarity as life has pounded and hammered away, shaping your personal truth and self-concept. Until now, it may be that all of the hammering and pounding and shaping took place outside of your awareness. Like the fleas in the open jar, you may not have even been aware that you had a choice. Well, you may not have been aware then, but I'm telling you now that you do have choices, you do have power; now you know.

You don't have to just mindlessly go along with this life chain you have both inherited and passively contributed to. You can begin to shape its links, actively and consciously. You need the tools, you need guidance on where to start and what to do, but with a little help, you can do it. You are worth it, and you can do it!

I want to start providing you with that help by looking at how the world gets inside your head and changes your self-concept from a solid, authentic self-regard to a less confident, less focused image and belief about you. Let's look at how you conspire with the world to create changes in how you see your self at your most core level. Let's also take a hard look at what links are in your existing life chain. Once you've done those things, once you've found your way back to the you that has been buried under a mound of world experiences and self-pounding, hang on. Hang on, because you aren't going to believe what is about to happen in your life as you claim the power of refining your personal truth, knowledge, and personal power.

I'm not going to give you a "new" personal truth or a new "authentic" self-concept, because I don't have to. What you need is there! It has always been there; it has just been buried so deep you didn't know how to access it. Your personal truth, your self-concept, just needs to be "cleaned up" and rid of all the junk and misinformation that you have internalized for so many years. You soon will know exactly how to do just that. I have often said, "You either get it or you don't!" It's time for you to get it. Part of "getting it" is coming to realize that if you are currently deciding who and what you are, based on where you have been and what messages and results you have accumulated, you are always living with a backward focus.

Our focus in this book will include a look back into your history, but only for the purpose of targeting for elimination the distorting experiences of the past. These are the contaminants that you must eliminate from your here-and-now self-concept if you are going to have an authentic existence, one that gives you the ride you are looking for in this life. We must then adopt a forward focus, looking at where you are going instead of where you have been. Your future is a place and time of much greater interest to me as I work to impact your concept of self and your experiences in life.

It is the forward-looking view that affords you great power, because that is where you can create so much more, so much that is authentically you. Right now I will guarantee you that you are spending too much life energy worrying over and being controlled by what has already happened in your life. Why? Because the links in your existing chain are events that are over and done with. Those events have gone by; they are of little consequence at this point. As with a rocket taking off from Cape Canaveral, everything you see trailing behind—the flame, the smoke, the steam—everything that is *behind* the rocket is "spent" energy. Spent energy has no value. It got you where you are, but it's of absolutely no value in the here and now. It's over; it's done. It got you where you are, good or bad, but where you go from here is up to you. It doesn't matter what the links in your chain have been. It doesn't matter what the tail on the rocket was or wasn't. The only time is now and the choice is yours.

I'm not just going to tell you to "be free" of your past. That's no big news flash. What I am going to do is help you identify, exactly, precisely, what specific past experiences have had what effect.

I am then going to show you precisely how you can deal with those experiences in the here and now, in such a way as to take your power back. Then and only then will you be able to stop being a passenger in life and start driving—and driving with passion.

4 YOUR TEN DEFINING

MOMENTS

"If there is no wind, row."
— LATIN PROVERB

TEN DEFINING MOMENTS

When I was in the fifth grade, my family and I lived in a tidy little neighborhood in the suburbs of Denver, Colorado. Nobody on our street was high society, just a lot of small tract houses, but it was a quiet, comfortable environment; new school, people swapping stories on the porch after dinner, and everybody's house was the same: three bedrooms, one bath, and a single-car garage. School was humming along pretty well for me that year. I had a close-knit group of friends, was making good grades, and had found my passion in athletics. In fact, sports were becoming the big deal for me; I found that I was comfortable in the thick of competition. As the school year drew to a close, I was awarded Athlete of the Year for the school, together with the award for sportsmanship. Very affirming events for me, because it was the first time I had ever won anything, except for a Mexican hat dance ribbon I got in the fourth grade. (I won that for getting less dizzy than my partner, Linda Snider, who later came up behind me, hit me between the shoulder blades, and proceeded to beat the crap out of me for making her look bad!)

At the very least, I was feeling pretty good about school in general, and the fifth grade in particular. Looking back, I have to say this was a time of real innocence for me. I had no problems to speak of, other than not turning my back on that "she-wolf" Linda Snider. I was glad to be me, glad to be living where I was and doing what I was doing. It was a simple time and I guess the lens that projected my self-image up on the wall was clear and in focus. That was all about to change, not in some dramatic, newsworthy way, but in a way that was important to me because it would involve me.

I've come to learn that for most of us, the events that shape our lives are typically events that, but for our personal stake, are of little interest and of little drama. But once you add that element of personal involvement and personal impact, once you add that relevancy, events that barely even hit the rest of the world's radar screen take on considerable significance. Remember: If it's important to you, then it's important, period. What was about to happen to me would hardly be noticed by anyone not personally involved, but it would shape a part of my self-concept to this very day.

Now, according to my mom, I've never, ever started a fight in my life. But also attending our little school that year were some kids who all lived together in a rough neighborhood several blocks away from my house. They were in the sixth grade, just a year older than I was, but a foot taller and a foot broader, it seemed. One day at recess, these "sixth graders from hell," as we called them (never where they could hear it), started picking on a bunch of the younger, smaller kids, including me and a couple of my buddies. The verbal abuse escalated, and then a couple of them grabbed my friend Michael by the neck, got him in a headlock, and threw him to the ground. They started pushing and shoving the rest of us all at the same time. I don't remember a whole lot after that. I mean, I remember hitting one of them in the face with a basketball, as hard as I could. I remember hitting one with a swing. (My dad always said, "Son, if they're bigger than you, just pick up some 'difference' and even things out a little bit!") The whole thing exploded into the biggest, most chaotic playground brawl you can imagine. No one involved was big enough to really do any damage, but to all of us it was an epic battle of indescribable proportions. I didn't start it, but I can remember being fairly passionate about finishing it.

Eventually, we were hauled into the principal's office and my homeroom teacher was summoned. As I stood there at "the judgment seat," my nose bleeding, my shirt ripped, chunks of gravel embedded in my cheek, and with a huge knot on my forehead, I recall feeling a sense of relief. It surely was what an embattled soldier feels when he learns that reinforcements are on the way. I was relieved that Mrs. Johnson, who, of all the adults at the school, knew me the best, was coming to my aid. She would be my protector and advocate. Knowing what she did about my character, my sportsmanship award, my loyalty to my friends, and my peaceful nature, there could be no doubt that she would quickly get to the bottom of it all, and would speak up for me before the principal. I didn't check these things off in my mind; I felt them, and it filled me with a sense of calm. Mrs. Johnson was coming to make everything all right.

What happened next was a defining moment in my life. Mrs. Johnson walked in. She looked at the principal, she looked down at me—and she flew into a rage. For the first few moments of her tirade, I couldn't even make out what she was saying. I was astonished. Apparently, she was humiliated that one of "her" students had been in a fight. The verbal abuse I'd just heard on the playground was nothing compared to what she heaped on me. She never stopped to ask what had happened; she made it clear that she didn't care what had happened. She just blistered me with a torrent of angry words.

Some of those words, I will never forget. "Oh, you're Mr. Tough Guy, aren't you?" she said. "You don't take guff off of *anybody*, do you?" Didn't she realize how big those kids were? Didn't she know what they had done? Didn't she owe it to me at least to ask what had happened?

At first, I was stunned and hurt. Then it was as if something clicked in me. I saw with sudden clarity that Mrs. Johnson was not my friend at all. I saw that, far from taking up her responsibility to protect me from bullies and to find out the truth, she was going to protect herself first. She had an agenda for me that ignored my safety and my well-being. It ignored my need to be who I was to myself and my friends. The message was clear: "Don't you make waves in my world, young man. You do whatever I need and expect you to do to not complicate *my* life; to hell with yours!"

In a flash, it hit me right there in that principal's office that I could no longer assume that life was fair. It was not fair. It was not objective. It became clear to me that the person I had to look to was me. The only person who "had my back" was me. Inside, I was saying, What are you thinking, lady—have you gone insane? But what I said aloud was, "No, you're right, I don't take any guff from anybody. And that includes you!" The principal immediately suspended me from school for three days, earning him a prominent place on my s—list, as well.

That singular event, that defining moment that I labeled as "betrayal," would prove to change who I was inside. Call it the death of innocence, the maturing beyond naïveté, or just a wake-up call that the world was not my personal oyster, but it changed who I was inside. In that five-minute span, the world wrote on the slate of Phil McGraw. Was it a big deal? Probably not to Mrs. Johnson or the principal, or those sixth graders who spent half their school year in the detention hall, but it was to me. To me it was a defining moment.

Fast forward almost one full year. At the same school, I had another teacher named Mr. Welbourne. Mr. Welbourne was a big guy, huge. He taught art, among other things, a decidedly "sissy" class to my sixth grade sensibilities, and one that seemed totally out of character for him, since he had hands the size of hams. One morning after a heavy spring snowfall, lots of people, including several teachers, were late getting to school. Those of us kids who had made it on time were sitting in the art room, waiting for "Bigfoot" to arrive. Minutes passed. There were hunks of modeling clay sitting on the tables, and we got bored looking at the clock and one thing led to another. It seemed almost a requirement of nature that we start flicking bits of clay at one another. Peel off a little bit, roll it up, and flick it. We got pretty good at it. Soon the air was thick with little projectiles of clay, just whizzing around the room. I was particularly proud that I had landed two direct hits in the back of Vicky's hair without her even knowing it.

That's when Mr. Welbourne walked in. Not surprisingly, he got mad at us. There was no denying we were flicking clay, which we shouldn't have been doing. I fully expected a lecture, being made to clean it up, and maybe even a lost recess. But Mr. Welbourne just lost it; I don't mean he kind of lost it, I mean he went nuts! I had the misfortune of sitting right by where he decided to have this little "Bates Motel" psychotic meltdown, and before it was over, he yanked me out of my chair, shook me like a rag doll, grabbed me by my right arm and my right leg, hoisted me over his head like a barbell, and bellowed, "How would you like me to slam you down on the floor? I oughta crush your head and break your neck, you little smart-ass!"

Pinned in his grip, the room spinning below me, I absolutely believed he was going to do it. Welbourne was like a man possessed. My arm was bleeding where his fingernails dug into my flesh. I thought he was going to break my back at an absolute minimum. His eyes were wild. Spit and slobber flew from his mouth. It was the first time in my young life that I actually thought I was going to die.

In my terror, I remember looking expectantly at the door. Somebody, please help me, I thought. Finally, I was able to form the thought in words that were audible: "Somebody, get this freak off of me, do something!" Understandably, the entire class was frozen in their seats in shock and disbelief.

After what seemed like an eternity, another kid, this doofus named Karl, dashed out of the room, probably more to save himself than to get help. Fortunately, he had a head-on collision with another late-arriving teacher, who deciphered his panic and crying. The commotion brought several teachers running at full speed. After much yelling and screaming, and a fair amount of wrestling around, Mr. Welbourne was "talked down," and I was released, shaken but not seriously hurt, aside from a few bruises and skin tears. I remember Mr. Welbourne sitting there on the floor, staring off into the distance as they took me to the nurse's office. We never saw Mr. Welbourne again after that day, and the vice principal and assorted substitutes finished out the year teaching his classes. I assume he was fired or sent wherever you send psychotic maniac teachers who attack students and offer to break their necks; nobody ever told me, and I frankly didn't give a damn, as long as it wasn't around me.

Let me tell you, once again the world had taken out its marker and written on the slate of Phil McGraw. I'm fifty years old, and both of those moments are as real and immediate for me as anything I've ever experienced—two defining moments in my life. Neither of these moments made the six o'clock news, nor should they have. They are not wildly dramatic, although I think I could make a pretty good case for the second incident. I could cite thousands of much more traumatic life events that I have heard about in the lives of others; so could you. I include these particular events here because they were important to me. They aren't at the top of my list of ten defining moments, but they did make my list. I include them here because I want to emphasize my point that if certain events in your life are important to you, if those events have shaped you, then that is enough to qualify those moments as "defining" and therefore worthy of your full consideration. Those two moments, however trivial they may seem to others, changed me. Those two moments, however trivial they may seem to others, altered my concept of self and how I have approached life until this very day. I do not have to defend or justify how or why; they just did. I attended that school for three years and attended others for many more years. I attended thousands of classes for hundreds of thousands of minutes, but those two events, spanning not more than probably five minutes combined, stand out from all of the others with distinct and unmistakable clarity.

As I said earlier, in the span of your life, not every moment can be recalled and singled out. Nevertheless, just as with me, there have been events, moments, in your life that have defined and redefined who you are. The event enters your consciousness with such power that it confronts the very core of who and what you conceived you were. It is no exaggeration to say that, before such an event occurs, your self-concept is A; after it occurs, your self-concept is B. A part of you is replaced or modified by that piece of your history, something new that will always be with you. You will forever after define yourself, to some degree, by your experience of that event. It is those events, those moments in the time of your life, that we must now identify and evaluate.

Assuming you are forty years old today, you have lived a total of 14,610 days. You probably cannot separately distinguish in your mind 14,600 of those days, but ten of them you can and already have. These moments, on those particular days, stand out for you, the same way that a house stands out from the background in a painting.

A renowned psychologist named Alfred Adler observed this tendency we have to form mental pictures of ourselves based on our history. He noticed that our minds condense all of our experiences around those happenings that are most important. One of Dr. Adler's favorite techniques was to ask the patient what their earliest recollection was. However the patient responded, Adler would complete the patient's description by saying, "And so life is." His point was that this relatively small portion of the patient's life was critical to their present perception of self. It was his belief that those recollections were at the core of each person's personal truth. He was right.

For example, one woman told of being chased by two dogs when she was a little girl. Eventually she outran them, but although she was safe, she was still afraid. While the experience of being chased was obviously in her past, years later, in her present life, she reported that she viewed the world as an angry and hostile place. Although she thought that she was agile and competent enough to handle it, she remained afraid. What Adler realized was that the woman was telling a childhood story that had come to epitomize her entire life. As such, the episode still caused her the deepest emotional turmoil. Clearly, based on results, that story was for her a defining moment. In his words, "And so life is."

As I look back at my own defining moments in elementary school, I can see pretty clearly how those two episodes altered my concept of self; I recognize the consequences that they had in my life. First of all, it should not be surprising to learn that I have always been leery of those who are in positions of authority in my life. That's just become part of who I am. Whether my perception and interpretations of those events are accurate or not, they are real to me. An argument could be made that I deserved at least most of what I got. But, to me at that age (and now, for that matter), I don't see it that way, and if it's real to me, then that is reality. Please understand: I have been blessed by some outstanding teachers along the way, and I have always tried to be on guard against making any other teacher or authority figure pay for the shortcomings of Mrs. Johnson or Mr. Welbourne. Whenever I'm asked, "Who are your heroes?" my unhesitating answer is, "Teachers who do it right." Nevertheless, since those two episodes in Denver, I have never, ever been completely at ease in an academic environment or any other in which someone has assigned authority over me in any way. That is now part of my self-concept.

Bottom line: On the continuum that runs from paranoia at one end to naïveté at the other, I'm a good ways from paranoid, but I am absolutely a country mile from naïve and accepting. Having been what I believe to have been emotionally and physically violated, I am committed to being self-reliant and self-protecting, and to never let it happen to me again. I refuse to be helpless. I don't give anybody "the benefit of the doubt." And I am fully aware that there is a direct, unbroken connection between that approach to life and what happened to me in grade school. Those two happenings are among my ten defining moments. Are they examples of positive or negative defining moments? I'm not sure; they just are. They were clearly negative experiences at the time, but I'm not at all sure that they weren't pretty good wake-up calls, as well. I know I wouldn't wish either moment on any child I know, but I think I did create value from them. I suppose opinions could differ on that, but still, they happened, they changed me, and that is for sure.

Some of our defining moments are decidedly negative, while others are emphatically positive. The positive moments powerfully affirm our authentic selves, inspiring us with an awareness of our own capabilities. They lift us up to a place from which we can see all kinds of possibilities for ourselves. We take from them the kind of emotional and spiritual energy that can sustain us for a lifetime.

I recall another classroom story, one that a very dear friend shared with me one day when I was telling her about this chapter of the book. I related my harrowing experiences of the fifth and sixth grades and she said that she had been just as powerfully impacted in the third grade but in the complete opposite direction. I was so moved by the story that I asked her if she would share it with my readers. These are her words written for this book:

"I always liked school because, aside from my church, it was the only place as a child growing up that I remember feeling valued. I loved books. They were an escape, a way for me to believe that I could become anybody and do anything. Books presented a possibility to me.

"So when Miss Driver, my third grade teacher, assigned us to read *Honestly Katie John* (a fifth grade–level book, I don't mind telling you!), I was mucho excited to take on the challenge. We had two weeks to read and turn in our book reports; I was done in less than a week! Miss Driver was so proud of me and my work that she stood before the class and made much to do about it. Of course this did not fare well with my other classmates, who turned on me for supposedly making them look bad. But it didn't stop there, she didn't just compliment me in front of the class; she told *everyone*, including all the teachers in the teachers' lounge. When I moved on to the fourth grade a full year later, my fourth grade teacher, Mrs. Duncan, said, 'Oh, I know you, you're the girl who reads and turns in your work early.' Life altering moment! In that one moment in time, I was changed. I realized that when you work hard, when you do things well, people take notice, people remember you and value you. In my young mind, I also made the important connection that it was only because I had loved the book so much, that I had found it so easy to do the work and turn it in early. I was so passionate about the book and wanted to be so much like Katie John that I actually went home and tried to give my black girl self some freckles! So *another* life-altering, defining moment: Do what you love, do what you have a passion for, and life becomes so very much easier."

The friend that told me that story of third grade passion and clarity was Oprah Winfrey. Oprah says today that it was absolutely one of the proudest and most defining moments of her life. A zest for learning had led her to a definition of self that was based on a powerful connection to a personal truth that had its roots in that classroom. From that point on, she believed that she could do anything if she worked hard. She knew that hard work and creating value by being who and what you authentically were could create respect and great results. As the years passed, she was repeatedly sustained and energized by the recollection of that day the papers were returned. When people told her that she, a black woman from the Deep South, should not even think about pursuing a career as a TV reporter, she remembered that day. When the possibility of her hosting a morning talk show came up, and people said, "An overweight black woman with almost no experience? I don't think so," she remembered that day. She recalled the little voice inside the third grade girl that had whispered to her as she sat down to write, "I can do this because I love it." She never forgot the lesson: that with the determination to put her God-given talent to work, and the willingness to try as hard as she could, she could accomplish anything.

When you think about your capacity for remembering, you probably recognize that that ability is both a gift and a curse. As humans, we are poor historians of facts, but we are superb in emotional history. Memory gives us the ability to travel back in time, but our ability to recall facts is far from accurate. By contrast, we reexperience the *feelings* connected with an event with extraordinary efficiency. For example, remember any Christmas in your life, and I will bet you that you not only remember the emotion you felt at that time, but that you also experience that same emotion now in the present! If you were extremely excited about getting a bicycle then, you'll get excited now. If Christmas morning came and there was no bicycle under the tree, you will feel the same disappointment now that you felt that morning. Like it or not, that's the way we work, and so it will be with the recollection of your defining moments.

I once worked with a fifty-two-year-old patient who identified a powerfully defining moment that happened when he was six years old. Richard was traveling cross-country on a train with his mother. Early in the trip, he needed to go to the bathroom, and after convincing his mother that he was a "big boy" and could go to the men's room by himself, he made his way to the bathroom at the far end of the car. On entering, he locked the door; the problem was that when he got ready to leave, he couldn't get the door open again. No matter how hard he pulled on it, the door wouldn't budge. Against the roar and clatter of the train, Richard's calls for help were useless. Panic rose in him, and his cries became desperate screams. No one could hear him.

After what seemed like hours, Richard finally figured out a way to pry open the door and he escaped. Still trembling, he returned to his mother. Speaking of that incident years later, Richard vividly described the fear and anger he felt—and continued to feel. He remembered how angry he was that his mother had not come to his rescue. So began a life of almost total self-reliance: Richard never again trusted another person to help him or accepted help when it was offered. And to this day, he is claustrophobic, breaking out in a cold sweat when he's confined in a small space like an elevator or closet.

The point is that, although the terror that Richard the *child* endured may have lasted ten minutes at the most, Richard the *adult* still feels the urge to scream; he says he still tastes the salt in his saliva when he thinks about what happened.

Now, this incident could have happened at any time in Richard's life, so what makes it such a remarkable and critical piece of his life story? It's impossible to know for sure what earlier experiences— about being betrayed, about some loss of control—were folded into that episode on the train. There may have been any number of other lesser incidences of fear or anxiety of abandonment that were percolating around inside Richard before he stepped into that bathroom. But for whatever reason, it was that moment of definition that brought it all spewing forth in the panic he remembers. With overwhelming power, that moment in time concentrated all of his emotional energy, all of his attention, all of his nerve endings, into one episode. In other words, Richard's experience may have just been the straw that broke the camel's back, with regard to an insecure life. It may have been a representation of all of his other anxieties. Either way, it is a defining moment that had shaped him for forty-four years. Whatever those earlier experiences were, the restroom incident was the culmination of everything that had gone before. *And it has been a determiner of everything that has happened in Richard's life since then.*

Your and my defining moments are the outlines of our lives. If we do not have even some awareness of them, we are blind to ourselves. When we don't know our defining moments, life becomes unpredictable, irrational, needlessly confusing. We wonder why we do the things we do and hope that tomorrow will be better for us. Although we may know that we've had a bunch of interesting events in our lives and memories of them emerge from time to time, those memories seem random to us, disconnected from each other and from anything going on in the present. Our attitude becomes, So what?

CONDITIONING WHO WE ARE

While it may be true that rewards and punishments teach us what to do and what not to do, it is the defining moments that shape our internal behaviors. Defining moments anchor our emotional reactions to the world. They determine the feelings and reactions we have to the inevitable stresses we encounter throughout life.

Defining moments are so important that, in many cultures, they have been deliberately provided for as a matter of ritual. For example, the ancient Egyptians would put a person under the floor, in a container of water that allowed him barely enough space to breathe. After a day or more, the person would be removed, with the theory that whatever mental incidents he reported would be his significant, defining moments. Many Native American tribes send their adolescents out into the wilderness for the purpose of enduring some life-or-death circumstance, such as killing a bear or spending the night without food or shelter on top of a mountain. Sun dances and sweat lodges replicate dangerous conditions, enabling the participants to grasp the seriousness of the situation and to make memorable decisions for themselves.

By contrast, our culture takes a "hands-off" approach when it comes to our defining moments. For better or worse, we leave it to fate or chance as to when and how these events are identified, let alone dealt with. Consequently, we have a society of people whose lives are dominated and controlled by life experiences they don't have a clue about.

Bottom line: Planned or unplanned, ritualized or not, you have had defining moments in your life, and you must identify them if you expect to reconnect with your authentic self and take control of how you feel about you and what you create in your life. Your defining moments can be the door that opens your authentic self. By that I mean that your defining moments have elicited a response from you, but your response may not be an authentic part of who you are. In fact, your defining moments may have blinded you to your power and strengths by evoking overwhelmingly negative emotions and fear about yourself or the world. It is time to haul your defining moments out into the sunlight. It's time for you to get some bright-line, no-kidding understanding of what have been the major influences on what you have become and how you think about yourself.

THE CHALLENGE

In psychological terms, you are about to do some "recollecting." You are recollecting when you remember an occasion in terms of at least two ways: first, an incident, and second, a result. You remember falling down (incident), and the next thing you remember is your mother holding you (result); you remember the dog biting you, and you cried; you drew a picture, and the teacher told you it was good.

By themselves, memories pass quickly. Maybe—just maybe—you remember your first butterfly, your first taste of ice cream, your first bicycle. But when that memory has consequences, it becomes a life story. It's those *consequences,* the connections between the incident and the result, that make the memories useful. They become small stories that you refer to later in life. When you feel insecure, you remember the story about falling down. When you're afraid of being alone, you recall the story, and the fear, of being bitten by the dog.

The following exercise is designed to discover what those important stories are for you. Let these questions help you recollect. I have grouped the questions in age brackets, so the answers will be easier to remember, but be aware that defining moments are not age-specific: defining moments shape your interactions with the world, regardless of when in your life they occur.

For this exercise to be useful, you must require of yourself the most detailed and thorough memory you can muster. Features, facts, circumstances, and emotions must be as clearly described as possible for you to come away with the depth of information that you need. For example, I will be asking you about physical aspects, such as where you were at an exact moment; what you were smelling or tasting; how your arms were positioned; what your breathing was like; and so on.

I'll also challenge you to recall the emotional and mental states you were experiencing. So get ready for questions like, "What emotions or change of emotions did you have at this time?" "Were you confused or eager when this moment happened?" "Did you feel as if you were going to die?" "Were you in a mental fog, or were you clear-minded?" "Did you feel love or hate?"

Don't feel uncomfortable, however, if you do not have recollections of defining moments for each age. These events happen at different times, often many within a small period, depending on the circumstances of our lives and our personal challenges during those times. And don't feel bound by the short description I've provided as to each stage. The point is simply to stimulate your thoughts with some general observations about that stage. Those general observations may or may not apply to your particular experience of life.

Now get some form of journal that can hold many pages of work and that is intended to be TOTALLY CONFIDENTIAL AND FOR YOUR EYES ONLY.

As with the other exercises in this book, you don't necessarily have to block out a huge chunk of time for doing all of these questions at one sitting. They can be done piecemeal, age group by age group, as time permits. But they do require 100 percent of your concentration and focus while you are doing them. Find a quiet spot that affords you some privacy, a comfortable place to sit, and some uninterrupted time. In other words, turn off the damn television and send the kids to bed or out to play.

Ages 1–5

Typically, recollections of these years and their outcomes focus on interactions with other family members or the early trials of growing up, like playing games, going to nursery school for the first time, or learning to sleep in the dark. Learning about the aging process—noting that some people are old and others are younger—may also prove to have been important. Now begin writing about whatever recollections of these years stand out in your mind and heart. We are looking for defining moments, so if you already have a clear target event in mind, go right to it and start answering the questions below. If you are not clear on a standout moment, don't assume there aren't any; just start writing and recollecting. You might surprise yourself and discover a moment that you had suppressed or were in denial about. Be sure to note as many details of each incident as you can. Use the following questions to guide you to those details. If you will try to observe each event as if you were a third person, a reporter who is writing things down in your behalf, this process will be easier for you.

Taking up the first moment you have selected, relax and allow your mind's eye to roam freely over all of its details. As you reexperience that incident, let all five senses play a part in your search for information.

Consider these questions:

1. Where are you at this moment?
2. How old are you and what do you look like?
3. Who is there with you, or who is supposed to be there with you?
4. What is happening that makes this moment so significant?
5. What emotions or changes of emotions are you experiencing at this time? Loneliness? Anger? Fear? Confusion? Joy? Power? Helplessness?
6. How would you change this situation if you could?
7. What is your mental/physical experience? Are you in a mental fog, or are you clear-minded? What do you smell? Taste? Feel? Are you happy or sad? Are you in pain? Weak? Paralyzed?
8. If you could speak to someone at this moment, who would it be? What would you say?
9. What are you saying to yourself?
10. What do you need right now more than anything else?

Once you've written answers to these questions for one important incident during this life stage, do it for another incident in the same stage. Take whatever time you need to recollect and write down as many of these moments as possible. Then, for each event, answer the following in writing:

1. How do you feel *now*?
2. What emotions are you *now* having?
3. What are you telling yourself about these events *today*?
4. What power and self-determination, if any, did you lose to this event, if it was a negative event? (If it was positive, what did you learn or gain?)

Ages 6–12

These are typically the grade school years, when the teacher replaces the parent for the first time and you have a lot of sibling types to cope with. Although you may have been "top dog" in your family, you now have to prove yourself with this new group. Were there defining moments for you in these years? Look back at the ten questions we used for ages one to five, and answer those same questions with reference to this age bracket.

Remember to write your answers with as much precision as possible. Then answer in careful and thorough writing:

1. How do you feel *now*?
2. What emotions are you *now* having?
3. What are you telling yourself about these events *today*?
4. What power and self-determination, if any, did you lose to this event, if it was a negative event? (If it was positive, what did you learn or gain?)

Ages 13–20

Turmoil and frustration often characterize the teenage years. This is when we learn about being an adult, breaking away from the family, and finding out what a "big deal" there is about sex. New motivations enter your life. Social relations become more important than food. There may be an acute sensitivity about whether you belong to the "in" crowd, however that group is defined for you. Love can be a major source of confusion. Forms of initiation or "rites of passage" may mark the struggle for adulthood. With varying degrees of focus and concern, your thoughts turn toward your future.

What were your defining moments from these years? Recollect them; then write them down, using the ten questions to stimulate your thoughts. Include as many details as you can. Remember to identify the people who are involved.

As you reflect on these times, once again:

1. How do you feel *now*?
2. What emotions are you *now* having?
3. What are you telling yourself about these events *today*?
4. What power and self-determination, if any, did you lose to this event, if it was a negative event? (If it was positive, what did you learn or gain?)

Ages 21–38

This is typically the stage in which people begin their lives as citizens of the community and take on the responsibilities of jobs and families. We begin the tasks of learning how to be parents ourselves and how to become a partner in life. We are often confronted at this stage with our lack of knowledge on a number of fronts, such as power and self-discipline. The challenges we face may give us a newfound admiration for our parents or the other role models we recall from childhood.

Let the same ten questions prompt you to write a detailed and thorough recollection of these years. Write answers for as many defining moments from this period as you can. Again:

1. How do you feel *now*?
2. What emotions are you *now* having?

3. What are you telling yourself about these events *today*?
4. What power and self-determination, if any, did you lose to this event, if it was a negative event? (If it was positive, what did you learn or gain?)

Ages 39–55
This age span is usually a time when you begin a new era of your life. You are usually settled into some vocation and you have a pretty good idea of what life will offer you in the future. Wealthy or not, you may be living in a situation where you know you will be there for a long time. You have done most of the things you needed to do in order to participate in the community. Now begins your time, the time in your life in which you can pay more attention to yourself.

Allow your mind to travel over these years and see what comes up. For each recollection, consider the ten questions and respond to each in writing.

As you look at the answers you've written:

1. How do you feel *now*?
2. What emotions are you *now* having?
3. What are you telling yourself about these events *today*?
4. What power and self-determination, if any, did you lose to this event, if it was a negative event? (If it was positive, what did you learn or gain?)

Ages 56 and Beyond
While the age of fifty-six is by no means the end of life, for many this age brings thoughts of retirement from work and release from the responsibilities of the community and family. We begin to lose some physical vitality and are confronted with more limitations. Many of the defining moments in this stage of life emerge in the context of relationships, turning over responsibilities to others, and getting to know others in more intimate, less competitive ways.

What recollections stand out for you from these times? Again, I remind you that these memories do not have to do with the issues that I've presented, but with *what stands out for you*, regardless of the time or place. As you think of these moments, answer the ten questions as before.

Finally, once again answer the following in writing:

1. How do you feel *now*?
2. What emotions are you *now* having?
3. What are you telling yourself about these events *today*?
4. What power and self-determination, if any, did you lose to this event, if it was a negative event? (If it was positive, what did you learn or gain?)

CONNECTING THE DOTS

Before you go on, look back over your writing. Examine those age brackets again and see if there might be a defining moment that you have overlooked. By the same token, is there a defining moment that you have avoided talking about?

Remember that monsters and ghosts work in the dark. This work that you're doing is designed to help you flip the switch and turn on the floodlights. So have the guts to get all of your defining moments out there, on the page. Refusing to do so, putting your head in the sand rather than confronting those moments, means that you are cheating yourself and your loved ones.

If you have done an honest and thorough job of these exercises, you have defined some very important times of focus. You have identified moments that have been extremely important to your experience of life and to the development of your self-concept. These are the building blocks upon which all of your perceptions about life stand. Now is the time to link up your defining moments and see what emerges as the foundation of who you have become.

When you try to look at and evaluate your entire life, it can be overwhelming: so much time to consider, so many things to recall.

Instead of asking you to undertake that daunting task, what I want you to do now is evaluate your life and the impact it has had on who you have become by reviewing *only* those key, defining moments that you have just detailed. Let the following steps provide you with a structured approach to getting a handle on this important personal history:

1. **List your defining moments; then describe each defining moment in one brief paragraph.**

Here's how it works. Look at what you have written for your first defining moment. Come up with a title or summary statement of that defining moment, using one sentence or phrase: Mine might be called "The time Mrs. Johnson chewed me out."

Next, underneath each title, write just one short paragraph that captures the gist of what happened. You can use what I've written about my run-in with Mrs. Johnson as a guide, although it's quite a bit longer than what you need. The point is to consolidate or condense the event into one paragraph. Boil it down to its essence.

You may end up with exactly ten paragraphs (one for each of the ten defining moments); you may have more defining moments, or fewer. What matters is that you capture all of your most important life events and identify the people in them.

2. **For each defining moment, identify the "before" and the "after" in your self-concept.**

What aspect or dimension of your self-concept was involved in or affected by that defining moment? Maybe it was your confidence. Maybe the defining moment had an impact on your sense of peace, your hope, ambition, joy, or love. Whatever dimension was affected, name it in writing.

Now, for each dimension, write down where you think you were on that dimension:

- immediately *before* the defining moment occurred,
- and then *after* the defining moment occurred.

In other words, if the defining moment affected your self-confidence, how were you different, in your self-confidence, before and after that defining moment? Think of these as before-and-after "snap-shots" of one element of your self-concept.

Let's use my Mrs. Johnson story as an example. Before that inci-dent, I had no real understanding of my need or my ability to self-protect. Protecting me was a responsibility that I assumed belonged entirely to other people, meaning adults. You could say I was pretty much the typical, happy-go-lucky fifth grade kid. My approach was "go along to get along." I was like a duck: If it didn't rain, I would walk. When it came to my need to protect myself, and my ability to do so, I was totally ignorant. My thinking was that I was just a kid; adults, teachers, and parents took care of things like fairness and safety.

By contrast, after my defining moment, I recognized that my imagined "free lunch" was over. I had both the obligation and the ability to self-protect. I could no longer expect others to do it for me and what's more, I learned that standing up for myself and what I be-lieved to be right would not always be really popular with those who were running an agenda that didn't include me and my interests. After I had been kicked out, and as I was escorted down the school's main hallway and out the front door, supposedly in shame, I was thinking, I did the right thing. I stood up and defended myself and my friends against some kids and adults who were in the wrong. I just got kicked out of school, but *I am not ashamed.* I would do it again. I also took note of this: that not one single kid who was star-ing at me, as I was ushered out, had judgment in his or her eyes. They knew, and I knew they knew: One of them, one of us, had taken a stand.

3. Write a paragraph to describe the long-term residual effect of that defining moment.

How has that defining moment affected you, long term? What you're looking for here are aspects about yourself—qualities or lack of qualities—that have developed as a direct consequence of that event. Your paragraph might begin, "As a result of this defining moment, I believe that I have lived my life with the tendency to be X, or with an approach to living that is governed by a self-concept that includes Y." My own paragraph, for example, might start out like this: "As a result of my experience in fifth grade, I became somewhat cynical, but also very self-reliant. I don't have a blind trust of authority. I firmly believe that if I don't stand up for myself, it is very possible that no one will. I recognize that I cannot expect anyone to 'carry me' through life," and so on. Put some precise language around the parts of yourself you acquired as long-term consequences of the incident. How has it defined you?

4. **Write down how and why you think the defining moment either clarified or distorted your authentic self.**

As an example of the approach you might take here, I can tell you that my own experience in the fifth grade clarified for me that I was a good and decent person with a degree of courage about my convictions. It showed me that, when the chips were down, I would do what I thought was the right thing. It's not that I engaged in a lot of "hooray for me" aggrandizement. I just came away with a quiet confidence that I was okay. I had never really been down in the "foxhole" with myself before; I had never really had a test of character. That defining moment allowed me to sort of bond with the person who was me. "We" (me) had been to the wars, with our back to the wall, and we learned something about ourselves (and others) in that defining moment. I saw that in a conflict of them versus me, the me would survive. The tremendous sense of peace I got from that discovery was a very affirming message to me from my authentic self. Negative event, positive effect.

5. **Review your interpretation of and reaction to the defining moment. Decide whether or not you believe your interpretation was and is accurate or inaccurate.**

Look back over your answers to Questions 2, 3, and 4. As you review those answers, do so with the advantages of your present-day perspective. Examine them with the time, objectivity, maturity, and experience that you lacked when you were in the midst of the defining moment itself.

Now ask: Has my interpretation of this defining moment been accurate? Or have I exaggerated or distorted it in some way?

For example, with respect to my being punished in fifth grade, I might acknowledge that at least some of what I got I deserved. Therefore, I might need to "dial down" somewhat the enormous outrage that I felt as an eleven-year-old. Understand: My adult perspective doesn't cause me to deny that episode as a defining moment; if it was, it was. But the benefits of time and adulthood do help me see that I was not entirely a victim.

Take some time now to check your characterization of your defining moment. Were you really the victim you believed you were? Was the victory, or the loss, or the outcome properly characterized by you, to you? If you've been BS-ing yourself about this defining moment, now is the time to acknowledge that—in writing.

6. Write down whether this is something that you think you should keep or reject with regard to your concept of self. Include one paragraph as to why.

Your task here is to evaluate what you took away from the defining moment. If your "take-away" from it has been negative, be honest enough with yourself to say so. If, on the other hand, a painful ordeal has taught you something worthwhile and positive about yourself, then be honest enough to acknowledge that. Whether the results have been negative or positive, write some explanation of why.

For example, as difficult as my defining moment was for me, as an eleven-year-old kid who had never talked back to an adult or been defiant a day in his life, I can see that it instilled in me a high degree of self-reliance. It awakened in me an acute awareness of my duty to protect myself. And it forever erased my blind faith in people with assigned authority. Those are the things I would write down in answer to this question. I wouldn't want to relive the moment, but at the same time I see that it called into action some traits that have served me well, thank you very much.

Suppose, however, that that defining moment had an entirely different effect on me. Suppose, for example, that as a result of it I had become some kind of paranoid rebel, unable to function in any kind of social system or relationship because I had become a self-righteous crusader, seeing a hidden agenda in every person I ever encountered. If a life filled with social upheaval and misery appeared to me to have roots in the defining moment, then I would answer this question by saying so, in writing. And I would make it clear that aspects of my self-concept attributable to this defining moment were *not worth keeping.* I would conclude that this event had not unlocked a part of my authentic self, but had instead become part of my fictional self, in that it was the residue of a world that had corrupted my accurate and balanced thinking about myself.

7. Reviewing these defining moments as a whole, what has been the bottom-line effect on your concept of self, having lived through them?

(Remember that you need to answer Questions 1 through 6 on pages 118–121, for each defining moment, before you are able to do this Question 7.) Your goal here is to identify the *overall trend or pattern* in the ten or so defining moments that you've identified. Looking at all of them as a whole, would you say that your defining moments have affected your life positively or negatively?

As a young man, Benjamin Franklin used to test his decisions and review his life events this way: First, he would draw a big T shape on a piece of paper; then, down the left side, he'd list all the positive aspects of the decision or action and down the right he'd list the negatives. This two-column list invariably helped him reduce seemingly complex problems to their essence. I urge you to use the same technique here. Extract from what you've written the words that describe what you have carried with you, through life, as a result of your defining moments. You are looking for characteristics that you attribute to those moments. On the left side of your T, for example, you might list positive qualities like "kindhearted," "generous," "thoughtful"; on the right would go the negatives, maybe "fearful," "hesitant," or "bitter." Don't stop filling up this T until you have thoroughly reviewed all of what you wrote for Questions 1 through 6.

I'd be willing to bet that, when you look at your T chart, you see some things about your self-concept with great clarity. For many people, looking at the chart is like having a lightbulb switch on; it's an "Aha!" moment. "No wonder I'm so mad at the world all the time." "No wonder I can't sustain a lasting relationship with the opposite sex." "No wonder my relationship with my kids is so awkward and difficult." Honestly and thoroughly engaging in this inventory of your defining moments will bring your self-concept into sharp-edged focus. Your fictional self will be more apparent. And you'll be a substantial step closer to reconnecting with your authentic self.

There is work yet to do in that process of rediscovery. In the meantime, however, trust that you are on the right track. Consider those words, "and so life is," for what they mean in your life. Yes, you have had defining moments. Yes, their consequences have flowed through innumerable moments in your life since then. But remember, as well, that you are in control. You are the manager of your own life. Whether "and so life is" means forever for you is a matter for you alone to decide.

5

YOUR SEVEN

CRITICAL CHOICES

*"I was seldom able to see an opportunity
until it had ceased to be one."*

—MARK TWAIN

YOUR life demands choices. Day in and day out, someone or something is expecting you to make some decision. Choosing is a fact of life that you cannot escape: what do you want; where do you want to go; are you going to buy this car or that one; should you just live together or take the plunge and get married; should you tell your mother what Uncle Bill did to you when he visited last Christmas; should you try drugs or just say no; should you believe what the kids are saying about what happened; is it time to put Mother in the home; do you take this job or figure a way to stay home with the kids; should you believe in God? Choices, choices, choices and no way to avoid them. If you're honest, you know there have been times when you have stepped right up and made certain choices with conviction and clarity. At other times you "chickened out" and hoped somebody else would just make the decision for you, simply because you didn't have the guts or the energy to face the pressure. What you may not have realized is that even in "not choosing," you were in fact making a choice. No matter how fast you run, no matter how much you try to hide, you cannot not choose.

Like everyone else in the real world, some of your choices have worked out really well, and some of them have proven to be total train wrecks. Unfortunately, all of your choices, good and bad, have the power to be hugely significant in your life. The right to choose is both a burden and privilege and it all started at a very young age.

At first it's nothing more than, "Do I eat my peas and carrots?" All too soon, it becomes so very much more. As you get older, bigger, stronger, and "smarter," the gravity and impact of your choices goes way up, and so does your ability to screw up and *really make it count*! As obvious as that should be, it always amazes me to hear parents trying to rationalize the behavior of their own precious, little, future serial killer by denying the fact that he has been a knucklehead from very early on: "Billy was difficult, sure. He had some problems with anger in grade school, but never anything big. He didn't get all screwed up until he turned fifteen. We just don't know what happened. He was never in trouble with the law before! He just seemed to really go downhill overnight!"

Well, guess what, "Ozzie and Harriet"? Most five-year-olds *don't* have showdowns with the cops, beat up teachers, smoke dope, steal cars, and get busted. That's not because they wouldn't if they could; it's because they're only *five years old,* so they can't. At five years old, their only ability to express rebellion or maladjustment is to throw a tantrum, pout, or set the cat on fire. What happened is that, just like you, his ability to make bad choices that matter, and then act on them in some powerful way, went vertical when he got old enough, big enough, and strong enough to behave with impact. It wasn't that he wasn't messed up enough to do really dumb stuff; it just never occurred to him to steal your money and your car. He didn't have the ability to act at that level. It's the same deal with you. As you get older, you carry a bigger stick in your life and that of those around you. Your choices count from day one and that impact—legally, morally, physically, financially, and socially—does nothing but go up with age. Choices are a huge deal in how and why your life is what it is. That includes the ones you have made, whether young or old, and the ones you will make.

In short, unlike your defining moments, some of which you had no control over, the choices you have made and will make in your life are 100 percent your responsibility. Some of these choices are absolute "bell ringers" that have changed your life in some monumental and lasting way. It is those choices that we must revisit and get real about.

The challenge of this chapter is simply this:

Identify the seven most critical choices in your life and how your self-concept has been shaped by the results of those choices.

If you've been following my thinking throughout this book, you well understand that your self-concept is the product of some give and some take with the world. It involves the impact of certain events, choices, and people *and* your internal processing of those events, choices, and people. All three categories work to shape your concept of self, but the primary focus here is to help you identify the impact of those choices you have made, some of which you are living at this very moment. Some of these choices and your internal reactions to them have created major results that have distorted your perceptions of self and created defects in your expectations about and interactions with the world.

You will recall my saying that you have been an active participant in the process of creating a self. That is, when you respond internally to what happens in your life, you are exercising an internal choice. We will talk more about these internal responses later; for now, just recognize that internal responses, just like your external behaviors, are a matter of unavoidable choice. This all means that you, through your own decisions and choices (both internal and external), have created both contributions and contaminations to the development of your self-concept. There's no time like the present to take stock of these inputs.

As with the events that we talked about in Chapter 4, Ten Defining Moments, most of the choices you have made in life run together; they blur. We are faced with so many day-to-day, routine decisions that it would be difficult for most people to list all the choices they had to make yesterday, let alone throughout their entire lives. Nevertheless, as with your defining moments, there are a surprisingly small number of choices that actually rise to the level of life-changing ones. I'm talking here about these seven most critical choices that have shaped your life, either positively or negatively. These **seven critical choices** have been major factors in determining who and what you have become. Identify and understand these choices and you will unlock an amazing amount of information about you and your self-concept and you and your future.

Whenever I think about critical choices, I can't help thinking about my high school friend Dean, and hearing his words, "My God, what happened?" During our entire high school careers in Kansas City, Dean and I were inseparable. We took classes together, played sports together, ate together, and spent weekends chasing girls together. We both found work as laborers—"grunts" would be a more accurate label—at a warehouse downtown. The hours were terrible, the work was worse, but the money, such as it was, allowed us to indulge our passion for tinkering with cars, going on dates, and having a pocket full of cash. It was pretty intoxicating to a couple of kids from, shall we say, the less-than-fancy side of town.

As senior year arrived and many of us started thinking long thoughts about college and beyond, Dean had fallen in love big time with a girl at our high school. Before long, he was talking to our shift supervisor at the warehouse about a job that had opened up elsewhere in the plant. Compared to the work he and I had been doing, this new position was a "grown-up" job. It meant significant responsibility. More importantly, it came with a "real people" salary:

maybe nine or ten thousand dollars a year, which in those days was all the money in the world to a poor boy. Within a few days after our graduation, while the rest of us were planning for the next "preparatory" phase of life, Dean had made a choice. He was through preparing; it was time to start living. Immediately after graduating, Dean seemed to have it all: a nice apartment, a killer stereo, and a shiny new pickup truck. His wedding date was just around the corner. At the farewell party that he threw for all of us "kids" later that summer, we all admired Dean's pickup, revving the engine and smelling that new smell; we looked around his apartment, amazed that an eighteen-year-old actually owned *furniture;* and we pretty much just drooled with envy for Dean. Soon I packed my luggage (three pillowcases), and off I went to school, dead broke, but bright-eyed.

I didn't see or talk to Dean for several months. Our paths had parted into two dramatically different worlds. Soon, word trickled through the grapevine that Dean had lost his great job. Naturally, we wondered about Dean and his new bride, but the demands of college prevented us from wondering for very long. Not long after that, we heard that Dean's marriage had also fallen apart. By the time I caught up with him again during a visit back to the old stomping ground, about ten years had passed and Dean was now the night manager at a convenience store. He was single, still living in an apartment, and driving the very same pickup. We laughed about old times, I shared with him a little bit about my practice, and he kidded me about being "Dr. McGraw," saying that he "wouldn't let me treat [his] dog." I said living with Dean was surely an uncommonly affirming experience for the dog, as seldom was a mutt the smartest one in the house. After we had traded good-natured barbs and caught each other up on the details of our lives and families, Dean fell silent. Finally, he said, "My God, Phil, what happened? You and I were almost twins in school, a pair of bookends. We made the same grades, we blew off the same classes, we ran from the cops together, we walked the same halls and had the same friends—hell, we were like peas in a pod. Now ten years later I'm working the night shift at the local 'stop and rob,' and you're a damn doctor! What the hell happened?"

As much as I would have preferred to just stare at my shoes at that point, I remember answering, "Well, what happened was that you made your choice and I made mine. You did what you did and I did what I did. When you choose the behavior, you choose the consequences." Ten years before, he had chosen marriage and the "grown-up" job, while the rest of us had chosen college; he had chosen the "grown-up" salary, while the rest of us had chosen to live like paupers for the next four years; he had chosen a seemingly secure position, while the rest of us took the risk that our opportunities would multiply once we had diplomas. Now we had those diplomas and Dean had a stack of pay stubs from a number of dead-end, no-future jobs. As much as he might now have wanted to go to college, he was too far in debt to even consider it. In other words, the choice he made at eighteen, the choice to have a little bit now rather than a whole lot later, was outcome determinative. Now, college is not for everybody and his decision could very well have worked out for him, but it didn't. He could have wound up running the whole place, but he didn't. Like I said, when you choose the behavior, you choose the consequences. Dean would surely put his choice to take immediate gratification, in the form of right-now marriage and money, at the top of his list of seven critical choices.

It is time to identify the various crossroads that you have encountered in your life: what choices you made at each, why you made the particular choice you did, and what you think have been the results for your life. What alternatives did you *not* choose and what would have been the results of those alternatives? Finally, you need to recognize and distinguish choices you made for yourself, versus those that you *chose* to have made for you.

In approaching this task, and so that we can work with the information later, it may be useful for you to consider some of the "whys" behind your choices. What factors came into play when you were faced with a choice? When you start looking for your seven most critical choices, keep in mind that you, like all people, have various motivations or needs that drive each and every one of your choices. In fact, you are driven by a hierarchy of needs, such that unless and until a more basic need is met, you cannot and will not be motivated by the next level of need. Below is a list of that hierarchy of needs:

- Survival
- Security
- Self-Esteem
- Love
- Self-Expression
- Intellectual Fulfillment, or
- Spiritual Fulfillment

Notice that first among them is the need for your very survival. Life itself must be protected before you will be motivated by any other need such as security, self-esteem, or love. This is important in understanding why you choose some of the things you choose and ignore some of the things you could have chosen. Let's examine each need or motivator.

Survival

Regardless of whatever else was, or is, going on in your life, your most critical need is and always has been survival. It is the most basic of all instincts, and it is with this very powerful force that you first began your presence on earth. Don't "pooh-pooh" this one; it is a big, big deal, because you start making choices and therefore getting shaped by the results of those choices from very early on.

When first born, you were, of course, totally vulnerable. A community, in this case probably a family, hopefully valued you, protected you, and cared for you, but at a price: The price was that you had to conform to the values, patterns, and demands of that community to insure that you would be embraced by them. You had to eat the way they did, behave the way they did, learn to speak their language, and accept and adapt to their environment. Early on, most choices were, of course, made for you. Even once you were old enough to begin making conscious decisions, choosing not to follow the rules of that community could have made you the outsider, the enemy. It could have left you vulnerable and subject to punishment. Again, this is a big deal. It suggests that you may have been conditioned very early on to make choices that were primarily motivated by fear.

Think about how that early experience and the need to have the approval of others, in order to peacefully survive, may have carried over into other areas and choices of your adult life. It may well be that you learned to make choices based on whether or not the decision and associated action would please others; not please you, but please others. If that tendency began as a motivation powerful as your very survival, just think how deeply ingrained it may well have become. A fear of displeasing others, rather than a philosophy of questioning and requiring justification for how things are, can be a huge life choice that you may not even be aware of having made. You may well have been conditioned to give your power away and make your own individual wants and needs secondary in determining the choices you would make, because you sensed or convinced yourself that conforming was essential to your very survival. You may well have convinced yourself that you would jeopardize your job and income and therefore your ability to maintain food and shelter, if you didn't stay quiet and compliant—obviously powerful motivators if in fact that is what you believe. If you have gotten so distorted in your thinking as to believe, for example, that you "just couldn't go on living" without the presence of your spouse, then the survival need would motivate you to do or tolerate amazingly irrational things in order to "survive." The fact that the threat to your actual survival is not an objectively genuine threat is of no consequence, because again, if you believe it, then that is for you reality. Moreover, if this is your belief, no other need will be addressed, because as long as you believe your very survival is threatened, that need will dominate, and your choices will show it.

Security

Once your survival needs are satisfied, the next level of need that can motivate your choices is the need to find some basis for emotional security, in addition to your physical security. The number one emotional need for all people is the need for *acceptance or belongingness:* the emotional satisfaction that comes from external approval, from feeling that you are part of a couple, organization, or peer group. Again, this is a *huge* influence on what you choose for yourself. For example, if this need is predominant and you feel that true individual expression might bring criticism or even rejection, you might very well choose conformity rather than expression. You may very well have developed a pattern of ignoring your own thoughts and feelings, instead opting to substitute someone else's judgment for your own because that met your need for emotional security. That behavior is not so farfetched; if you think about it, politicians do it every single day. I don't think a damn one of them has ever had an original thought. Instead it's, What do they want to hear; tell them what they want to hear or they might reject me at the next election. Your personal choice to do the very same thing with the decisions in your life may have been based on very similar logic. Many of your choices may have been made out of concern for what other people might think and the hope that by complying with what you *think* they want, you will win their approval and acceptance. Problem is, you and what you want or need gets ignored as a motivator in your decision making.

Love

Studies of newborn babies show that unless we receive love, our survival is in jeopardy from the first days of our lives. As we grow up, if we are not convinced that we have it, we will go through life trying to find it. There is a certain way in which we need to be touched, held, and regarded behaviorally and emotionally. If we feel deprived, even from an early age, and before we have the vocabulary to describe it, we will be driven in our lives to find it. That drive can be so powerful as to dominate our thinking and motivations and therefore our choices throughout life. Some of your most critical choices in life may have resulted from your need for, your search for a love that, whether real or imagined, you felt was elusive.

Self-Esteem

Once we have satisfied our survival needs, have attained a basic sense of security, and feel loved, we relate our decisions about life to self-esteem. Unfortunately, most people haven't got the foggiest idea of what *self*-esteem is all about, because they've been chasing after other people's versions—that is, external sources of esteem—all their lives. For many, self-esteem or self-worth is too often measured as a function of what one accomplishes, accumulates, or extracts from the world in the form of titles, trophies, or acknowledgments. Too often it can mean a particular car, house, dress size, golf score, or bank account.

This craving for esteem, if it is measured by an external yardstick and or worldly "stuff," can be elusive, fickle, and as addictive as any drug. Research with adolescents has shown that consistently boosting kids' esteem externally, such as with random, "just-be-positive praise" or a particular title or position in school, is not a good idea: Children can end up as a bottomless pit, wanting more and more, even going so far as to commit illegal acts to gain it from their peers, all because the external never really "hits the spot," and so they just keep trying to meet a need from the outside that can only be met from the inside. The more your internally defined self-esteem is lacking, the more you are vulnerable to external influence. In short, if you aren't "squared away" within yourself, they can "get to you" from the outside. The world will pick on self-doubt like it is an open wound. As a result, you can find yourself making decisions driven by a need to build how you feel about yourself, but from all the wrong resources. Simply put, if you don't love, believe in, and accept yourself, you will try to find someone else to do it for you. Seeking that validation so desperately from someone other than yourself can have a huge effect on the choices you make.

Self-Expression

Sooner or later, if we feel that our more fundamental needs have been met, we begin to start making choices based on the need to express the gifts that are uniquely ours. If we feel that our life is safe, our acceptances are secure, and we have the confidence of good self-acceptance and worth, we turn to more esoteric needs. We feel the urge to make our mark on the world. We may feel that we have to teach, train, design, or create. We may feel the need to write or draw or paint. We may feel we have to have children or travel the world to express ourselves. We make the choice to go into our own business, rather than being "just a number" in a megacorporation. Driven by the need to "be" who we uniquely are, we choose to be in the country with nature or in the city, shakin' and bakin' in the business world. This need is so great in many people that they will renounce everything that is familiar and predictable—their jobs, their position in society, even their families—to write their novel or become an actor. The need for self-expression can be an enormous drive from within, prompting choices that often puzzle friends and family.

Intellectual Fulfillment

Choices in this area are driven by the desire for answers: to the acquiring of knowledge, both general and specific, and the pursuit of answers to profound questions. As with the other needs in the hierarchy, once this level of functioning is met, it can become powerfully consuming. The search for an answer can consume some people, and all of their choices can be driven accordingly. Once other needs are met, some just take a totally cerebral approach to life and their choices show it. When such is the case, choices are often one-dimensional.

Spiritual Fulfillment

Choices here are guided by a vision or goal beyond personal interest. Many regard this level of functioning as being highly actualized, because it transcends everyday life as you may make choices that are designed to deal with someone or something that you perceive as greater than yourself. You make choices that reflect that you realize that material and ego needs are often transient and may only be momentary. You order your decisions so that your spiritual needs, while difficult to measure by objective means, are focused upon. It shouldn't be hard to understand why these choices are often not the focus of your life if you are dealing with more immediate needs, such as survival. It is sometimes difficult to invest in the spiritual pursuits when your energies are absorbed in feeding or protecting yourself or your children. I'm not saying that that is right or that it is universal cross-culturally; I am just saying that it "is." Those with deep religious convictions would disagree with this pursuit being only at the top of the hierarchy. My response is that those with a deep spiritual focus, in the absence of well-met needs at the other levels, have transcended the worldly measure of whether those needs are met or not, and are in fact "evolved" in their choice making.

Those are categories of needs that may have been at work in your seven critical life choices. As you seek to identify your seven critical choices, I trust that these motivations will help point you to what were your most significant choices, as well as why you made them.

THE ROLE OF CHOICE

We don't begin life with the privilege and responsibility of making choices for ourselves. Typically, we don't even begin to differentiate ourselves from other living forms until the age of two. Your dependence on your parents or other adult authorities means that, during your crucial years of growth and learning, they were the people who made your choices for you. Questions about what to eat, what to wear, what your living environment would be like, and which schools you'd attend were probably answered with little or no input from you. The adults in your life worked these things out and they did so either with your interests in mind—or not. They may have heavily influenced your choice of friends and your ultimate choice of a career. In fact, if you had agreed to all the "wants" they wanted for you, you might still be busy helping them implement a long program of deciding the rest of your life.

Too often, parents forget that one of the most important aspects of our growing up is learning how to make choices for ourselves. It is a skill to be learned and one that is exercised with confidence when the authentic self is the platform from which one makes those choices. What rules or guidelines did you learn as a child that equipped you to make good decisions? What did your parents teach you that served as a framework for your saying yes or no to the options you have had in your life? Did they instill in you a sense of confidence about your ability to make choices for yourself? Unless your parents identified it as an explicit target, a goal that they consciously incorporated into their child rearing, then whatever skills you have today as a decision maker you have learned by trial and error. Tragically, some people never learn these skills at all, because they live with the fear and doubt of a fictional self that operates without substantive connection to you and your strength.

Helen's story is typical of the American experience of growing up, even if the details are unique to her. Helen and her brother, Robbie, ten years younger, were raised by two very ambitious parents. When I say they were ambitious, I mean that like a lot of parents, they loaded up their children with ambitions they themselves could not fulfill. I don't recall what particular glory Robbie was supposed to achieve, but Helen was destined to be a major Hollywood star, according to her mother. When Helen was still a toddler, her mother would rewash and iron Helen's clothes during Helen's nap, I suppose so that she would be presentable if a big-time movie director happened to stop by that afternoon. There were speech lessons on Mondays and Wednesdays, singing lessons on Tuesdays and Thursday, and either gymnastics, ballet, or tap the rest of the week. As her school years progressed, Helen would regularly miss important assignments and tests because, in her mother's words, "she's number one on the list for a part in that new TV sitcom, you know," and they were flying out to California for yet another audition. The bottom line was that her parents had determined all of Helen's choices by the time Helen was ten minutes old.

You might guess the rest of the story. Mothers do not always count on their daughters changing the script, but they do. Although Helen landed a few bit parts here and there, and got some "nibbles" from some celebrated names in the movie industry, she was sick of the whole business, both emotionally and physically, by the age of eleven. It was as if her soul and body could no longer endure the struggle to live a fictional life. Her authentic self cried out for release.

But who was Helen, really? She could not allow herself to rebel against her mother openly. Remember the list of needs that we discussed at the beginning of this chapter. Outright revolt would have jeopardized Helen's needs for survival, security, and love. Instead, she rebelled inwardly. At about the time Helen's mother knew that she had lost control of her daughter's life, the drug habit began to take its toll. In other words, now there was nobody in charge: Her mother could not run her life, but neither could Helen. Helen was in no shape to take over at that point. She had never known the power of making her own choices and she did not understand consequences. So began years of being dependent on drugs to "resolve" her lack of self-esteem and her ignorance about how to make choices. Consistently, the choices that Helen made from this point on were destructive ones. She never learned better. She died at the age of twenty-nine, still not knowing her own will.

Sadly, letting others make our choices for us is a growth industry. The prospect of making a wrong choice can be so tough for some people, so frightening, that they will yield to other people their power to choose. Or, not realizing not choosing is a choice, they will sit idly by. There are plenty of people like Helen who, rather than turning to drugs as she did, forfeit their power to a gang or a religious cult, where all decisions are dictated by a single leader. Psychic hotlines and spirit mediums generate huge profits from people's fear of making decisions on their own. In a variation on the same theme, some people dread leaving the military because they are terrified of the new choices they would face in civilian life; they have developed a "comfort zone" that equates contentment with being told what to do. Other people seek help from counselors or clergy, but then say to them, in effect, "Tell me what to do with my life, and I will obey." And it will be no surprise to learn that lots of people look to marketers and advertisers to make their choices for them, from sunup to sundown—a job that those industries are more than happy to perform.

What I am challenging you to do, instead, is take ownership of your own decision making. Step 1: You can't change what you don't acknowledge and acknowledging the most important choices that you've made so far in life is a crucial step toward positive change. Without this review, you will continue to make choices without any awareness of what is driving them or what you are setting yourself up for when you make the choice. This lack of awareness can only lead you still further from your authentic self, because it denies the priorities that you have within you. Without knowledge of what you are, and the choices that have led you to a fictional, world-defined, parent- or employer-defined existence, you are lost. By identifying your seven critical choices, understanding why you made them (that is, what needs drove those choices), and the results they led to in your life, you will gain important insight into who you have become in this life.

You may find that many of your choices have had negative consequences; others have been positive. Your task now is to get them down on paper and to distinguish one kind from the other. Prepare to get real and get honest with yourself about the choices that have led you to where you are, right now. There is no room for victim thinking here. We are dealing with life influences that *you* made through the choices and decisions *you* chose.

THE CHALLENGE

As with the written exercises you have done previously, you are about to do some "recollecting." Remember what that means: You are recalling, first, an incident, and second, a result. In this case, the incident you should focus on is the particular *choice* that you made at a given time in your life. The result, the set of consequences that followed that choice, will be what lifts the decision to the status of a **critical choice.** In other words, when you look at that decision with eyes wide open and you do an honest appraisal of the consequences that have flowed from it, you see that a critical choice is one that has affected your life, for better or worse, up to the present day.

Also remember that choosing not to act is, in itself, a choice. That means that in taking stock of your critical life choices, you must keep a lookout for moments when a choice was called for and you chose not to act. As an example, a woman who, tragically, was molested as a child, might need to acknowledge that she made a choice to conceal that fact. When she could have spoken up, she chose not to. Because that choice may have prolonged her pain, because it has so clearly affected her present self-concept, she has got to acknowledge it—I'm not saying punish herself for it, and I'm not saying that to do other than be silent would have been an easy choice; I am saying that, easy or hard, it was a critical choice, so she must identify it. You cannot change what you don't acknowledge. Similarly, a talented entrepreneur might need to acknowledge that he allowed himself to spend years working as a faceless cog in a company that he hated, rather than step up and challenge himself to do something different. (I've already confessed a similar critical choice in my life that cost me ten years.) Deciding not to end a harmful relationship, or try for a scholarship, or ask for a raise, are the kinds of choices to bring out into the open. *Not* acting is a choice that you need to own.

Another reminder: Your critical choices may certainly include positive decisions, moments whose consequences have affirmed or inspired you and which continue to give you satisfaction today. These are the decisions about which you say, "You know? If I had it to do over again, I would do it *exactly that way.*"

So: What are the seven choices that have most profoundly shaped your outlook on life? Let the following questions help you recollect. As in previous exercises, I have grouped the questions in age brackets, so the answers will be easier to remember. Likewise, I have set out some categories for you to consider as you reflect on your decisions during each period of your life. However, treat these age brackets and categories as suggestions, not requirements. I assure you that, like defining moments, your critical choices are not age-specific, nor are they limited to one area of your life. Their "ripple effects" continue through your life, regardless of when they occurred or in what area.

Again, use your private journal here. Find a quiet spot that affords you some privacy, a comfortable place to sit, and some uninterrupted time to do the following exercises.

Here are the life dimensions or categories that I invite you to consider. Do not feel that you must restrict yourself to this list or that you must identify at least one critical choice in each dimension. Instead, simply let this list stimulate some ideas for you as you write. Your critical choices may have occurred in the following areas or in others:

Personal Life
Physical Life
Professional Life
Family
Education
Spiritual Fulfillment

Social Life
Relationships

It may also be helpful to take a look back at the material you wrote for the exercises concerning your defining moments, since some of those defining moments may be directly linked with a critical choice. As an example, you may recall my mom's decision to move into our home not long after the death of my dad. First, there was the defining moment (the death of my father), and then her critical choice (to move in with us). The same formula may hold true for you, too. Let your defining moments lead you, as appropriate, to your critical choices. There may be some complete overlap here, as well. In other words, a critical choice may well have turned out to be a defining moment.

Recall the various age brackets:

Ages 1–5	Ages 21–38
Ages 6–12	Ages 39–55
Ages 13–20	Ages 56 and beyond

For each age bracket listed above, do the following exercises:
Consider: Was this age bracket one in which I made a critical choice? If so:

1. **What was the choice?**
   Write a sentence that describes it. An example: "When I was eighteen, I chose to get married and go to work."
2. **Why did you make it?**
   Write a paragraph that explains what prompted you to make the choice. Identify as many factors as you can recall. Feel free to use the list of needs set out earlier in this chapter. As an example, this paragraph might start out with something like: "I thought I was in love. I had never done particularly well in school, and my family didn't have much money, so college just

didn't look like an option to me then. Working at the plant looked like real security. I got big self-esteem from being able to buy a new pickup truck, move into my own apartment. I liked being liked by the supervisor, and envied and admired by my high school friends."

3. **What alternatives did you give up by making this choice?**
   Write a paragraph that describes what the "cost" of the choice was. An example: "By going straight to work, I was choosing not to go to college. By getting married, I was giving up the opportunity to date other people," and so on. Obviously, there may be a certain amount of speculation involved here; but do the best you can to examine what "might have been," had you not made the choice that you did.

4. **Where were you, in terms of your self-concept, immediately *before* this choice, and what was your self-concept *after* this choice?**
   In other words, if the critical choice affected your self-esteem, how were you different, in your self-esteem, before and after that critical choice? What aspect or dimension of your self-concept was involved in or was affected by that choice? Write those observations down.

   Maybe the critical choice had an impact on your sense of self-control, your anxiety, ambition, pride, or fear. Whatever dimension was affected, name it in writing. Just as for the exercise you did for your defining moments, think of these as before-and-after "snapshots" of one element of your self-concept, this time with respect to that critical choice.

5. **Write a paragraph to describe the long-term residual effect of that critical choice.**
   How has this critical choice affected you, long term? Again, what you're looking for here are aspects about yourself that have developed as a direct consequence of that event. Your paragraph might begin, "As a result of this critical choice to

get married and go to work, I believe that I expected everything to come easy to me after that. I made no effort to come
up with a 'safety net' for the possible loss of my job and I
started living on assumptions. I became financially irresponsible, believing that the job would always be there for me, and
that I could continue to expect increases in pay. My expectations for my own life got narrower and narrower." Let your
writing speak to the consequences of your choice. How has it
defined you?

6. **Write down how and why you think the critical choice either
clarified or distorted your authentic self.**
The task here is to determine whether the choice led you away
from your authentic self or closer to it. Did it contribute to
your joy, peace, and satisfaction? Or, as a consequence of that
choice, did you give up some of those things? What did you
learn about yourself as a result of that choice? Write a short
paragraph of explanation.

7. **Review your interpretation of and reaction to the critical
choice. Decide whether or not you believe your interpretation
was and is accurate or inaccurate.**
As you did with your defining moments, test your reactions to
your critical choice using the benefit of time, objectivity, maturity, and experience. It may be that a critical choice for which
you have regularly blamed yourself has been distorted, in your
perception, into something it was not. Your paragraph should
answer: Has my interpretation of this critical choice been accurate? Or have I exaggerated or distorted it in some way?

At this point, you should have completed one set of seven exercises for *one* of the age brackets shown on page 141. Now go back,
take another look at those age brackets, and decide which bracket
you want to address next. As you have just done, ask yourself, Was
this a period in my life when I made a critical choice? If so—even if

you just think the answer may be yes—let me encourage you to get going with Question 1 again and work your way through all seven questions. Recall the focus of this chapter: You will have completed your homework for this chapter when you have conducted this "self-audit" for a total of seven critical choices.

6 YOUR FIVE PIVOTAL PEOPLE

*"He who seeks for applause only from
without has all his happiness in another's
keeping."*

—OLIVER GOLDSMITH

THE fear-induced, self-destructive determination that so many
people demonstrate in suppressing who they authentically are is a
never-ending source of amazement to me. When you think about
how much life energy people devote to denying who they are and living who they aren't, you can't help being awed by the tragic enor-
mity of it. What a waste of talent and energy! As we get into the
complexities of adult living and try in vain to "dance" for so many
masters, the drain of crucial life energy just gets worse and worse. In
the complex lives we create with kids, parents, spouses, jobs, church,
friends, and every other demand source, it can seem like you are trying to hold *ten* of those "childhood beach balls" underwater all at
once. Trying to be so many things to so many people, oftentimes
when none of them are even almost who you really are, can absolutely wear you to a frazzle. You are who you are and the more
you try to ignore that reality, the higher the cost to you. You can be
your own worst enemy, creating emotional and physical breakdown.

The disconnect shows in estrangement from loved ones, physical exhaustion and illness, frustration, and inner turmoil. As if we don't do a good enough job of losing touch with our authentic selves and sabotaging our own lives by settling for what we don't want, we frequently and tragically get "help" from those we encounter along the way. These "helpers" are among what I call the **pivotal people** in your life. Maybe those people include your parents, spouse, or siblings. Maybe the pivotal people in life include teachers, friends, and coworkers. Whoever these people are in your life, some of them are genuinely positive influences and some are horribly negative. But make no mistake: Certain other people do have a huge impact on the formation and content of your self-concept. Moreover, these people can determine whether you live consistently with your authentic self or instead live some counterfeit life controlled by a fictional self that has crowded out who you really are.

You have encountered hundreds, maybe even thousands, of people in your life who have had an impact, yet research has shown that there are as few as *five* truly pivotal people who have left indelible impressions on your concept of self and, therefore, the life you live. Our goal in this chapter is to identify and examine these people and their roles in your life.

In one of my seminars some years ago sat a woman who appeared to be about sixty and in outward appearance was the picture of success. My initial impression of her, sitting there in the second row, was that she was somehow solid or "hard," a powerful woman. She looked as if she might have stopped by on her way to a board meeting. The seminar was a weekend event, but she had clearly chosen not to dress down for it. Her dark suit was elegantly tailored, crisply pressed, and very expensive looking. Every strand of her silver hair appeared to have been set in place with deliberation and care. Her large hands were manicured and a platinum bracelet gleamed on one wrist. Even more striking was the fact that she said not one word for the first two days of the weekend seminar. The program was designed to be a highly participative journey of self-discovery and self-disclosure. Yet no matter how vocal the rest of the group became or how intense things got, this lady sat stoically, her hands folded in her lap, her jaw set, her gray eyes resisting contact with anyone else's. At those points in the seminar when I normally would have solicited responses from each person in the room, I chose to bypass her. It was obvious to all of us that she wasn't going to say anything until she was ready.

At about 10:30 in the morning of the third and last day, after a series of heartfelt, "unburdening" disclosures by a number of people in the room, there was a pause in the program as we got ready to move on to the next phase of the session. It was in the midst of that pause that this woman got slowly to her feet. Everybody immediately stopped what they were doing. All eyes turned to Claire, our silent lady of detached composure. All of us sensed that we were about to hear something vitally important. She placed her hands on the back of the chair in front of her, gripping it so tightly that her knuckles were white. Finally, staring straight ahead, she spoke.

"His hands were heavy," she said, in a voice that betrayed her apparent strength. "His hands were rough." She paused. "His strap was vicious."

I recall that it took an effort of will on my part to break the spell she had unwittingly cast, but I encouraged her to go on.

"My mother was married to a man who beat her," she said. "I was always so scared, so afraid that he would kill her. I wanted to help. I wanted to make him stop, but I couldn't. He made me sit on a cane-back chair and watch him as he beat her with his fists, his belt, and sometimes a broom handle he had broken her leg with once when I was not around. He told me it was so I could 'learn some respect.'

"Sometimes my mother would look at me through swollen and bloody eyes and shake her head, telling me not to move or get involved. She knew that I, too, was in danger. She was afraid that I would somehow provoke his anger toward me, as well. Once, when I threw myself on top of my mother and cried and begged him to stop, he immediately started beating me along with my mother. I felt so helpless. My mother and I couldn't help each other—we just had to take it and take it and take it! I was a little girl when it started, only seven years old. I am now sixty-four years old and I can still feel the fear. I still get dry-mouthed and sick to my stomach in one second when I think about it."

Now her tears began to flow and her voice was filled with so much pain that it was difficult to listen to.

"He beat me for the next fourteen years. Nothing was too small or trivial to set him off. He would lay that strap across my backside and thighs until I bled. When he was beating me, he would scream vile and ugly things: 'You little bitch, it's all your fault. You make me crazy with your whining and crying and constant money spending! I hate you for what you've done to me! I hope you're happy, you filthy little whore!'

"I felt so guilty. I would go for days without eating anything, because I knew our problems were because I cost so much to have around. I could never bring friends home, because I was terrified of what might happen. At school, I would do anything to keep my legs from being seen. No one was going to see the marks that his strap had made on my body.

"It's strange to say it, but because of him I learned to withdraw from my body. Whenever he beat me, I would lie there on my stomach, with my face buried in my hands, and it was like I wasn't there somehow. It was so humiliating, so degrading that I just had to 'go away' in my mind. I stopped being there anymore. It was like the real me was hovering above the bed, watching what was happening."

Standing there by herself, she now looked surprisingly fragile and small. For the very first time, she looked around the room. She studied each of us, one face at a time, as if she had just read a news report in a foreign language and she needed to know whether a single person there had understood her. She looked for the judgment she had expected should her secret ever get out. She hung her head in shame, clearly wishing she could take back the truth that had been so carefully hidden for six decades of her life. Another participant, a woman in the same row, approached and placed a consoling hand on her shoulder. She stiffened at first, then relaxed a little.

"I've made a success of my business," Claire said finally. "We deal in scrap metals, and we do very well. I have succeeded in an industry dominated by men. But for sixty years of my life, that's how I have dealt with every crisis, every moment that was the least bit emotional: I have pulled out of myself, withdrawn. I've been emotionally unavailable for my children. Their father left me not long after my youngest son was born. I'm here because my children begged me to come. They don't know why I've always been so 'cold,' as they put it. I'm here today for them. And for me. I don't want to die this way, having never felt, having never lived, having never shared.

"I have been emotionally 'checked out' for sixty years, do you see?" Then she whispered, "I'll be sixty-five in July. Please, God, someone help me get free of this horrible burden. It has been so very long. This is my *last chance*."

That was part one of what became a very moving journey for her back to her authentic self. Through the remaining hours of that seminar, and again in another session later on, we focused on teaching her that she could safely let her guard down. Within minutes of her first comments to the group, for example, every person in that room had approached her, and as they placed an affirming hand on her hand or arm—acts of physical kindness rather than pain—she had responded, first with fear, then with acceptance. There had been tears and murmurs of encouragement and quiet embraces and she began to "check back in" to her authentic self in a powerful way. We taught her that she could be vulnerable with people who would not hurt her. We helped her see that she must not feel shame for actions she had no part in and for which she bore no responsibility. With time, she discovered that she must not take ownership of her stepfather's pathology by "splitting" into a separate personality. She learned that she could take her power back from this man who had so cruelly controlled her life while he was alive and still dominated it in death.

The epilogue to this story: Once this woman reclaimed her authentic self, it was as if floodgates had opened. Years of pent-up affection, her inborn gift for loving and caring for other people, just erupted from her. Her overjoyed children received a mother they had never known before. She became a volunteer facilitator at subsequent workshops and her passion for it was a sight to behold. Her own experiences taught her who in the room was most resistant, most "cold," most in need—and she latched onto those people as her particular project. At seminar after seminar, she became a kind of mother hen, clucking and embracing and loving the stoniest souls in the room until they melted. No matter how shut down, backed up, or embittered they were, she would not let go. She knew from experience where they were and she went in after them. She absolutely was not going to leave anyone behind.

What this woman's experience demonstrates is that, just as our self-concept is shaped by a series of defining moments and by a small number of critical choices, it can also be profoundly influenced by this handful of **pivotal people** whose actions resonate, for good or ill, throughout the rest of our lives. In her case, a diseased and twisted stepfather set in motion her desperate withdrawal from life. His brutality caused her to slam shut her emotional window. In a tragic and wholly undesirable way, he became pivotal to the development of her self-concept. He buried her authentic self, a self that was previously marked by young and fresh hope, optimism, and joy. He buried it beneath a cruel barrage of pain and rejection, denying her value and using her instead to vent his sickness of mind and heart. He became pivotal by poisoning a young and impressionable girl in such a profound way that it altered her for a lifetime—almost. Every person who has ever lived, you included, has a short list of these pivotal people. Once acknowledged, once identified as the source of such powerful impact, the effects that these people have had on you can be dealth with, but not until you get real about the role they have played in your life.

It is also the case that the pivotal people in your life can be those who give you words of encouragement at critical times, who open up opportunities you didn't know existed, who unravel for you a problem you thought had no solution. They can be people who step up at critical times with great acts of courage and support or can in a thousand humble, simple ways demonstrate their love and concern for you. Sometimes they are the people who recognize in you a particular talent and inspire you to develop it. They may even be people you don't know very well but whom you watch from a distance, and the way they live their lives challenges you to live yours with the same qualities. They can be people who love you when you are not very lovable.

Pivotal people can be found in unexpected places and in unexpected stages of your life. They may be people whose influence is connected to the authority they exercised, in a caring and responsible way, during your growing-up years. On the other hand, they may include someone you encountered today. The influence they've had in your life may be the result of years of steady guidance, day in and day out—or it may be the result of a single act that they themselves would be unlikely even to recognize. Perhaps they entered your life only for a short time before moving on, yet you still carry, today, the effects of that encounter.

Perhaps predictably, I've observed that successful people—meaning those whose lives are peaceful, well balanced, and satisfying—tend to identify more heroes or role models among their five pivotal people. By contrast, people who live with pain in their lives tend to single out those whose influence was just as significant, just as dramatic, but who were their tormentors. It is also possible, and in fact not at all uncommon, that a successful person may attribute a great deal of positive characteristics to someone whose influence at the time was entirely negative or destructive, yet the person accommodated or adapted that negative experience in a healthful and positive way. In other words, some of the jerks in your life may have actually toughened you up; they may have made you work hard to escape and in the process you may have come to appreciate meaningful alternatives. I'm not saying, "See? It was all worth it. It builds character, you should thank them!" That is absolutely untrue. Cruelty and pain are not legitimate teaching tools, no matter how tough or committed they may have made you. What I am saying is that the problems certain pivotal people may have inflicted on you may have, over time, tested and refined some of your finest qualities and brought them to the surface. The "tuition" was likely way too high, but if this is the case in your life and you found a way to create value from the pain, then maybe you have found meaning in your suffering.

With all these considerations in mind, then:

Who are the five pivotal people in your life? Who are the five people who shaped the self-concept that controls your life today, both positive and negative? Who has written on the "slate of you"?

As you think about this question, it may be helpful to look back at the writing that you did for the previous chapters on defining moments and critical choices. Your answers there may instantly reveal who belongs on your list of five pivotal people. If not, perhaps the mental associations or connections that are triggered by those writings call some names to mind.

You may find this exercise will be a breeze; you may have a hard time limiting yourself to just five names. Alternatively, you may find it very difficult to come up with that many. Wherever you find yourself, though, remember who you're looking for: These are people who have played a unique and substantial role in creating the person you are today. Think of them as five individual links in the long chain that leads to who you are, at this moment, as you read this paragraph. Every link in that chain is a critical element of it. In other words, if any one of these five people were to be removed from that chain, the you at the end of that chain today would be someone substantially different, a person you might not even recognize.

As before, take your journal and carve out some time alone to do this writing. You'll want to be relaxed yet focused as you do the following:

- List the name of one pivotal person in your life.
- In two separate sections under that person's name, write first a description of the person's actions and then secondly, the influence that that person has had on you.

In section one, first identify, with as much detail as you can, that person's conduct or behavior that you now see as pivotal. You will want to use "action verbs" in order to make it as concrete as possible: for example, Claire, my seminar participant, might begin by writing, "For fourteen years, he thrashed my mother and me with a strap, destroying my sense of self, my sense of value, my sense of dignity." Someone else, writing about an adult friend, might begin, "She loved and cared about me when I wasn't very lovable. She was coming in the door, when everyone else was on the way out. She stood by me when it would have been so much easier not to." Write as long and as detailed a description as you need to and can. You will be amazed at what flows from your pen.

In the second section, describe the effects that you attribute to that action. What consequences flow from the pivotal person directly to your present-day self? Examples might begin: "Because I could not bear the humiliation and pain, I 'checked out' of life, and withdrew from anything that involved my emotions, even when my husband and kids were yearning for my emotional self." Or: "Her words of encouragement, spontaneously offered and never judgmental, have caused me to believe that I must have something worth loving or else such a fine person wouldn't have been there for me. She gave me the patience to make it through some of the toughest times I've known and I've tried to emulate her character in the things that I do today."

The value of this exercise depends upon your giving a voice to connections and consequences that you may never have expressed in words. By that I mean that the *cause-and-effect relationship* between the behaviors of each of your five people, and the results in your own life and self-concept, demand your closest attention as you write. This will be information that you will need to come back to as we go on, so take the time now to do an honest and thorough appraisal, in writing, of *all five of your pivotal people.* Don't be afraid to write down your acknowledgment of a pivotal person's impact on your life for fear that it will galvanize or justify it. I'm not teaching you to play the victim and blame others for who and what you have become. We will soon be dealing with your power to reclaim the power that is yours, but for now realize that you cannot change what you do not acknowledge. Be real, or you will forever be stuck due to misdiagnosis of what cancer is eating away at your authentic self.

An important caveat here is that the people who have been pivotal in your life may not fit neatly into either "black hats" or "white hats." Someone may have had a profoundly negative influence on your life, while at the same time having qualities that you appreciate and admire. I recall one patient's telling me, for example, how much she admired her father for his extraordinary work ethic, his willingness to take on two and even three different jobs in order to support his young family. He arrived in the United States knowing almost no English, having little money and no "network" he could turn to for help; yet within a few years, he established a comfortable and secure lifestyle for his wife and three daughters. On the other hand, she told me, her father had also been a stern and difficult parent. In talking about it as adults, the three sisters discovered that he had never once told any one of them that he loved them. (And I promise you, no matter how much he may have thought he showed it, every one of those girls needed to *hear* it.) Moreover, the academic and career expectations that he placed on all of them were incredibly burdensome, creating emotional and physical stresses that each daughter was still dealing with well into middle age.

Certainly this woman could acknowledge her gratitude and admiration for her father's sacrifices and for the life he had created for them in America. At the same time, however, I can tell you that he will always be on her list of pivotal people, both because he drove her so relentlessly and because he deprived her of the praise she so desperately needed, and for which she still hungers.

Another possibility is that some kind of turnaround occurs in the life of the person who was pivotal. It may be, for example, that an abusive, alcoholic mother creates for her daughter a childhood filled with terror, loneliness, and instability. Eventually, however, the mother successfully completes some kind of recovery program and carries through on her commitment to stay sober. Recognizing the trauma she has created in her daughter's life, the mother actively seeks out ways to repair the relationship; she asks for forgiveness and does everything she can to become the mother she would have wanted for her daughter. In those circumstances, the daughter might well decide that her mother has been pivotal for wholly positive reasons. She doesn't pretend there weren't lots of dark years growing up. She vividly remembers the pain her mother caused. But none of that should prevent the daughter from identifying her mom as pivotal, if that's what she concludes about the love and character that her mother has demonstrated.

The lesson is that your pivotal people may be admirable in all kinds of ways, yet they may have influenced you in an unmistakably negative fashion. Similarly, a person whose "rap sheet" might be riddled with all kinds of bad deeds may, with a kind word, a gesture of sacrifice, or in some other manner, have affirmed and uplifted you in a life-changing way. You should not think of "pivotal" as meaning 100 percent negative or 100 percent positive.

Do not move on until you have written your responses, for both sections described above, as to each of your five pivotal people.

Time now for a critical question:

Were *you* on the list of the five pivotal people in your life?

If not, why not? If your own name does not appear anywhere on your list, consider what that means. It may mean that your self-concept has been molded and shaped primarily by other people. It means that you attribute your most basic, core characteristics to the actions and behaviors of others. For better or worse, you have yielded your power, entrusted it to someone else. Maybe that someone took good care of what you entrusted to them. Maybe they didn't.

Doesn't it make sense that your own name would appear on your list of five pivotal people? Let that be your goal for the remainder of this book. You are about to turn to that area in your self-concept where your greatest power lies. As you go forward, taking up a series of tools that can dramatically improve your experience of life, think of what you're doing as becoming a pivotal person. I'm challenging you to take the steps necessary to put yourself in position number one, "A," top of the list, first in the lineup of those who have and will determine the course of your life.

INTRODUCTION TO

INTERNAL FACTORS

"We have met the enemy and he is us."
—WALT KELLY AS POGO

I F you have honestly and thoroughly applied yourself to the exercises in the preceding chapters, then you know a great deal about your history. By completing an inventory of the external factors—moments, choices, and people—that have most profoundly affected who you are today, you've taken some huge steps forward in understanding your own self-concept.

But I will also acknowledge that, at this point, you may be reeling. You may be in pain. In fact, it would be a strange thing if you had completed your exploration of your external factors and felt nothing at all. That's because, as you revisited your defining moments, critical choices, and pivotal people, you were almost certainly coming face-to-face with a number of the sources of the pain you have in your life right now.

But be encouraged. You have found the bottom; here comes the power. By that I mean that your external factors are what they are: they're over; they're done. You can't change your history. But you *can* change your responses to those external factors. You *can* change what you do in response to that history. What you're about to learn about your internal factors will give you the power to create those changes.

Since it is a law of life that you cannot change what you do not acknowledge, it is important that you learn exactly, precisely what your current concept of self is made up of and what you are doing to either contribute to or contaminate that concept, every day, all day. Just as you've examined the external factors that have impacted your concept of self, now it's time to do a detailed audit on your internal factors: that is, how you have reacted internally to those key events, as well as how you tend to approach the world generally.

As I have said, you respond not to what happens in the world, but instead to your interpretations of it. Those interpretations—your perceptions and reactions—are the stimuli that you actually respond to, as opposed to what events have actually taken place in your life. Those interpretations take many different forms. They can be immediate and transient and they can be deeply ingrained and long lasting. Either way, they contribute to that chain of events that leads to your present self-concept and you must understand that, in examining your self-concept, you cannot skip a link in the chain.

Suppose, for example, that you were fired from a job. That was an external event to which you had some internal reaction. It is that internal reaction to the firing that impacts your concept of self, not the actual firing itself. Let's say your internal reaction is, Hey, I really hate getting fired; not good, not good at all. But, I know in my heart I did a good job and I'm a talented person. This just didn't work out. It was, however, a good learning experience and I will use it to my advantage so I don't screw up my next job. You're being realistic, yet you're not likely to suffer a huge blow to your self-concept. On the other hand, maybe your internal reaction is, I am such a loser. I blew it and got what I deserve. That job was too good for me and I was in way over my head. They just saw right through me. Now, with that internal reaction, your self-concept will definitely suffer.

One external event, two very different outcomes. Those hugely different internal reactions create the possibility of two resulting impacts on your self-concept. Hence my point: You respond not to what happens to you externally, but instead to how you internalize it. That means you have a tremendous power to influence and control your concept of self. I'm not preaching rah-rah here. I'm talking about your internal dialogue, the real-time conversation you have with you, about you. You have to be honest with yourself, but you do have choices and before we're finished, you will learn how to make them constructively. Bottom line: It's bad enough if negative things happen in your life, but it becomes disastrous if they result in your kicking your own ass, making them worse.

Just as with your external factors, the key to understanding your internal responses lies in knowing where to look and what questions to ask. We are going to do just that in the upcoming chapters, where we will examine five categories of internal activity:

Locus of Control
Internal Dialogue
Labels
Tapes
Fixed/Limiting Beliefs

I gave you a sketch of each of these categories of internal activity earlier, but without much detail. In the chapters that follow, we're going to "drill down" into each category, applying it as precisely as possible to your particular circumstances. We're going to find out the exact nature of your personal content, at both the conscious and unconscious level. And we're going to accomplish this with the precision of independent, structured observation. Remember, these internal factors are where your real power, your real opportunity to impact your concept of self is located. Pay superclose attention because this is not just some semantics game. This is where the rubber meets the road in the control of your self-concept and your life.

We need to begin by addressing what for many people is a point of confusion. When I start talking about internal factors, your understandable reaction may be, "He's asking me to examine my thinking, about my thinking," which sounds like a good recipe for a headache. It can sound really circular and impossible to do. Trust me, it's not. I'm not going to send you to the mountaintop without a map, asking you to contemplate your self and your essence. I *am* going to ask you some very specific questions and, once again, I am going to ask you to write your answers in your private journal. Your writing your answers is extremely important, because it gives you a measure of objectivity. Confusion comes from trying to observe yourself and your thinking without writing things down; it's like trying to see your own face without a mirror—which *will* give you a headache, I promise. By contrast, when you write your answers down, you gain an external perspective of internal events. Your writing will become the mirror that reflects what is going on in your mind and heart.

There's another concern we need to address right away. You may be thinking, Hey, I just don't think that much about myself. Maybe I'm just not that smart. I just don't think that all of this mental activity is going on within me.

Wrong! I guarantee you all of this mental activity is going on within you, but some of it (not your internal dialogue, which happens in real time) may be happening so fast, so repetitively, and be so well-rehearsed and overlearned that it is virtually automatic. When you have been over and over a process many, many times, you no longer consciously break it down into steps or thoughts.

Think about driving your car, for example. You don't have to think about what to do. You don't even have to look or think about putting in the key. There are muscle memories and habits that are so ingrained that you do it automatically. The same is true with your thoughts. You can go through labels, tapes, and fixed or limiting beliefs at incredible speed. You can think through a series of self-observations and judgments faster than you can blink an eye. It can happen so fast that you may not even be aware that you are doing it.

To grasp how internal factors can affect you, you've got to understand their speed, how automatic some of them can be. A good example of automatic, superhigh-speed thinking is someone who has a snake phobia. I'm talking about the kind of person who has a huge, *irrational* fear of snakes, versus the rest of us who may not love them or go out of our way to hold them but yet don't want to jump out of the window if we think one might have come through the room once a year ago. I'm talking about people who panic at the very thought of a snake, who try desperately to escape any circumstance in which a snake even might be present. Their fear is so debilitating as to be totally paralyzing.

Now if you sat this person down and asked him or her to tell you everything that is scary and hateful about snakes, he or she might say, "They're terrible! They are slimy, mean, and vicious creatures from hell. They can bite me and poison me and kill me. They have devil eyes. They're cold and sneaky. They crawl in your mouth and out your eyes! They make you scream and cry and wet your pants or worse. They are just horrible, cold, and clammy creatures."

These statements would be that person's **tapes** about snakes. Now suppose that, while he or she was still sitting there, you suddenly dumped a bunch of snakes in front of them. There wouldn't be enough time to process all of the words, "They scare me. They are slimy. They can bite me and kill me. They have devil eyes, and so on." They couldn't possibly think that fast—as you know from having seen or experienced this kind of thing in your own life.

The instant this person perceived the physical reality of a snake, they would instantly yell, "Snake!" and immediately lose all rational control. They'd go into a panic flight to get out of there, diving under the table or jumping out a window and hurting themselves in the process. Now the point is that the term "snake" is a summary term for the collection of beliefs they have internalized about snakes. The term becomes a symbol that represents a whole cluster of horrid fears about snakes, so that they do not have to go through a whole list of five or ten paragraphs about why snakes are bad. All they need to register is "snake," and they can instantly understand "bad deal" and out the window they go. This symbol or summary term is so overlearned, and it happens so fast, that that person's body and mind go into automatic pilot. The same is true with you. Instead of "snake," however, your term might be "loser" or "trapped" or "useless."

When I say "overlearned," I mean the reaction or thought has become a kind of shorthand. It's similar to the way prisoners tell jokes and stories while they're in the lockup. They tell them over and over, so many times, that they develop a shorthand for each joke: They can summarize an entire ten-minute joke by simply saying a number they all know. One prisoner will call out "Forty-one," and everyone will laugh, and another will call out "Twenty-nine," and they laugh again. They know what every number means. Through repetition, the jokes have been condensed down to summary terms and the collective information is packaged automatically into a single word or number.

Peggy was a special friend of mine who took a lot of pride in being independent and had developed a very successful business on her own. She came to me with a request to help her get ready for her *fifth* marriage. She confessed that she was totally in love with her husband-to-be, but she had also been totally in love with her previous four husbands and things had not worked out. Obviously she was afraid of another disastrous relationship and she thought that if she had some good advice, something she had not heard before, she would be better equipped to make this one work.

Instead of giving Peggy advice, I asked her first just to slow her thoughts down and relax. Then I asked her to close her eyes and imagine being married to her husband-to-be and to tell me what messages were going on in her head. Once Peggy started listening to her internal mental activity, she started saying things like, "I hope that I am wrong that Harry will not be as weak as my father and can support me. Harry sure is sweet, but I wonder how smart he is, since his job seems so lackluster. I am sure that it will be all right, because I will make it all right."

I wrote these statements down as she said them and when she was ready to review the session, I asked her to read them. She was shocked by what she had said and by her obvious fears, beliefs, and attitudes about Harry. These tapes and fears may or may not have been present in her past relationships, but they were certainly apparent with this one. Clearly, by telling herself that Harry was weak like her father, and that she expected that she would be disappointed and would have to be strong for herself, she was already preventing herself from being vulnerable with a husband she could not respect. In all likelihood, if she kept those messages in her head, she was headed straight for another divorce. And all of this was happening so fast in her head that she had no conscious idea that she was setting herself up for failure. How about you? You, too, have automatic thoughts, but not just about snakes and husbands (they *are* different, by the way). You also have these high-speed thoughts and internal reactions about yourself and they are so overlearned and happening so fast that you are not consciously aware of how they affect your behavior and your concept of self. We must learn to slow these thoughts down and listen ever so carefully.

The question arises: If these thoughts happen so fast, what can I do about them? Peggy's experience offers some answers. Among the incredible abilities that you have as a human being is the ability to go put your mind into slow motion, to hit the "slow-mo" button and cause everything to go into a steady, deliberate pace, so that you can hear what you are thinking and write it all down. The way you do that is first by getting very quiet and very still and second, by answering some hard questions about how you think and organize what you believe about yourself, in specific areas and categories. By doing that, you begin to challenge your internal processes. You start to test them against some modicum of conscious reality. Once you identify what is going on inside your mind, you can change it.

I believe that as we conduct this internal audit, slow your automatic thinking down, and record it all in writing to create objectivity, you are going to be absolutely amazed at how you have been setting yourself up to feel and act the way you do. Through this audit, you are creating access to powerful influences on your concept of self. You are going to find that so much of this content is at odds with your authentic self and is the basis for the life that you are passively and reactively living.

By putting a microscope and a bright light over these internal events, you can now observe, evaluate, and challenge what, until now, has been insidiously sabotaging your very existence from the inside out. In order for you to find your path back to your authentic self, you must become aware of these internal perceptions. You must learn how your internal processes have formulated your fictional self, only then can you fix what is negatively influencing your concept of self. If the oil pressure in your car drops, the problem is in your motor, not in the oil gauge. If you are living a fictional life that you neither designed nor wanted, the problems are in your internal reactions, not necessarily with the world events that have happened to you.

You will always be challenged by the external factors in your life. The electricity may be turned off. The repairman will be late. You may not get promoted. These events may not seem so critical when you look at them objectively, but if your internal reactions to these adverse events are toxic enough, they may eventually cost you your health. I tell you this to insure that you take all of this very, very seriously. You may not be able to change what happens externally in your world, but you can definitely change how you react to and internalize it. That is clearly a task worth doing. Let's start the audit and identify your targets for change.

7 LOCUS OF CONTROL

"The best place to find a helping hand is at the end of your arm."

— SWEDISH PROVERB

STOP. For this chapter to be meaningful, you need to do some homework first. I want you now to take the two "self-tests" found in Appendix A and Appendix B. You're going to find that this chapter is highly interactive, but you need to have your results from those tests before you go on. Take as much time as you need to answer all of the questions in both tests. Remember that honest self-appraisal is the key. We'll be dealing very directly with what you do in those self-tests, so don't cheat yourself by not doing them. Once you have finished both tests, come back here.

Okay, if you have taken both test, we are ready to go! In one of my "past lives," that would be before I came to my senses and pulled my head out, I helped direct a pain clinic in which we treated people with chronic and debilitating physically based pain. We once had two patients in the program with strikingly similar profiles. Both men were truck drivers, both were from the same town, both were married, they were close in age, and they had the identical diagnosis: protruding disks in the lower back, with severe pain irradiating down the left leg. Two patients that, although very much alike physically, proved to be dramatically different in some very important and outcome-determinative ways.

At his first appointment, Steve described for me his bouts with intense pain and his deep, reactive depression. He nonetheless wanted to be actively involved in his treatment and asked me to provide him with reading material—books, articles, anything—that might explain his pain syndrome and could help him understand why and how he was continuing to suffer with this chronic and life-altering problem. He said that traditional medical treatment had proven unsuccessful and that he believed that there "just has to be something that I can do to help myself." After some uncommonly in-depth questions and discussion, Steve's appointment came to an end and he headed home, loaded up with the kinds of documents he'd asked for.

Ten days into his therapy, Steve told me had reached two conclusions: first, that his pain emanated from a chronic imbalance in his muscles; and second, that this muscle problem was in turn being kept alive by his emotional stress and imbalance. He described the long-term stress he had accumulated from feeling overworked and overburdened year after year and by his recent frustration with his nagging pain. He also told me that he suspected his many battles with depression were complicated by a family history marked by frequent bouts of depression and anxiety.

Steve then said he had decided he, himself, could reverse his condition by improving the behavioral and emotional balance in his life and consequently his muscle tension. He believed it was now within his power to break the cycle of pain. True to this prediction, he came back in a few weeks to report that he had reduced his pain to a more moderate level, one that he described as manageable. A year later, in a follow-up visit, Steve looked upbeat and relaxed. He said his pain had improved even further, to the point that he would now describe it as very mild. He said that it no longer disrupted his life to any appreciable degree.

Although Don had the identical back problem, he was a study in contrasts. On Don's first visit to the clinic, he let it be known that he wasn't there willingly. He said his wife "just wouldn't let up" until he agreed to come by, so here he was. For the rest of the visit, about all Don would say was, "I hurt and I want somebody to take care of this pain. The doctors I've been to are all worthless. I should be getting better treatment than I have." What really got my attention was his parting comment as he headed out the door: "If it wasn't for bad luck, I wouldn't have any luck at all. First my back gets screwed up. Then I get a bunch of Mickey Mouse from the doctors." He shook his head and said, "Story of my life, what can I tell you."

After that first visit, several of the clinic staff had predicted "zero improvement" as Don's probable outcome from completing the rehabilitation program. And they were right. At no point during the program did Don make any effort to take charge of or even understand his condition. Rather than "work" the problem, he continued to dwell on it. He said he simply could not perform any kind of work, either inside or outside the home. He did not feel that anything helped his pain. In fact, in his view, the treatments only made it worse.

Don concluded that we were all wasting our time. He said it was obvious he had just gotten a "bum deal" from life, and that was that. Ultimately, what Don got from his treatment was exactly what he was looking for: nothing.

Two different approaches. Two very different results.

The one question that human beings probably ask more than any other is, Why? Why did this or that happen? Why did something not happen, or—if it did—why now? Why me, instead of someone else? Why did the accident happen to me, not the next car? Why didn't I get that raise, that promotion? Why, why, why?

From all that you've read so far about "internal factors," it should be clear that they deserve a great deal of your attention. A big part of what I'm asking you to do in this book involves bringing your internal factors into the sunlight, taking stock of your interior reactions to and interpretations of your experiences. And to do that right, you need to understand, first, the particular mind-set that you bring to the whys in your life. Think of it like this: Whenever you reach for a pencil, your being right-handed or left-handed predisposes you to reach for that pencil with one particular hand. You've done it the same way thousands of times, from the time you were a child. In the same way, when you are faced with one of the many whys in your life, you have a characteristic style or attitude of reaching for that answer. You have a predisposition to answer that why question the same way, time after time. This pattern of response, unique to you, is a characteristic that is called your **locus of control.**

"Locus" means "location," as in place. Locus of control is concerned with *where you tend to assign causation for the events in your life.* It's your accustomed viewpoint about where you perceive control to be. As things happen from moment to moment and day to day, your locus of control identifies and describes who or what you think is responsible. It's how and where you assign blame for your difficulties and credit for your accomplishments. In fact, your locus of control tells you not only what you think are the causes of your problems and your victories; it even determines where you tend to look for those causes in the first place.

Everyone, without exception, carries around this "perceptual set," this way of interpreting and assigning causation for the things that happen in his or her life. You may not be consciously aware of it, but it is there. It is down deep, at the bedrock of your self-concept. That's why we've got to address it first, before any of your other internal factors. Your belief about what or who you believe is in control of your life strongly influences the self-talk you have about yourself and the world you live in. It is a powerful and durable factor in how you interpret and react to events and opportunities. It means you are answering certain simple, but critical, questions in a predictable way.

What's your way? What does your locus of control point toward when I ask you questions like the following: Who or what is in charge of your life? Who is responsible for the results in your life? To whom or what do you look for answers or help when facing a challenge? Who is in control when things go wrong? When things go right, who gets the credit?

An illustration from the business world may help. If you've ever been in a situation where you had to convince someone to do something, you know how important it is to talk to the decision maker. You want the ear of the person who's got the authority to say yes or no. Pretend for a moment that you are a business operation called You, Inc. If I were going to consult with the business of You, Inc. if I had an appointment to create positive change throughout You, Inc. I would need to know who or what you believe is in control of the operation. Who's the decision maker, the person who'll be most directly involved in creating that change? Who's going to take the responsibility for making it happen? Where is this person *located*?

If in response to those questions, you said, "Beats me. I know *I'm* not in charge," then I would be wasting my time talking to you. I wouldn't bother talking to you if your answers showed me you believed you were like a passenger on a runaway train, a passenger with absolutely no control over what happened, when it happened, or for how long. If, on the other hand, you let me know that you were the person in charge of You, Inc., the engineer running the train, then you would definitely be the place to concentrate my efforts.

You've got to know what you believe about your role in the hierarchy of you. Identifying the standard way you answer life's most basic questions is a crucial step toward your authentic self. With that in mind, let this chapter help you identify and understand your particular locus of control.

You may recall that, in general, people's locus of control is either internal or external. For the sake of efficiency, let's use the term "internalizers" for those whose locus of control is internal, and "externalizers" for those whose locus is external.

INTERNALIZERS

Internalizers operate from a self-concept that says, "Anything bad that happens is my fault. Anything good that happens, I make it happen." In other words, whatever is going to be, good or bad, "it's up to me." To explain the outcomes in their lives, internalizers look to their own actions, inactions, traits, and characteristics. They almost always point to something they did or did not do as the primary factor in the outcome of any event. In some way or another, the event was "caused" by them.

For example, when an internalizer does poorly on a college test, she says, "I'm just not smart enough to do well; I haven't got the brainpower." Or she might say, "I bombed that test because I didn't study hard enough." Either way, her explanation would center on elements *specific to her,* and, therefore, elements that she controlled. Now suppose she scored well on the test. How would the internalizer explain her success? Right: "I'm smart," or "I worked hard and prepared well." Again, aspects of herself and her control.

EXTERNALIZERS

Whatever bad happens, the externalizer takes no ownership of it. Whatever good happens, the externalizer takes no ownership of it. In her view, someone or something else is behind all the results in her life. It might be the government. Maybe it's her mother. But it's certainly not herself.

I read a study once that assessed various occupations on a scale of "highly stressful" to "not stressful." Of all the jobs that the researchers looked at, by far the most stressful was bus driving. Why? Because there is nothing as stressful as having responsibility for events, yet not having any appreciable control over them. Think about it: Bus drivers are responsible for sticking to a schedule that is beyond their control. They can't control the traffic, they can't control their passengers, and they sure don't control the road construction that they've got to deal with on the way. Externalizers think of themselves as bus drivers on the route called life. They are stressed-out, uptight, and anxiety-ridden people and they're convinced that almost nothing along that route is within their control.

For example, if an externalizer did poorly on that same college test that the internalizer took, whose fault would it be? The teacher's, perhaps. Maybe bad friends who kept him up partying the night before. He might say the test was just too hard or it was "unfair." He never thinks for a moment that he failed because he was lazy, ill prepared, or unfocused.

Similarly, if the externalizer does well on the test, it's because "that test was easy," or the teacher was generous with the grades. The externalizer's habitual response, his "perceptual set," means he cannot give himself much credit, if any, for a successful grade. The story of his life is the story of other people and outside forces. His self-talk will predictably be a very victim-oriented one. Whatever happens, bad or good, the responsibility is someone else's.

CHANCE

For all their differences, internalizers and externalizers have this in common: Both of them identify someone or something that they perceive to be responsible for the outcomes in their lives. Whether "it's always me," or "it's never me," both of them have a deep-seated belief that there is a reason and a direct cause for everything that happens.

But there is a third category of people who we haven't talked about yet; call them "chance" people. In these people's perceptual set, every result or outcome is due to fate, accident, or just plain luck. For them, the expression "s___ happens" isn't an amusing bumper sticker; it's a creed, a philosophy of life. Chance people do not believe that they nor anyone else have any input or control over the results of their lives. They've got no idea why things happen the way they do. Accidents happen randomly. We are blessed randomly.

A good example of a chance person is a slot-machine gambler in Las Vegas. Other than inserting a coin and pulling the lever, this person has absolutely no control over the outcome, which is entirely dependent upon the machine.

People who measure high in the chance factor may believe in God, but not as one who makes things happen on a day-to-day basis. They certainly don't believe that they are part of a larger, purposeful plan. Things just happen and there is nothing we can do about them. Consider, for example, their attitude toward death: In their view, death is a random, wholly unknowable event that will not change schedule, regardless of how much you take care of yourself, how smart your doctors may be, where you live, or any of the hundreds of other things that could possibly affect your health. When your number's up, your card gets punched. There's no point in trying to influence or even change when and how you die. It just happens.

Let's look more closely for a moment at this issue of physical health, since it opens up for us a useful way of understanding more about the relevance of locus of control. Simply put, the question is this: Do you attribute the condition of your health to hard work (exercise, eating right), good doctors, or luck?

When internalizers get sick, they are likely to believe that they had some part in the onset of their illness. They take responsibility for getting sick and they will also take responsibility for getting well. For example, some patients with heart problems will declare that they got sick because they got too fat or did not exercise enough. They might feel that they had put themselves under too much stress or were smoking too much. By the same token, they would view their rehabilitation as part of their responsibilities, as well. They would take on the majority of accountability for healing themselves, including changing their lifestyles and faithfully taking their medication. Those are the internalizers.

Externalizers, on the other hand, might lie there in the hospital bed, blaming their heart trouble on any number of factors other than their two-pack-a-day habit or the two jumbo cheeseburgers they'd enjoyed every night for the past ten years. They might blame their parents ("I have terrible genes") or they might blame God. You might hear an externalizer explain how he was "hexed" by an enemy, doomed by the environment, or targeted for attack by a government agency. And as you might expect, they cannot be held responsible for their recovery. Rehabilitation, after all, is a job that belongs to doctors, nurses, and physical therapists—not to them.

Not surprisingly, the people who fall under the chance category are the most difficult to help. They take no personal responsibility for their recovery, they have no faith in any treatment, and they see no reason for setting goals or for trying to get better. Lacking a reason for effort, they have little or no motivation. The onset of disease is an accidental occurrence, a card played from the game of chance. Nothing and no one is responsible, other than the accidental combination of events. It was just the luck of the draw. You were in the wrong place at the wrong time.

Consider again my two patients at the pain clinic, Steve and Don. It's fairly obvious that Steve's quality of life is now much better than Don's. But the point of that story is not so much to prove "who was right" as to demonstrate how locus of control *can and does create results* in your life. Because Don had a mind-set that his problems came from bad luck, a raw deal, he ignored powerful resources at his disposal. In other words, even when opportunities to get better were within reach, he didn't see them. His "radar" wasn't scanning for those resources or opportunities, because he considered them irrelevant. He believed he was cursed with a bad back and that there wasn't really anything he or anyone else could do about it. His self-concept, dominated by a mind-set of "chance" regarding the key events in his life—in this case, his health—doomed him to a painful life that I have no doubt he is living today.

As important as your health is, make no mistake: The issue at hand is about far more than your health. Understanding and addressing your own locus of control has implications for your physical well-being, certainly, but it touches on *every* other area of your life. It directly influences the content and quality of every moment that you live.

Where you place the causes for the events in your life affects all of the big things: your career, your effectiveness as a parent, your marriage, and, yes, your health. If you are consistently and repeatedly attributing events in those areas to the wrong causes, then there can be no doubt that you are living a fictional self. And you are probably "misassigning" even the smallest things. My younger son, Jordan, bounced into the house the other day, looking as if he had conquered the world. I knew he had been preparing for a major test, so I assumed that he'd done well. I asked him, "Hey, how did your test go, did you slam or get slammed?"

He answered, "I did the slamming today. I kicked butt! Dad, it was sooo *easy.*"

I sniffed out a definite "teaching moment" here, time to help Jordan groom the ol' self-concept. (God has a special place in his heart for kids who have to grow up with a psychologist for a parent.)

I said, "You mean, you studied hard enough that you knew the answers. The test seemed easy, because you had the information, right? Instead of giving the test the credit for doing well, you can give the credit to the effort you made in studying, right? I mean really, you even skipped *The Simpsons* for this one!"

After looking at me as if I had sprouted an extra eyeball and after probably initially thinking Jeez, Dad, give it a rest! he eventually nodded, looked insightful, and said, "Yeah, I guess so. You're right. I did bust it pretty hard for two nights in a row!"

He had decided the test was easy. But aren't they always easy, when you're prepared? Easy or hard, it's the same test; the one who makes the call is you. If you are a chance person, you might say, "I lucked out on this one," or "I was unlucky." The externalizer would attribute his or her performance to how hard or easy the test was.

The internalizer would attribute the outcome to how well he or she studied to know the information or, more generally, how smart they are overall.

In which perceptual category do you place yourself? Where do you assign responsibility for your performance in life? Are you making your life choices based on your responsibility or someone else's? Are you waiting around, hoping that whoever you've assigned to manage your life will be smart enough to do it well?

Time for a reality check. Since I tend to speak a great deal about your being responsible for the way your life works, you would probably assume that I would vote for the internalizer as the person most likely to succeed on the road to authenticity. It is true, as I've said many times, that you create your own experience. I strongly believe that most things in your life are internally controlled. But I also trust that, in reading this chapter, you've spotted the defects in every locus of control. Neither the externalizer, the chance person, *nor* the internalizer can claim to have the perfect viewpoint. There are flaws inherent in all three.

For example, a woman is not to blame when her husband abandons her and their three children to run off with some cute bimbo at the office and does so without any warning whatsoever. His spineless, immature, and cruel conduct is not a matter of her control or responsibility. If she's sitting around a year later, still numb with grief, saying, "It's my fault," then something is wrong with her perceptions. She is inappropriately internalizing. She's taking ownership of behavior that isn't hers. Yes, I believe anyone's authentic self is one in which you would naturally want to take control of your life and your reactions to the events that happen to you, but be realistic about what you can control and what you can't.

Suppose you're enjoying a baseball game when, two thousand miles away, your elderly parent drops dead at home of a sudden heart attack. You'd be wrongly internalizing that event if you said, "Oh, if only I had been there, Dad might still be alive. I blame myself for what happened." Excuse me? A few seconds' logical reflection should tell you that that death was certainly not under your control. Yet I hear people say this kind of thing all the time and so do you. This is negative internalizing behavior. People blame themselves for accidents their children might have on a playground. At the extreme, unstable people we often label as psychotic might even blame wars on themselves. They take on the whole world's problems as their fault. We recognize the fallacy of that extreme thinking, but are often guilty of the same and only slightly less bizarre type thinking.

People's tendency to fall into this negative internal attribution is a weakness that lawyers sometimes exploit. How many times have you heard some lawyer make the claim that you and I and all of society are responsible for the way the young murderer has turned out in life? It's not his fault; it's yours—so take ownership of it. Teenagers use the same gimmick when they try to make their parents feel guilty because they don't have as good a car or dress as their friends. Mom or Dad, you must be to blame.

Nonsense. If you buy into this stuff, if you choose to internalize events and behaviors that you do not control, then you're setting yourself up for years of depression and needless pain. And when you think about this kind of reaction, there can actually be a streak of arrogance in it, some egotism: It's as if you're saying the sun can't rise without your permission, that the planets orbit at your command. I mean, let's be rational here. There are things you can control and things you can't. Don't lay claim to things you don't own. To do so is to put your self-concept in the crosshairs of undue criticism and therefore subject it to taking a beating in the confidence department. Give yourself a reality break here; there are enough things for which you are clearly and undeniably responsible without your taking on things over which you have no control.

What about the externalizers? Can their locus of control create problems for them? Clearly, yes. Negative *external* attribution can be extremely destructive. For example, a binge-spending externalizer, on the verge of financial collapse, might say, "I guess that God just wants me to go bankrupt. It's God's will." Imagine the consequences that flow from that kind of thinking. If you were an externalizer and one of your parents died, you might perceive that some major force was responsible. You would probably become angry at that outside force and rage at its injustice. You might say, "Why does God despise me? He has punished me in the worst way. I can't imagine what I've done to deserve this pain." Inappropriate blame never addresses the heart of the problem. If you misdiagnose a situation, you will also mistreat that situation and fail to do what is actually and realistically called for. Again, the challenge is to be rational and genuine with regard to what your self is telling you. The authentic self is based in accurate knowledge of who and what you are and are capable of controlling. It is the fictional self that is grounded in guilt, manipulation, and expectancies that will mislead you. The biggest step and one we will soon be working on is beginning to listen to what you are telling yourself and evaluating the lens through which you are viewing the world. Remember, to be authentic in your thinking you must deal with facts and only the facts. A self-concept that is distorted with an inappropriately external locus of control will be compromised dramatically.

Similarly, scoring high on the chance scale cripples your self-concept and sets you up for obvious problems. If your approach tends to be, "What difference does it make?" then you're likely to spend your life on the sidelines. Chance people, not surprisingly, strike others as being lazy and uninvolved in life. They miss crucial opportunities to make a difference in their own lives, to align themselves more closely with their authentic selves.

Whatever justification you might offer for adopting an internal or external locus of control, there is none for the chance approach. That's because there are no real accidents in life. Living as if you have no self-determination is living on a false premise and nothing but a fictional self-concept would ever try and sell that logic. It means you are forfeiting your capacity to change. Ignoring every opportunity to become who you are, you instead live in a state of continual chaos. There is no authenticity in a life left to chance.

IDENTIFYING YOUR LOCUS OF CONTROL

I trust that you are becoming comfortable with the concept of locus of control. By now, you probably suspect which kind of locus is at work in your own life. But let's find out for sure. We are going to turn now to the questionnaires that you have completed and start drilling deeper into your personal data.

We'll start by taking a look at your results from Appendix A, the questionnaire on health issues. This questionnaire will help you identify who or what you feel is responsible for your health conditions. Your responses to the questions for each section generated a score in the range of five to forty. For each section of the test—Internal, External, and Chance—your score places you into one of three categories: low, average, or high, in accordance with the following chart:

Section I: Internal Locus of Control

Scores

5–12   Very low attribution of your health to internal responsibilities

13–20   Low attribution to your health to internal responsibilities

21–32   Average attribution of your health to internal responsibilities

33–40   High attribution of your health to internal responsibilities

Section II: External Locus of Control

5–10   Very low attribution of your health to external sources

11–15   Low attribution of your health to external sources

16–21   Average attribution of your health to external sources

22–40   High attribution of your health to external sources

Section III: Chance Locus of Control

5–9   Very low attribution of health to chance

10–17   Low attribution of health to chance

18–25 Average attribution of health to chance
26–40 High attribution of health to chance

Now let's consider the specific meaning of your scores. In light of what you've just learned about the chance approach to life, it will not surprise you to know that the factor that best predicts poor health in the future, and the failure of rehabilitation, is a high level in the chance category. If you are in the high end (26–40) for this perceptual style, you are basically telling yourself that you have no trust in yourself or anyone else to be the guardian of your health. You're saying you're at the mercy of any germ or trauma in the universe and you have no weapons to fight them. If this is your profile, you are probably very passive when it comes to the management of your health (remember Don from our story).

If you have little or no belief or trust in yourself or anything else, you will probably not put any faith in any health-related resource. You may not see any point in changing your diet or quitting smoking. Take note: This dynamic of chance is not about "self-discipline." It's different from not wanting to change your habits just because you don't want to discipline yourself. Chance is a self-concept of *powerlessness:* You see no purpose in discipline and therefore have zero motivation to change.

What are the health implications for an externalizer? A high score (22–40) on the external scale implies a highly dependent reliance on powerful others or powerful things, for your state of health. Like those with a chance locus of control, if you are an externalizer, you are apt to be way too passive in maintaining your health. Instead of relying on the "luck of the draw," you rely on doctors or others to "fix" any health problems you may encounter, rather than avoiding them by responsible behavior. The old adage that "an ounce of prevention is worth a pound of cure" is the bane of the externalizer's existence. Any time you give your power away you are at the mercy of forces you do not control. Suppose, for example, that two or more of your doctors hold differing opinions. In the confusion and conflict between the two, you're likely to panic and be totally lost as to what to do. It is never a good idea to substitute anyone's judgment for your own. As an externalizer, your vulnerability in that situation is huge.

If you had high chance or external scores for health, you might want to consider our country's top killers: heart disease, cancer, diabetes, homicide, suicide, and automobile accidents. What are the lifestyle choices that affect those outcomes? The major determinants of heart disease are poor diet, lack of exercise, high stress, and smoking. Stress, smoking, and diet issues have also been implicated in cancer prevention research. Although there are major implications for genetics in diabetes, the biggest issues there are, again, diet, exercise, and stress. Stress is even more clearly linked to homicide and suicide. And when it comes to automobile accidents, the major factors are high speed, alcohol intake, carelessness, and failing to use seat belts.

Looking back over all these factors, ask yourself: Who controls these things? Are you the one in charge of these choices or are you letting something or someone else make them for you? Bottom line: Most major health issues can be influenced by what you do or don't do. Like it or not, a lot of the cause and effect is in your hands. The health professionals who treat you may have greater knowledge about your disease, but you have greater knowledge about you. Over the long haul, you have more power over your body and mind than anyone else. And you have more of the responsibility. A higher internal score is therefore often productive.

Now you know something about where your locus of control is with respect to your physical well-being. Let's look next at your scores on the questionnaire in Appendix B. As for the health questionnaire, your responses here generated a score in the range of five to forty. For each section of the test, Internal, External, and Chance, your score places you in one of three categories: low, average, or high. Look at the following table of scores to determine the specific meaning of your scores.

Section I: Internal Locus of Control

5–20   Low attribution of authentic self to internal source

21–32   Average attribution of authentic self to internal sources

33–40   High attribution of authentic self to internal sources

Section II: External Locus of Control

5–15   Low attribution of authentic self to external sources

16–21   Average attribution of authentic self to external sources

22–40   High attribution of authentic self to external sources

Section III: Chance Locus of Control

5–17   Low attribution of authentic self to chance

18–25   Average attribution of authentic self to chance

26–40   High attribution of authentic self to chance

If you scored in the top classifications for internal and in the lower levels of chance, then you hold yourself responsible for positive change in your life. You are willing to ask yourself the tough questions that need to be answered for you to regain clarity and authenticity.

If, on the other hand, your highest score was on the external scale, you need to address the validity of your self-concept. You need to start investigating what has taught you to give up your control of self. Don't think that I am dogging you because you did not fit neatly into the "best" scenario. As we have seen, there are downsides to internal attribution: Sometimes we cannot control everything that happens and it becomes a false, arrogant belief to hold otherwise. Nevertheless, in those cases where you *can* control the external world, you should do so. You need to go on the alert against the negative aspect of external attribution, which is the classic "victim" role.

If your highest score was chance, we need to talk. You need to decide, right now, whether you're going to come down on the field and get in the game or whether you're going to sit in the bleachers for the rest of your life, waiting to get hit by the ball.

Is your decision really all that difficult? It's your life, why would you want to be a passenger?

In examining your locus of control, we've been talking about the particular style with which you interpret and respond to the events in your life. I trust that, by this point, you have a clear understanding of which of the three styles best describes your approach to life. Knowledge is power and knowing what your style is will give you a new measure of power in your life. It is a critical first step in addressing your internal factors.

As we proceed through the chapters that follow, you'll start to be more conscious of your tendency to answer those whys in your life in a patterned fashion. You'll recognize opportunities to question whatever your personal tendency and locus of control is. You'll begin putting the cause of an event where that cause belongs, rather than reaching for that why in your old familiar way.

I hope you've seen, too, that arrogance and victimhood are twin impostors that dwell within your fictional self and can jerk you around at every turn. Mistakenly internalizing causes means that you'll be arrogantly claiming ownership of everything that happens in your life, good or bad, without regard to the facts. Quit doing that. You cannot change the fact that your parent died, your spouse left you, or that a hurricane is happening in Florida. If you insist otherwise, you'll be rebuilding your fictional self. Once again, you'll be drifting away from your authentic self. Distinguish the things you can control from those you can't.

As for those things you *can* control—which is most of them—you are starting to see that you can no longer play the victim. It's like that old saying, God don't drive no parked cars. You cannot continue to sit in the parking lot. Your authentic self is summoning you and it's time to get moving. Let's continue to work through whatever may be keeping you from doing so.

8 INTERNAL DIALOGUE

"No one can make you feel inferior without your consent."

—ELEANOR ROOSEVELT

WHAT DISTORTED PERCEPTION IS LIKE

In an experiment some years ago, a group of scientists asked their student volunteers to wear special eyeglasses that inverted the image: the lenses turned everything upside down. For the first few days of the experiment, the students were stumbling around like my Uncle Bob did every time he got knee-walking, commode-hugging, big-white-phone-in-the-sky drunk, at every family reunion I ever had the misfortune of attending. The students were bumping into desks, walking into corners as they changed classes, falling flat on their faces, and generally having a difficult time. Because they knew how things *really* were, their brains rejected this new, bogus data—at least at first.

Then something odd happened. After just a few days, the students began to accept their fictional, upside-down world as the real one. Their brains became accustomed to the distortion. They weren't even questioning that up was now down and down was now up. By the end of just one week, they were getting around perfectly fine.

"Hmm," said the researchers. They decided to prolong the experiment for a full month. By the end of that month, the students reported that the eyeglasses no longer posed any problem at all. They said they considered their orientation close to normal. They could read and write almost as easily as they had before the project; they could accurately gauge distances; and they were even able to navigate long flights of stairs as smoothly as their "right-sighted" peers.

What this experiment suggests is that we will quickly adapt to our perceptions, even if we're looking at the world through a lens that completely distorts reality. Given enough time, we soon treat a profoundly faulty perception as normal. Pound people with enough data, enough input, and you can convince almost anybody of almost anything. We have seen dramatic examples of this throughout history: brainwashing in prisoner of war camps, indoctrination into cults, and the absorption of our children into street gangs. People young and old, smart and dumb, sophisticated or not, have had their views, their realities, their values altered by a relentless deluge of distorted data. People who once had a clear view of life, a strong sense of right and wrong, strongly held priorities and values, nonetheless begin to accept distortions as the truth. A perspective that is way wrong starts to look right, often with tragic results.

How much of your own self-concept is based on this kind of distorted thinking? The point of this chapter is that you, too, may be getting brainwashed, in a way that is just as devastating, if less sensational, than being sucked into a cult. While you may not be headed for a cult or a street gang, the most powerful "brainwasher" you will ever encounter is you. And if you're being fed a bunch of bogus information about who you are and who you aren't and are buying into it, your world could be totally upside down and you may not even know it. If your self-concept is compromised and causes you to let some mean-spirited and destructive "jerk" pound on you as a part of your daily life, if you are talking yourself into believing that you are some kind of loser, you're screwing up big time. This chapter focuses on how that happens, how it gets to you, and what to do about it.

FILTERS

As we look at the world and ourselves, we do it through a set of filters. Think about what a filter is. A filter is a mechanism that lets
some things flow *in*, but screens other things *out*. Depending on
what the filter is made up of, it can also alter whatever is looked at or
passes through it. Sunglasses are a good example of a visual filter.
But, obviously, I'm not talking here about some physical apparatus
that we can put on and take off, like a pair of glasses. In fact, the filters I'm talking about are not really visual in nature; they are internal
and are mental, emotional, verbal, and perceptual in nature.
Through them, we process and assign a weight and meaning to every
event in our lives. Some things flow in, others are screened out, but
everything is affected. Our filters affect not just what we "see," but
what we "hear" and believe.

Now, because we trust ourselves to be honest and because we
think we don't lie to ourselves, we tend to believe that our filtered
perceptions are an accurate depiction of reality. Whatever passes
through the filter, accurate or not, is what we tend to believe. As a result, if and when our filtered perceptions lie, we get suckered big
time. We walk around believing that an upside-down world is the
real one. So here's a warning: When it comes to any of your *untested
and unchallenged* perceptions, you should be afraid, be very afraid.
You could very well be seeing your self in a distorted light.

I say that because our perceptual filters have the unfortunate tendency of being highly sensitive to the negatives, while screening out
the positives. It's just human nature.

All of us are subject to distorting the truth or missing the truth,
particularly when we are dealing with a situation in which we are
physically or emotionally threatened. For example, research shows
that a person being held at gunpoint will fixate, not surprisingly, on
the weapon, as opposed to a door or some other opportunity for escape or safety. Why? Because negatives invariably scream louder
than positives and the more extreme the negative, the louder it

screams. We tune into the negatives, the threats, and the problems because we are programmed to self-preserve, so if someone or something is perceived to threaten us (a gun), that threat can and will drown out all other events and inputs. The fear of the weapon galvanizes your attention, completely overwhelming and excluding any other data. The building could have fallen down around you and you wouldn't have known it. Such is the power of the human mind when it becomes fixated on a negative.

Let's move to a more likely scenario, one that may be much closer to home. In your life right now, there may be lots of people who believe in and encourage you. Your "supporting cast" may number in the hundreds, yet I'd be willing to bet that if you have even one or two critics—one or two naysayers—those "noisy" few can command your full attention, often drowning out the effects of all of the positive input. Why? Because it hurts to be rejected, criticized, and attacked and we pay attention to pain. As with the robber's pistol, your filters are sensitized to painful threats and you see those threats to your self-concept more vividly and memorably than you see anything else. Just as importantly, they linger: Those negatives tend to stay with you for years. Think about an actor on the stage: hundreds of adoring fans can be respectfully and adoringly rapt in their attention, yet one heckler can dominate the performer's entire experience and memory of the night.

In Chapter 3, I told you that your past reaches into your present and programs your future. Your filters explain a lot about how that happens. For example, if even some of the people in your life have caused you significant pain, you may internally react in a way that it "gets to you" and causes you to ignore the more positive majority and view the world through a filter that sees *all* people as a threat or a potential harm. Maybe you have wrongly concluded you got hurt because you deserved it (inappropriate internal locus of control) or, at a minimum, that you must accept it. Either way that negative history changes who you are; you let them convince you they are right and essentially you join the critics in dogging on you.

If, on the other hand, your experience of the world has been nurturing and supportive and that is what you choose to internalize, you are likely to anticipate new events through a filter that is positive. You tell yourself that you can handle what comes and that you will succeed. How you live and interact with the world is naturally influenced by *what you think you are seeing,* which in turn is totally a product of the filters through which you see, hear, feel, and think about the world.

In other words, your filters are largely a product of your past experience, yet you drag them with you, every second of every day, as you travel through your current life. Maybe the filters were, in fact, accurate in some past situation, but do they still fit? Or are you judging the present based on some event that is over and done with? Are you judging the people you meet today based on what they do or who they are or are you instead judging them based on what others have done in your past?

As any of those college students could have told you, a distorted life feels more and more natural the longer you live it. Put another way, a lie unchallenged soon becomes the truth. And we, of course, live consistently with the "truth." The fact is that, unlike those students in the experiment, you've been interpreting the world, and your place in it, for a lot longer than a month. Your filters almost certainly feel "normal" to you. But what if, just like a prisoner of war or a cult member, you have been bombarded with false information about you for so long that you finally just started believing it and living as though it were real? Things may look perfectly normal by now, but are they? Or do they only look that way because it's been so long since you had an unobstructed view of who you are and what you really care about that you don't even recognize what's real anymore? Have you simply forgotten? Maybe your life has seemingly become such a struggle of daily "survival," what with bills, kids, marriage, job and family, guilt and turmoil, that your filter is so contaminated with problems that nothing else gets through. Maybe you tell your self that there is just no use in trying to get what you really want.

Bottom line: If it's one or all of the above, if you fail to test the perceptions that flow through and from these filters, you could make serious errors in judgment, because your perceptions, born from history and a fear of pain, may very well *be flat wrong* and you could be ignoring what is really out there for you. And when it's your life we're talking about, you don't have room to *be flat wrong*.

With all of that in mind, let me state as clearly as I can the focus and challenge of this chapter. Your self-concept is at risk, because you are most likely misleading yourself with all kinds of misinformation that you currently accept as "true." You are probably wearing "upside-down glasses." Therefore:

- You need to realize that you respond not to what happens but instead to your perception of it.
- You need to test those perceptions (your filtered information), rather than treating your assumptions as facts.

INTRO TO INTERNAL DIALOGUE

The analogy of filters is a helpful way of thinking about perception and about how you color your perceptions of self and the world. It's a useful concept, but it's also just that, a "concept." It gets us only part of the way to a working understanding of how the way you perceive things affects your self-concept and life. To demystify the process further, by clarifying what actually happens within you, we need to get real about your self-talk. That's because, as information flows through your filter, it takes the form of words. It becomes a dialogue, a conversation that you have with yourself. (By the way, it's not "crazy" to talk to yourself, unless you're doing it out loud while you're standing in line at the grocery store or, really, anytime if you're saying really stupid stuff!) The negatives that you fixate on and internalize; the self-criticism; the distorted views of yourself and the world: All of that is expressed in this **internal dialogue.** So if we're going to stop and take notice of your filters, we have to address what you talk about when you talk to yourself—which you do, every waking moment of your life.

Internal dialogue is the real-time conversation that you have with yourself about everything that's going on in your life. It encompasses all of your self-talk—every syllable of it, whether positive and rational or self-destructive and negative. Internal dialogue is what you are saying to yourself, about yourself, and about the world, right now; everything you were saying to yourself before you picked up this book; and everything you will say to yourself once you put it down. In other words, your filters are actually a voice, a voice that no one hears but you. For future reference, that also means that no one can control it except you!

Your internal dialogue is really a subset or portion of your overall thinking. Here's what I mean. Taken as a whole, your thinking includes any number of necessary thoughts, but thoughts that are not necessarily relevant to your concept of self: for example, puzzling over a math problem or processing the printed instructions for a VCR or a swing set that requires "some" assembly (yeah, right!). That kind of mental activity, by itself, does not influence your self-concept and it's not the kind of thinking that I'm talking about. What we're concerned with here is the more pointed conversation you have with yourself that might very well run parallel to that other thinking, or just below the surface, when you are trying to put the swing set together or program the VCR.

For example, I can remember a very specific swing set I was trying to put together one Christmas Eve several years ago. I remember taking out all the parts, about fourteen zillion of them, and reading the instructions. Part of my mental energy was reading the instructions, but the rest—my internal dialogue—was screaming: You are so screwed here! You don't have a snowball's chance in hell of ever getting this put together by Christmas morning! You'd better get Scott (my brother-in-law, who has some kind of weird "engineering" brain parts I just didn't get) out of bed and over here or you are going to have some mighty disappointed kids! In other words, there was a two-track thought process going on. One track—my internal dialogue—had very little to do with Bolt A or Washer Z, but a whole lot to do with my self-concept.

Let's look now, in greater detail, at some other fundamental characteristics of internal dialogue.

Your internal dialogue is constant.

The time you spend with other people, even those who share most intimately in your life, cannot compare with the time you spend with yourself. You are with yourself twenty-four hours a day, seven days a week. And throughout your waking moments, your internal dialogue is active; you never stop saying things to yourself.

Your internal dialogue happens in real time.

Unlike those lightning-fast, overlearned, automatic thoughts that I will discuss in detail later, your internal dialogue happens at normal speed. If it could be somehow "broadcast live," you'd hear your internal dialogue unfolding at the same rate as any other conversation.

It's just as though someone were standing by your side and talking into your ear while you were doing whatever it was that you were doing. This may be a conversation that you don't "ponder" or deliberate upon or it may be so real that you actually speak it out loud! Its messages may be low volume, almost like a whisper, or they may come crashing in like a high-voltage current that is always "on." Its power can be deceptive: Its constancy and relentless flow can mislead you into thinking that you have no control over it.

Your internal dialogue triggers a physiological change.

As a result of every thought you have, there is a physical reaction. If your internal dialogue is telling you that you can't succeed, that you're about to embarrass yourself, the physical response might be sweaty palms, a tic, or an uncontrollable shiver; maybe your heart rate goes up. These physical consequences accumulate. As we will see, internal dialogue that is pessimistic and defeatist can be as destructive to your physical health as any injury or virus.

Your internal dialogue is heavily influenced by your locus of control.

Locus of control, which we looked at in the previous chapter, directly affects the content of your internal dialogue, whether your orientation is internal, external, or based on chance. So, for example, if you're an externalizer, a lot of your self-talk might sound like, I can't do this. Someone else will just have to fix it. If you're an internalizer, on the other hand, you might be saying, I cannot afford for anyone to screw this project up. Better just stay here till midnight and do the whole thing myself. No matter what the situation is, or what demands you are facing, your internal dialogue is likely to be influenced by your locus of control.

Your internal dialogue tends to be totally monopolistic.

Internal dialogue crowds out or drowns out any other data, from any other source, because, after all, this information is coming from you and you pay close attention to yourself, because you wouldn't lie to or mislead yourself—or would you? As a result, you may spend your time lost in the hustle-bustle and the frantic self-talk that goes with it. You may be condemning yourself for not keeping up or obsessing about what you didn't do or could have done better. You may be cheerleading yourself with an endless rah-rah session. Meanwhile, if your internal dialogue is really active, it can become so loud and pervasive that you fail to see important events going on all around you. You fail to hear what may be important messages from others. You might miss real opportunities for success or signals that you need to recognize in order to avoid danger. You lose awareness of your blessings. The rationally optimistic thoughts that you could be having get shoved to one side, simply because they aren't as loud, shrill, threatening, or demanding as your emotional self-talk.

Here's what may be the most troubling characteristic of all: **Your negative internal dialogue gets the loudest when you need it the least.** It gets the loudest when the pressure's on, because it flows at least in part from your personal truth. If your personal truth is riddled with doubts and anxieties, so, too, will it be with your internal dialogue. That dialogue, with all of its self-defeating messages, gets the loudest when you're in a confrontation with someone else. It gets the loudest when you're trying for that job: You're not smart enough; You're not good enough; You're gonna fail. It gets the loudest when you're deciding what you're willing to settle for in a mate, in a lifestyle, in a job. What you hear yourself saying is, Come on, what are you? Like, king or queen of the universe? You know, you just need to take what you can get and go on. Don't be putting on airs. That kind of talk, if you listen to it at such pivotal moments, can change your life forever. You end up being your own worst enemy.

THE COSTS

Those are the classic traits of internal dialogue. What are the costs that it exacts? What is the price you pay when your internal dialogue is endlessly negative?

Because internal dialogue is relentless and ever present, it can, in the aggregate, be a major life force. It can wreak a destruction that is cumulative, subtle, and slow. Imagine everyone going around with no shirts on their backs during the summer, not realizing that the sun is actually burning them. If you stuck an iron to their backs, they would yelp and scream and run. The sun and the iron are the same in terms of injury, but the sun is subtler. You don't even notice it. Similarly, if you were to step up to someone, look her in the eyes, and say, "You are a stupid, worthless bitch," she would recoil in horror and pain. Yet that is exactly the kind of thing that people say to themselves all day, every day, by way of their internal dialogue. Daily exposure to negative internal dialogue, like prolonged exposure to the sun, can be killing you, without your even knowing it. Ultimately, what you create for yourself is a toxic internal environment, one that grows by such indiscernible steps that it just kind of "sneaks up on you."

Remember from Chapter 1 that when I say "killing you," I mean it literally. When you are mentally and emotionally at war with yourself, it changes your physiology. It takes years off your life and makes you so much more susceptible to disease. How? Your immune cells are closely related to your nerve cells and there is instant communication between the two types of cell. For every thought you have, you have an instantaneous change in your physical body. If you are thinking negative and self-defeating thoughts about yourself, you will have a corresponding negative and defeating physiology. It might take the form of increased endocrine activity, chronic adrenaline arousal, elevated blood pressure, or even a heart attack.

In sum, internal dialogue is powerful medicine. You need to listen to your body because it damn sure listens to you. Your body speaks to you through your headaches, your painful back, your depression and anxieties, even your constant colds. It informs you and confirms what you are saying to yourself. And when you think about it, you see that these messages are your authentic self, crying out, "Help me out of here." If you are constantly tired, achy, sick, or in any way physically uncomfortable, you need to take a really hard look at what you are saying to yourself, day in and day out.

There's an emotional cost, as well, a kind of hardening of your psychological arteries. As we saw when the locus of control is out of whack, negative internal dialogue will cause you to overlook vital information that could otherwise be so incredibly powerful. You don't even recognize positive alternatives anymore, because, once again, your data-processing center has closed.

Think of it this way: When you've lost your keys and then you find them, do you keep looking for your keys? If you've been searching for an answer and you believe you have it, do you continue investigating? No. You call off the search. Now suppose your conversation with yourself runs like this: I am a knucklehead, I have always been a knucklehead, I will always be a knucklehead and no one will respect me. Once you begin believing yourself, why would you continue to process data? You might have ten experiences in the next week that run counter to your being a knucklehead, but your

data processing window is shut, so you don't see the contrary information. You don't hear it. If your internal dialogue is that you are a
knucklehead, and you believe that you are truthful with yourself,
then you absolutely will miss evidence to the contrary. You will miss
it, even if it's served up to you on a silver platter. And you certainly
won't go seeking out such evidence.

You might be in a job that is highly technical and structural and
makes a lot of people happy, but causes you pain in some way. Perhaps you have strong artistic gifts, but that job has you just connecting dots in a totally nonartistic fashion. It's easy to imagine the
internal dialogue that would cause you to start ignoring the pain.
You might blame your unhappiness on other things: your spouse,
the part of the country you live in, your lacking an education or the
right kind of education. For all the things there are to blame, it
doesn't occur to you that your frustration comes from your not
being true to yourself. You have already closed the door on that, so
you say, "I am doing the right thing." Your internal dialogue kicks
into overdrive, rationalizing and justifying the unfulfilling choice,
protecting you from the alternatives.

Result? The stimulus you are making is the response you get. Your
negative internal dialogue steers you away from the truth; it poisons
your self-concept; the frustrated, unhappy person that you present
to the world is the person that the world responds to; the world responds with more frustration and unhappiness for you. A negative
internal dialogue becomes a vicious circle of self-fulfilling prophecy.

Sometimes the toxic environment that your internal dialogue creates can rage in such a way that it doesn't "sneak up on you," but
hits you right between the eyes and creates disaster. I once treated an
executive from a Fortune 100 company named Greg who had
worked himself into a promotion that would soon require regular
public speaking engagements. He foresaw that he was going to be
talking to some pretty skeptical audiences about the environmental
impact of his company's activities. Before he came to see me, he had

tried to polish his skills and improve the mechanics of his speaking by enrolling in a Dale Carnegie course and joining a Toastmasters group. While his skills improved, his anxiety did not. I quickly surmised that his problem was not a lack of skill, ability, or motivation, but instead an interfering and destructive internal dialogue.

I got him to deconstruct a recent public speaking situation that had turned out terribly. He told me that as the engagement approached, he meticulously prepared both the content and the delivery of his speech. He rehearsed over and over and was confident that he was ready. He even went through relaxation exercises as he sat at the front table and visualized himself doing very well. That was all good and rational, but once he stepped to the podium, his internal dialogue started screaming. I asked him to recall for me his self-talk at the time. Here are excerpts of what he wrote:

> Oh no, I'm starting to sweat. These people aren't buying this a bit. They're staring at me like I'm trying to poison their children.
>
> I'm failing miserably. I can't do this. I don't know why I'm kidding myself. I just need to accept I'm not cut out for this. Seventeen people have stood up and walked out since I started. This is a disaster.

Now, you're probably thinking that Greg failed because he had negative self-talk and therefore set himself up to fail. You're right, but let's look closely at how that happened. Yes, his self-talk was negative. True to the mechanics of human behavior, there was a physiological event—sweating, trembling, and so on—that accompanied those negative thoughts. What's even more significant, however, is the interfering nature of the internal dialogue. Look at it this way. Greg started out having one hundred units of intellect and focus to deal with the speech that he was giving. But instead of focusing all one hundred of those units on the task at hand, he cut his resources in half. As he approached the microphone, 50 percent of

Greg was invested in this conversation he was having with himself, leaving only 50 percent for the task at hand, the delivery of his speech.

Think about that. How would you like to head out the door every day to face the challenges of your life, only *after* someone had first divided your intellect in half? In other words, instead of having an excellent IQ of 110, you'd have to deal with your world with an IQ of 55, which is at the retardation level. That's the kind of impact that an interfering internal dialogue can have. Was it any wonder, then, that when Greg stood up to deliver a complex speech, and he was operating with a 55 IQ, he didn't do so well? Greg's problem wasn't that he didn't know how to speak or even that he didn't know how to give an effective public speech. Greg's problem was that he was trying to do two things at once: listen to himself rag on himself and at the same time deliver a demanding speech. Once the problem was properly diagnosed, and Greg learned to manage his internal dialogue in the same way I'm going to teach you to manage yours, his problem was over and done with. Could he stop the internal dialogue? No, but he could challenge it and he could manage it.

So, where does your internal dialogue get its information? What are its sources or its "inputs"? Because we are a society of people who don't really know ourselves, we are highly vulnerable to input from all kinds of external sources: parents, peers, authority figures, newspapers, magazines, TV ads, Hollywood, and the Internet. If we really knew ourselves, who we were, what we believed, what we didn't believe, what we were all about, then we wouldn't be casting about allowing someone or something to define us from the outside in. My dad used to say: "Son, if you don't stand for something, you will fall for anything!" As usual, he was right. If you don't know yourself and "stand up" for who and what you are, then the door is open for you to be influenced and dragged away from who you really are.

We see and hear about this kind of input every day as it affects our children, when they get into drugs and other trouble because they let someone influence them to do things they would never initiate on their own. It happens because they aren't clear about who and what they are and, therefore, can't be sure that the proposed activity is not really "them." As applied to you, the input may consist of anything from a TV ad telling you to buy a new car so that you will be cool or sexy or successful, to the slick talk of some office "cool" jerk trying to get into your pants so that you can feel desired. All of these events trigger and then are interpreted by you through your internal dialogue. Dialogue A leads to one outcome, Dialogue B leads to a different outcome. The more those external people, TV ads, and other sources are able to influence us, the more our internal dialogue is reactive to outside influence, rather than reflective of who we know we are, the farther we stray from our authentic selves.

And please remember that when those external messages strike at our sense of value and worth, we tend to be especially vulnerable, much more so than when the subject matter is more concrete. As we have already seen, if someone tries to persuade you that you are a thief, they can't get to you, because **factually**, you *know* you're not a thief. By contrast, if they challenge something more abstract and subjective—your intelligence, your likeability, your sensitivity, worth, talent, or character—your ears perk up. You may adopt that message into your internal dialogue unquestioningly, because you don't have facts to refute it. In fact, you may absorb that message with such intensity and emotion that, like a complete dummy, you start to repeat it every time you start talking to yourself about yourself, even though you originally knew better. Somebody can give you some unfounded and unthinking criticism, commit some selfish act, or make some offhand comment, and damned if you don't let it get to you; the next thing you know, you've started "reactively" including it in your internal dialogue. Like the child falling in with "bad company," you might never initiate such negative internal dialogue on your own, but because you don't really, really know who and what you are, you are vulnerable to its getting a foothold when it is started by someone else. That's why it is critical that you stay committed to living in accordance with your authentic self.

THEMES/TOPICS/SUBJECT MATTERS

Although your internal dialogue is reactive, and therefore new in each and every situation, it will have certain predictable themes. Let's say you are convinced that you are just too heavy or that you just don't look good in your clothes. If that's the case, then your internal dialogue is likely to be pretty much the same whenever you enter a social environment, whether it's at work, the grocery store, a wedding, or (God forbid) the swimming pool down at the park, with that "skinny bitch" from next door "parading her narrow ass all over the place." You might be saying to yourself: I can't believe I am here. I look like a cow. How can I get the hell out of here? I could stand over there where nobody can get behind me. If I could just pull this jacket down a little more. I swear I'm going on a diet if it kills me. I am not about to let anyone see me eat anything. There *she* is. God, I hate her. I have an ass like a forty-dollar mule and everybody knows it. At least I'm boring and no one is paying any attention to me! How can I get out of here? Please, God, don't let them come over here. Oh no, here they come. "Hi, how *are you*? It's so good to see you!" Just beam me up, Scotty—this is horrible.

That's one example of how internal dialogue replays familiar themes. But because it is as unique and varied as people's individual DNA, the themes and topics of your internal dialogue are uniquely yours. In fact, a lot of your comments to yourself might not seem so bad, in isolation. Much of the time, your dialogue might be simply task-oriented, but heavily so, even to the point of putting considerable pressure on you. In the midst of your busiest mornings, your internal dialogue may be running right alongside, insisting, You've got to do X; don't you dare forget Y; You should; You really have to; You must . . . A snippet of your internal dialogue today might have been, I really need to get back to the office; This traffic is making me late. Maybe your internal dialogue is guilt-inducing, such as your putting yourself down if you sit too long and watch television or read the paper. The point is that your internal dialogue has particular themes; those themes are not always negative, but seldom are they neutral.

Your internal dialogue may include constant comparisons, fear, worry, anxiety, and pessimism. It may be a ruminative obsessing over everything from minutiae to major life events. You may downplay something that you really care about by generating a dialogue that is marked by a false sense of apathy. After all, if you "just don't care," it won't hurt if you don't get it, right? So, to protect yourself, your internal dialogue will convince you that you don't care. It will clutter up your mind with all kinds of BS, every time you try to do something that is not a lay-down, slam-dunk sure thing.

PAYOFFS

As you think about negative internal dialogue generally, and more specifically as you begin to take stock of your own, you may logically wonder, If it's negative, why do I keep doing it? If this behavior is toxic, then why do I persist in it? The first answer, as we've seen, has to do with the power of the negative. Just as the fear of that robber's pistol weapon overwhelms and excludes any other data, your tendency to "lock on" to negative information can cause you to miss everything else going on around you. Negative information can seem more vivid, more real, than even truthful information that is positive.

But you also need to keep in mind the **power of the payoff.** In any quest for understanding why your internal dialogue is what it is, you must be alert to what "payoffs" you are getting from telling yourself the things that you do. You will not maintain any behavior, dialogue, or thought pattern that is not providing you with some kind of reward or payoff. In other words, you don't choose your self-talk randomly; you choose it because, at some level, it "works" for you. At some level it pays you off or you wouldn't do it. No reward, no repetition.

Let's say your internal dialogue is stagnant in tone and message, telling you to just accept who and what you are. You may think you hate that kind of self-talk, but trust me: You wouldn't listen to it for one minute if you weren't getting something out of it. The question becomes, what is this payoff that has you doing that which you don't consciously want to do? Don't even bother telling yourself that you are the exception to the rule of payoffs. You're not an exception, because there are no exceptions.

Suppose, for example, Carol is thinking about going back to school and finishing her college degree, which got put on hold when she met and married her husband. Carol consciously wants to do it, but it isn't that simple, at least not at the level of her internal dialogue. To accurately predict the outcome of her efforts to complete her education and change her career, you would have to listen, not just to what she is telling you, but, more importantly, to what she is telling herself. If her internal dialogue is telling her that there are a number of risks or potential complications that come with more education, Carol may start getting nervous. Carol may realize that with a college degree she will lose her excuse for being in a dead-end, unexciting job. She will get into the much more competitive marketplace of the "high-powered" professional, meaning she will then potentially have to deal with a new set of demands associated with that more highly contested world. It just might be pretty darn scary and sitting tight, right where she "safely" is, can be a real payoff.

Now, this particular area of her life may never have been great, so her internal dialogue might be, I don't have a great job right now, but at least I have an excuse. I gave it up for him, otherwise I would be a star. If I were better educated like everyone seems to value, maybe I would have plenty of opportunities, but, then again, maybe I wouldn't. How embarrassing would that be, no excuse and no great job either?

Big risk—and the payoff for conning herself into not taking that risk is escaping the possible pain of not being accepted when she is out there with no excuse. As in Carol's situation, sometimes your internal dialogue can convince you that it's "just easier not to." Your

internal dialogue can complicate and sabotage even the most fundamental, important goals.

We need to talk more about this issue of risk. You perceive risks,
and therefore talk about them internally, in almost any change you
undertake. No wonder we are so stubbornly resistant to change.
Your internal dialogue can become self-defeating even if your problem is as simple as being stuck in a job that you despise. Simply to
consider going after that different job, a better job, involves risk: the
huge risk that lies in admitting that what you have is no longer what
you want. Once your internal dialogue acknowledges that, you can
no longer bury your head in the sand and hide in denial. Instead,
you're now faced with the stark reality that your work life is the pits.
Your internal dialogue can force you to feel like you have to "jack it
up" and do something about it—and that can create huge pressure.
If you admit the problem, you are forced to either continue living an
admittedly crummy life (pain) or reach for something more. If you're
reaching, if you're stretching and striving for something more, you
can definitely fail and you naturally fear failure.

This is where your internal dialogue can cause real trouble. When
the possibilities that life presents are interpreted through your internal dialogue as being scary and painful, it is easy to become paralyzed. Instead of getting real and confronting your life, you can
begin to lie to yourself and live a fiction. Your fictional dialogue becomes: This is really okay. I know it's not me, but hey, I should be
glad I have a job at all. I would like to contribute, but I don't believe
very much in myself. There's your payoff: You get to hide from the
truth and you avoid the fear, pain, and pressure of reaching.

In other words, the low self-esteem that internal dialogue can generate and perpetuate is for many people a very handy excuse. It is a
great excuse for playing it safe and not expecting very much from
yourself: Gee, I'd love to be a player and contribute, but I'm just really shy and don't have any self-confidence. Oh really! Well, how
convenient is that? You're scared, so we all get to drag your ass for
seventy years? I don't think so. Hey, everybody has doubts; how

about we challenge that internal dialogue, instead of letting it paralyze you?

If your internal dialogue is about your self-esteem, ask yourself whether that dialogue is getting you closer to what you authentically want or not. This world needs participants, not passengers. If you are nervous and fearful about life, and your internal dialogue shows it, you will be compromised. Everybody is nervous about different aspects of life. Everybody has self-doubt; everybody has fear; everybody has anxiety. But if you passively accept the excuses of your own self-talk, if you let it speak to you unchallenged, you will cheat yourself and everyone else in your life.

POSITIVE INTERNAL DIALOGUE

We've looked at a number of situations in this chapter where internal dialogue was hugely disruptive. Please understand: It's entirely possible for internal dialogue to be quite rational and productive. Those criteria—rational and productive—may need some explanation. They can help you to be clear about what positive internal dialogue is and is not.

Having spent almost my entire life involved in athletics—my earlier years in football, and more recently on the tennis court—I've been very blessed to have a number of coaches who recognized the importance of the mental side of the game and, specifically, of the profound effect that internal dialogue has in the heat of battle.

Paul Vishnesky comes immediately to mind. Paul is an excellent tennis player, a great doubles partner, but an even better coach. He has spent a lot of time studying psychocybernetics and self-talk and it showed in his teaching. He once told me, "If you miss your first serve, don't say to yourself, Don't double fault." His reasoning was, you do not want the last two words you process before you hit your second serve to be "double fault." Instead, he said, tell your self to "get it in!" a much more positive suggestion. He was totally correct, for all the reasons we have discussed. His advice was centered on the power of suggestion; it zeroed in on a precise moment of internal dialogue; it targeted a particular physical consequence. And, as I quickly discovered, it was highly productive.

As a result, whenever I play tennis, I monitor my internal dialogue with great regularity to make sure that the content is productive and rational. Whenever I'm in a tough game or a tough set, I find myself saying things like: Tough man wins. Be loose, be happy. You love this. He is hot and tired just like you. This will come down to who wants it the most. You don't *have* to win, you just *want* to win, so watch the ball, move your feet, and play proud.

Now, I don't know; maybe that all sounds weird to you, but it works for me. I don't have that conversation during a point where it could interfere; I have it between points. Because I have it between points, once the point begins and the ball is in play, I can focus completely and totally on moving my feet and hitting the ball. And you may have noticed that I decompress myself by saying I don't "have to win." Let's face it: I'm not playing at Wimbledon. I'm a bald-headed hacker who has a day job. So I use my internal dialogue to put things in perspective: I'm going to have a good time, and, win or lose, head for the shower, kill something and eat it, and start helping Jordan with his geometry homework.

We saw earlier that negative internal dialogue has physiological consequences: It can result in chronic adrenaline arousal, elevated blood pressure, and so on. It stands to reason, then, that if you are thinking rationally positive and empowering thoughts, each cell in your body responds with more positive and empowering energy.

Sports psychologists have been studying this mind-body connection for years. Their research has shown, again and again, that the thoughts we have about how we are going to perform a physical event determine how well we do it. Weightlifters lift more when they hold self-affirming thoughts. Swimmers swim faster and runners run faster. The testimony of Olympic athletes demonstrates how much importance they place on their internal dialogue. The things those athletes know are equally true for you, in everything you do, hence, the reason my coaches taught me what they did about my thinking. It's why I so readily adopted the advice of Paul Vishnesky to watch what I told myself on the tennis court. I am no Olympic athlete, but this stuff works for you and me, just as it does for them.

Now let's consider what positive internal dialogue is *not*. Positive internal dialogue, as I suggested earlier, is rationally optimistic self-talk, not unfounded rah-rah hype. Positive internal dialogue consists of thoughts, messages, and fact-based rhetoric that allow you to live in accordance with reality—not lies, assumptions, or opinions. Internal dialogue is truthful engagement with the world, not smiley-faced denial.

It's not a litany of "feel-good" mantras ("I'm good enough, I'm smart enough, and, doggone it . . ." You know the rest.). When you need to jack things up in your life and make a change, it does not say, "I am good enough as I am." The fact may be that you're *not* good enough—that you've been living like a lazy slug. If so, a rational, healthy internal dialogue would be telling you the truth, so you can do something about it. By having an honest conversation with yourself, you can identify something to put at the top of your to-do list. If you're a slug, admit it. If you're not a slug, then stop telling yourself you are. This is not rocket science here. You just have to start listening and start challenging your internal dialogue. Whatever the case may be, start talking about fact, not fiction.

You may know people, for example, who experience no fear whatsoever, even when they ought to. That is not even close to what I call a positive, healthy internal dialogue. I call these fools the "bulletproof people"—they think they're immortal. Their brand of internal dialogue is just as dangerous as the kind that unduly criticizes.

Look, this internal dialogue business is not an exercise in blind affirmation. It comes back to your personal truth and you know by now that that is a truth that you live. Lie to yourself and you *will* pay the price. Whether your personal lie is one of denial, self-derogation, or a bunch of rah-rah hype, it is still a lie. Your personal lie can be intentional or the product of distortions that have silently invaded your life. Nothing but candid truth that has survived the challenge of your honest self-appraisal will do. If your personal truth is to be riddled with self-doubt and self-incrimination and self-flagellation, you will live that truth as you go out into the world. If you know yourself to be confident, streetwise, and durable, then you will not necessarily be fearful, even in a high-risk situation. Your reaction will be the result of what you perceive about yourself. Stop dealing with self-opinion and start dealing with self-fact.

Knowledge is power. Positive internal dialogue allows you to know your history, yet move beyond it. It allows you to "rise above your raising." I think about my dad. As I've said, he was the first person on either side, my mother's family or his, ever to go to college. He rose above his raising. I'd be willing to bet that his internal dialogue, day after day, went something like this: Poor and uneducated is our pattern; that's who we are. Well, I'm rising above that. I'm fighting my way up off of this rung of the ladder. I'm fighting my way out of here.

Positive internal dialogue is what propels the Olympic athlete to a new personal best. It's as if the energy generated by all of that affirming self-talk is what carries him or her to another level of achievement. Afterward, the athlete can recall only that he or she was totally engrossed in the moment.

Positive internal dialogue is what Oprah factually took with her as the legacy of her experience in the third grade. Time after time, the message was the same: "If you do your best you will succeed and be valued." In my own case, it's the real-world, tested message of self-worth that I claimed with pride after being kicked out of school for defending myself and my friends.

Positive internal dialogue is wholly consistent with your authentic self and says, I don't have to earn my right to be here. The quality that I have as a unique human being gives me the right to be here.

TAKING INVENTORY

I trust that you're now ready to go on the alert as to your own internal dialogue, and to find out exactly what it is that you tell yourself. As before, you're going to need your journal and something to write with.

EXERCISE 1

Pick a day for doing this exercise, preferably a day when you don't plan to be doing anything dramatic or out of the ordinary. This should be a typical day for you.

Keep your journal or a small notebook and pen handy throughout the day. Make a series of appointments with yourself: Every two hours, stop what you're doing, take out the notebook, and simply jot down observations about the self-talk you've been having for the past two hours. Each of these eight or ten notetaking sessions need only take a few minutes. Write down what you've been telling yourself about:

- your appearance
- the work that you've been doing for the past two hours
- your job, more generally
- your intelligence
- your competence
- your skills and abilities
- your worth

If you find it easier not to wait for the two-hour mark, but instead to jot things down as you hear yourself saying them, then by all means, do it that way. The point is to develop a thorough understanding of one day's internal dialogue, without completely upsetting your daily schedule.

EXERCISE 2

Imagine that you are scheduled to make an important presentation at work tomorrow. A number of important customers or clients, as well as several of your coworkers and your boss, will be there watching. It's the night before. You're lying in bed, in the dark, thinking about the presentation. What are you saying to yourself?

Take whatever time you need to consider, honestly and thoroughly, the kinds of messages that would be going through your head. You'd be having a conversation with yourself, so what would you be saying?

Write down as much of this conversation as you can.

EXERCISE 3

Look back at the writing that you did for both Exercises 1 and 2. Do you see common themes or threads running through both sets of writings? If so, what are those common features? Describe them in writing.

EXERCISE 4

When you look back over your writing for Exercises 1 and 2, how would you describe the **overall tone** or mood of your internal dialogue? Is it positive, upbeat? Or is pessimistic, defeatist, self-condemning? If it is positive, is it rational? Or is it just some rah-rah, self-con job with no substance? Are there particular areas where what you've written sounds especially harsh or critical? By contrast, does your internal dialogue as to some areas of your life strike you as particularly upbeat and optimistic? Circle any writing that you think illustrates either especially positive or especially negative internal dialogue.

EXERCISE 5

Again, glancing back over your writing for both Exercises 1 and 2: What does your writing tell you about your **locus of control**? You completed some questionnaires in the previous chapter, specifically on the topic of locus—does this most recent writing add any new insight? Is your internal dialogue oriented externally, internally, or in accordance with chance? Write down your answer.

EXERCISE 6

As you look at your writing, answer this question: What kind of a friend are you to yourself, throughout the day? If you were a friend, whispering in your ear the messages you recorded in Exercises 1 and 2, what kind of a friend would you be?

You're the one who talks to you, all day, every day. What kind of a friend are you? Are you actively creating a toxic environment for yourself, contaminating your experience of the world? Or are the messages that you send yourself characterized by a rational and productive optimism?

9 LABELS

*"Every man stamps his value on himself
. . . man is made great or small by his own
will."*

—J. C. F. von Schiller

MANY years ago, a team of psychologists launched a research project using grade school students as subjects. The researchers were looking at how the social environment, and specifically the treatment one receives from those perceived as powerful and relevant, affects a person's self-concept. At the beginning of the school year, the researchers separated a class of sixth graders into two groups. The selection process was carefully randomized so that the two groups of kids would be virtually identical in terms of average intelligence, ability, maturity level, background, and so on.

The researchers then told one group that they were the Bluebirds, exceptional children who had been identified as having unusually high ability. They were told that the work that year would be challenging and the pace would be rapid, in keeping with their special gifts. Across the hall, by contrast, the Yellow Birds were told that they would have to work extra hard to keep up with their assignments; that they were going to face many challenges; and that the school year was likely to be a struggle for many of them, but that their teacher was going to try her hardest to help each one of them. The message to the Yellow Birds was basically, "You're marginally bright, and your achievements in life are going to be marginal, at best." Every other aspect of their experience was identical. All of the students, regardless of their group assignment, received exactly the same assignments, followed the same schedule, and took the same tests.

Thankfully, this kind of project would probably die today while still in the proposal stage: These days, you cannot and should not get approval for a psychological study that poses a risk of harm to the participants. Sure enough, although the artificial division of this class lasted only four months, the consequences were profound and went on for years. The Yellow Birds did, in fact, struggle and showed serious frustration and self-recrimination associated with their difficulties. Unfortunately, the troubles did not end when the label was removed. When the researchers again looked at these children ten years later, the kids who had been Yellow Birds had consistently earned significantly poorer grades, were much less successful in activities like sports and music, were more likely to have been in trouble with the law, and scored significantly lower on intelligence tests than did the Bluebirds. The Bluebirds were appreciably better performers on every single dimension measured. I want to be sure you get the gravity of what I'm saying here. These children, alike in every way, had hugely different outcomes in life, outcomes that were driven by nothing more than a label! Bottom line: Both groups of schoolchildren lived to the labels that had been placed upon them, early on. They didn't know it, they couldn't tell you that the label had changed their self-concept or that they were requiring less of themselves because of it, but it happened and it happened in a devastating way.

Labels are incredibly powerful influences in your life and I'm betting you may not be consciously aware of even a fraction of your labels, or the power of those labels, whether they come from the outside world or from within yourself. Your labels are so important because they are at the core of your fictional self. They are one of the ways in which the world has attacked your authenticity and messaged you on what is expected of you if you are to be a good "sheep." Maybe your most self-changing and limiting labels came from your parents, maybe they came from a cruel peer group or from teachers or coaches. Maybe they came from within you when you observed yourself messing up in life. Either way, whatever the source, you must acknowledge the existence of the labels, challenge the "fit," and confront the impact these labels have had on your concept of self. You cannot ignore these powerful influences if you are ever to get back to your authentic self. Labels are so powerful because they are prone to be internalized and accepted. If you accept these labels as the definition of you, you are changed at your most core level. Once you accept the label as valid, you replace your definition of who you really are with who the label tells you you are. Recall the question that I asked in Chapter 2: "Who are you?"

As we saw in that chapter, many people answer that question in terms of their jobs or their function. When you ask them, "Who are you?" they say, "I'm a loan officer." "I'm a plumber." "I'm a telemarketer." "I'm a mom." "I'm a professor." "I'm a real estate agent." That is, they describe themselves in terms of an externally defined role. They answer the question by telling you what they do, not who they are.

But there's a second, very important way that people answer that question, one they may never have actually put into words. By that I mean that no matter how you answer the question aloud ("I'm a businesswoman." "I'm a paralegal."), internally, you may be answering it very differently. Without doubt, you have a set of "social-mask" labels that you retreat to when meeting someone or presenting yourself to the world. You also have a set of internal labels that you apply to yourself as a function of the judgments you place on yourself, judgments that you would never disclose orally, but yet they are a key part of your personal truth. Internally, your answer to the question, then, is comprised of a separate set of **labels**, a set that can be incredibly unkind and scathing. Put simply, a label happens:

- When you allow someone else to define you based on how they *perceive* you.
- When you judge yourself and crystallize that judgment as a lasting self-characterization.

If you are living to a label, you have molded for yourself a fictional self-concept with artificial boundaries. Labels are generalizations or stereotypes and ignore who you really are. Whether the label is imposed on you from the inside or from the outside, you soon accept it as your own. In other words, either you or someone else may have told you years ago that you're a Yellow Bird, and you still believe them.

Labels are the icons of the self-talk or the internal dialogue you began as a child and continue to this very day. They may reflect the conclusions you reached when you measured yourself by some "yardstick" imposed on you by the world. Maybe the measure was popularity and you weren't, so your label was "uncool" or "nerd." Maybe it was money and since you had none the label was "loser." Maybe it was grades and your brother or sister made better ones, so you were labeled "not our best student." (That is so rude and condescending!) Unlike most of the other words you use, a label has an emotional "charge" associated with it; in short it's not just descriptive, it is *accusatory* and it stings. It is this emotional aspect that gives the label its devastating power.

Here's what I mean: As you learned to talk, you first learned the names of things only in terms of their physical properties and identifications. One of your first words may have been "ball." A ball is neither good nor bad. When your mom stood there over your crib, saying, "Ball, ball," she was just helping you differentiate that object from other objects. By contrast, what happened when you heard "bad boy" or "bad girl"? Her voice was different. Her face bunched up in a frown. You knew she was unhappy and you knew it had something to do with you. Those words she used became bound up in your own emotional responses to your mother and to the reference to you. That sting you felt meant that you could never hear "bad boy" or "bad girl" again in the same neutral way that you heard "ball."

As your vocabulary expanded, you learned to distinguish the bad words from the neutral ones. Maybe you learned what an "SOB" was or what a "sissy" was. "Failure" may have slipped into your self-concept, bringing with it the annihilation of self-esteem, wounded pride, and a longing for achievement. Maybe the label you heard was "hopeless," which you applied to yourself as meaning "useless" and "inept." Maybe the word "ugly" became "hateful" and "unworthy of love."

These abstract words, remember, are hard for us to challenge because they deal with subjective opinion rather than objective fact. As I said earlier, you could say with confidence that you were not a thief: That was a concrete distinction, no problem, no confusion, you have objective, credible data to rely on. But now, when labeled as "hopeless" or "loser" or "ugly," someone is attacking your worth.

Who are you to disagree? Maybe they're right, you thought: Maybe I *am* a loser. Maybe I *am* ugly. Resisting the label is difficult enough, if for no other reason than that it's so hard to quantify. Now stir emotional pain into the mix. It doesn't matter whether you heard the label once or heard it a thousand times: If you experienced the word at an emotional level, it became meaningful. Hurt made the word concrete. So thanks to its emotional sting, and because of—not in spite of—its abstractness, that label became even more vivid and real for you than a three-dimensional object like "ball."

If you were to look up "label" in the dictionary, you'd find it defined as "a term of classification." A label places us within a certain group of other people who supposedly are similar to us. The label also says that we are not like certain other groups of people. Everyone within the classification behaves a certain way; everyone outside it behaves differently.

When you think about what that means, you recognize that a

label is a kind of prediction. Bluebirds will always flourish in school; Yellow Birds will always struggle. Because you're a Sagittarius, you're going to do X in a certain situation. She's a Scorpio, so she'll do Y instead. You hear even smart people indulging in this kind of voodoo in order to reduce other people, and themselves, to a predictable set of boundaries.

High school tends to be a fertile breeding ground for our impulse to classify. There are the cool and the uncool, the jocks, the nerds, the beauty queens, granolas, freaks, dopers, and so on. These years are an acutely vulnerable time of life, when we are especially sensitive to social relations and we're hungry to know where we fit in. Our emotional sensitivity means that the labels we assume in high school may penetrate deeply into our self-concept. Expectations about our classmates and ourselves may "harden" to the point that not living up to one's label becomes unthinkable. We develop some very firm ideas about how other people "should be" or "shouldn't be." We don't want the "dumb jock" football star to make straight As, because that violates our desire for predictability. It's not right when the pencil-necked geek masters the guitar and becomes Buddy Holly; he was supposed to stay a geek. More importantly, we may become convinced, ourselves, that the prediction associated with the label that has been placed on us is the real thing, ironclad. We may become so adapted to our own label that we see any challenge to it as futile and even a threat. We can sometimes get comfortable with the fact that at least we have some identity. We may even actively defend it: "This is my box. Don't tell me to get out of it. I am the trouble-making rebel and don't you forget it!" You may fear that if you were to lose the label, there would be nothing to replace it.

The point is that when you were young and vulnerable, you may have bought into a classification that now blocks your way back to your authentic self. Remember that the world has an agenda for you and your authenticity is not anywhere on that agenda. The world loves labels. Labels are convenient. Refusing to live by a label makes you inconvenient.

IATROGENIC LABELING

As you get ready to identify the labels that may be at work in your own life, please understand that not all harmful labeling is motivated by hatred or by a desire for control over other people. There's a term, "iatrogenic," that describes harm induced by a healer. Iatrogenic injury results from good intentions. For example, the doctor prescribes a couple of extra weeks' bed rest and the patient develops bedsores. Or the patient loses some mental function, not because of his or her illness, but because the doctor cautioned that there might be some loss of mental function.

Similarly, iatrogenic labeling is destructive labeling that is actually motivated by kindness. A label that was intended to be helpful proves to be a lifelong disaster. Just because one has good intentions does not mean that the label can't be harmful.

Parents of handicapped children, for example, will sometimes communicate to their children that they lack the capacity to deal with a "normal" world. Understandably, the parents fear that their children will be bullied or hurt in that world. However, this desire to protect the child may give rise to an adult who is more handicapped by his or her self-concepts of weakness and fear than by any physical handicaps. The young Helen Keller's greatest obstacle may have been not her blindness or her deafness, but her overprotective father. Imagine the loss to the world if her entire life had been guided by his well-meaning but extremely narrow labeling of his daughter and by his desire to keep her shut away forever. Other kids have been told they have a "delicate constitution," or that they are "unusually sensitive." Any number of labels that might be placed on a child, with no malice at all, could nevertheless have awful consequences in the long run.

So you need to be alert to the possible effects of iatrogenic labeling in your own life. Look for *any* labeling that may have diminished your sense of self, boxing you into a lifelong sense of self-limitations, whether or not the labeling was done in a loving and protective way.

And let me quickly add that this is not an invitation to snarl at your parents for your sense of powerlessness. Yes, parents, teachers, or other authority figures may have assigned you some iatrogenic labels, but you have the responsibility for yourself now. Your task is to look inside, find those labels, and decide for yourself whether you want to continue using them or not. It's your choice.

LIVING TO YOUR LABEL

I once treated a forty-five-year-old woman who had about as poor a self-concept as anyone I have ever encountered. Beth Ann was the firstborn of four children. With three brothers, all younger but close in age, she was the only girl and, frankly, that was not a welcome circumstance.

Her father, Joe Bob, was a powerfully built man with a strong and overbearing personality and a chauvinistic value system that would have made Archie Bunker look like a liberal. Joe Bob was a "man's man" who spent all of his time hunting, fishing, and either playing or watching sports. He had wanted a boy, a "running buddy." When Beth Ann was born he did little to hide his disappointment. He treated his wife like "hired help" and as Beth Ann grew up, she was tolerated at best. As each of her brothers matured and became more able to companion their father, Beth Ann's role shrunk to nothingness in his eyes. He invested all of his time and energy in the boys. Beth Ann longed for acceptance and inclusion in his world, but was powerless to create it. His neglect of her did nothing but grow and culminated in outright resentment if she required or absorbed any time, money, or effort. The boys had the best clothes, sporting equipment, spending money, and, later on, nice cars. Beth Ann on the other hand was a modern-day Cinderella. She wore secondhand clothes, lived in a tiny room that doubled as a sun porch/junk room, and drove her mother's twenty-year-old station wagon. She had no privacy, no respect, and no attention from her father or her brothers. While Joe Bob would never think to miss one of the boys' school activities or games, he had never attended a single function of Beth Ann's, saying that it was just "silly girl stuff." Not surprisingly, Beth Ann labeled herself as inferior and as a second-class citizen. She labeled herself as second-class because, in the system that was this family, she *was* second-class. It is true that children learn what they live, and Beth Ann learned well.

"Living to the label," Beth Ann had been taught that she deserved very little and as a result, she expected very little. In every dating relationship she had, she was so passive and so subservient that she almost invited exploitation and was often seen as incredibly boring with zero spirit or spunk. Even when she came to see me, a professional who she was paying for counsel and input, she said she felt bad making me listen to all her problems. Having been labeled in this way by her father's treatment and, more importantly, having labeled herself in this way, she had foreclosed any other options or considerations of her self-worth. Her label controlled every thought, feeling, and action she had and she lived to it without exception. This label communicated by her father's words and deeds and then internalized by her had become the prison in which she lived. Every day that she conformed, the grip on her life became tighter and tighter until it was choking her spirit, to the point that she finally reached out for help.

How Beth Ann's father treated her spoke volumes, sometimes without him saying a word. As a result, she added to his labels when she condemned herself in response to the sting of his rejection. Her reaction was to doubt and abandon her true sense of self. Sometimes the reaction is less obvious but not less devastating.

Some people react to labels with complete and total conformance to the implied message and other times they radically react *against* the label by becoming extreme in rebelling in the opposite direction. Perhaps a person that has been put down and labeled like Beth Ann might respond with arrogance and a false sense of superiority. They may pretend vehemently that they couldn't care less about the acceptance that has been withheld from them. It's important to note that in both cases, whether you are conforming to the label or radically rebelling against it, the label is controlling you and dictating your life. It is easy to understand how such treatment of a young, vulnerable, and impressionable girl could control her thinking, but how does it persist when that girl grows up? Why would a mature, competent woman continue to be controlled by childhood labels? The answer is powerful, but not at all obvious.

Living to a label can only become a part of your personal truth and concept of self if at some level it is working for you. Living to that label, giving your power away, provides some kind of income—social, spiritual, economic, or otherwise—that can make even the most painful and inappropriate labels highly durable and stubbornly resistant to change. Somehow, someway, accepting the definition of that label provides you some currency or you wouldn't do it. Maybe it's an excuse to be passive or angry or play the victim, but whatever it is, you wouldn't do it without a reward, however sick that payoff might be.

Decidedly less dramatic than the Beth Ann situation, I have also encountered countless ordinary people who labeled themselves as "patients," not because they were sick or deformed, but because they received huge payoffs by living to that label. Calling themselves patients gave them an identity. Whether their disorders were real or imagined, whether they had legitimate disorders or were total hypochondriacs, it was a badge of how they wanted to be treated and how they wanted to treat themselves, giving definition to what they should do or should not do. They felt that by being "sick," they acquired the "honor" of being a patient, the same kind of honor that a wounded soldier might get on his return from a war. To the extent that their label got them that honor, they had no incentive to get out of bed. I used to marvel at how so many of my patients would take pride in their injuries or diseases. They would actually brag to one another about how sick or hurt they were. Their appointments became their reason for living. Once productive members of society, they were, by living to their labels, reduced to nonproductive parasites on society. They would hang around the hospital and compare notes but never plans to return to productive roles.

Their implied message was, "I'm a patient, so respect the label, rather than me. I am weak and limited in what I can do for myself or for others. Feel pity for me and give me respect, but do not expect anything from me." For many people labels, such as "patient" or "student," give the payoff of having a socially sanctioned "timeout" from the performance demands of the world. How could anyone expect someone to get up and go to work if, after all, they are sick and participating in some program of treatment? Very convenient if you're just plain lazy, don't you think? Problem is, once again it is totally fictional and living to that label completely ignores the authentic self and all the skills and abilities that are buried there.

For some people, holding onto a label simply offers that security of an identity. If you've got a label, then you are at least "something." Hey, everybody wants to be somebody, right? But what if you are so very much more than the label allows? Just as with Beth Ann, these everyday situations and labels can be very confining.

I'm reminded of my thirty-year high school reunion. The "pretty girls" may still have been pretty, but they sure weren't very interesting. Necessity is the mother of invention and although some of the pretty girls were pretty, smart, and hard working, some were not. Some were girls who had gotten picked for everything, had gotten by on everything, only because they were pretty. Result: They got really comfortable being "pretty." They never tried to become interesting or intelligent, because they believed they didn't have to. It was clear that that label, as comfortable as it was, had become a curse. They could no longer meet the "young and beautiful" standard, but they still struggled to focus on it as they lived in the past, totally contained and defined by the outdated label.

That is obviously another problem with labels; they are almost always backward looking. Labels describe where you perceive you have been, not where you are. If you give in to them, however, they can sure predict where you're going.

To focus on your accumulated labels is to look back rather than ahead. To focus on your accumulated labels is to allow your past to become your future.

What's true for the other internal factors is also true for labels: You distort information to support your labels. If you decide that your child is a hellion, that your boss is a jerk, or that you are a loser, you will be sensitized to and will eagerly collect every kind of information that supports those labels and reject any contrary data. You will put your "information radar" in confirm mode and will only scan for examples and will interpret all behaviors and interactions in a way that supports a relevant label and categorization. You do the same thing whether the label is applied to someone else or it is applied to you.

Just as with some of the former beauty queens at my reunion, if your label was and is that you are the cutest girl in the class, eventually, as you inevitably get older and your beauty fades, you're going to have to avoid mirrors and people who will tell you the truth or you will be very distressed. If you label yourself the quintessential mother and your children leave the nest to go off to college, your label and its boundaries will not serve you well. If, when perceiving and judging someone else, you say to yourself, That guy's an idiot, you will stop processing data, because you've already decided what he is. The jury is in: He's an idiot. No more questions. If the label, instead, is "I'm a loser," then you hold that label, "loser," in front of you every day. You may exhibit numerous "winner"–type behaviors, but your label will become a self-fulfilling prophecy.

I guarantee that if you have bought in to a bunch of labels, your radar will scan around and find support for them. You will live to the label. If you're like most people, you will shut the data-processing window and you will live that label. Why? Because—again, if you're like most people—you would rather be right than happy and your payoffs, however illogical, are powerful.

EXERCISES

It's time for some self-diagnosis. How do you label yourself? Did someone tell you that you were a loser? Have you, in turn, labeled yourself a loser? Somewhere along the way, did you accept a label in order to be accepted by a group? Have you labeled your life a dead end? If you have, what does that do for your life?

To pull yourself free from your fictional self, you've got to get your hands around the labels that may have entrapped you; evaluate them; and delete them. The following exercises will help you do just that.

EXERCISE 1

Simply list, on paper, all the labels you have been given. Starting as far back in your life as you can remember, write down every label you can recall. Your list will include some labels that you know had some influence on your self-concept and some that you have rejected.

EXERCISE 2

Copy the following three-heading chart in your journal. After you have listed all the labels you remember for Exercise 1, go back to your list and circle the ones that you believe were put on you by your parents.

Many labels come from such a long time ago that you may not remember when you first heard them, but try to remember the first time you felt the sting of these labels and what you were doing at the time. Fill out your chart with as much detail as possible.

Label	First Time Mentioned	Behavior
_____	_____	_____
_____	_____	_____
_____	_____	_____

EXERCISE 3

Go back over the chart you made for Exercise 2 and put a check beside any labels that you can sense to be part of your life today. Are you operating on the belief that these labels are true today and still reflect you?

EXERCISE 4

Now copy the following four-heading chart in your journal.

Look again at your original list from Exercise 1. Which of those labels were you given by **people other than your parents**? Do you remember when you received this label and what you were doing? Complete the chart with that information.

Labels	Given to You by	First Time Mentioned	Behavior
_____	_____	_____	_____
_____	_____	_____	_____
_____	_____	_____	_____
_____	_____	_____	_____

EXERCISE 5

This exercise requires three columns. Identify each column as shown below.

It is time now for you to remember which labels on your list have become part of your own labeling. Since our internal labeling often lies beneath our consciousness, this exercise demands your utmost concentration and focus. What you're going to list are the labels that you took away from some event, *as your conclusion about yourself*.

Examples: If you were hurt and dejected when a love relationship broke apart, did you then, and do you today, label yourself as a loser?

If you went through a bad divorce, did you and do you label yourself as a failure?

If you failed a test, did you label yourself as a dummy?

Is there some job or career incident that caused you to assign a particular label to yourself? What was the incident and what label did you take from it?

What are the self-labels that you carry with you?

For each self-label, try to remember those times that you knew that you identified with your label: in other words, when you accepted the label as a true statement about yourself. What was the situation?

Use the chart you've made to record all of this information.

Label	Time Occurred	Behavior
_____	_____	_____
_____	_____	_____
_____	_____	_____

PUTTING IT TOGETHER

We're going to deal with your answers in some detail later on. Right now, I want you just to look over the various labels you have come up with for yourself. Imagine that those labels are listed on your résumé. Now suppose you are looking at that résumé the way a future employer might. Is he or she saying anything like the following?

"Let's see, who do we have here? Okay: A fat, lazy drone—a worker bee with no ambition. That's super. Let's hire a *whole bunch* of those."

Absurd, isn't it? If those are *not* the labels you would want an employer to attach to you, then why do it yourself? Resolve that you will no longer conspire with the world in assigning limiting labels to yourself. Whatever the payoff you're getting from living to your labels, determine that you are going to move out of that comfort zone, once and for all.

10 LIFE SCRIPTS

"There'll be two dates on your tombstone
and all your friends will read 'em
but all that's gonna matter is that little dash
between 'em."

— KEVIN WELCH

IN the chapter on internal dialogue, you learned that you're engaged in a never-ending, real-time conversation with yourself. You learned that your self-talk has immediate and concrete consequences. If the internal dialogue is rationally positive, you are energized and strong; both your mind and body are functioning from within a "zone" that opens up new possibilities for achievement. If your internal dialogue is negative, you'll feel it, even at the level of the cells in your body. It both comprises and reflects your personal truth and, therefore, your self-concept. With everything you feel, say, and do, that contaminated self-concept will show itself as you present to the world all kinds of negative messages. The world will, of course, respond accordingly.

In taking stock of your own self-talk, you may have become aware that there is a certain species of that talk that is unlike any other. It's a self-conversation, but it has this distinction: While you may have the sense that it is filled with sour notes from your past, it seems to happen so fast that it is just kind of a blur. Unlike the rest of your internal dialogue, which takes place in real time and can be listened to at will, this embedded mental activity is tough to get a handle on. It happens incredibly fast and it is especially malignant. For those reasons alone, it demands a separate discussion and your special attention. This especially dangerous kind of self-talk is what I call a **tape.**

A tape is negative self-talk that you have rehearsed and repeated for so long and so often that it has become "overlearned." It has played in your head, hour after hour, day after day, month after month, year after year. Ultimately, a tape becomes so deeply ingrained that it becomes an automatic response: It can be unleashed without your even being aware that something has happened in your life to trigger it. Remember our earlier example of how quickly and powerfully snake-phobic people can react when someone yells, "Snake!"? When your tape is triggered, it can be screamingly dramatic or it can pervade your consciousness, silently yet with dominance. It's a reaction that is so powerful, so fast, that no other thought, rationale, or reason sees the light of day.

If some puppeteer were standing above you, controlling your every move, you would want to know it and know it now. You'd be shocked and appalled to learn that you weren't actually the captain of your own life, that you weren't choosing what you did and when. Well, that is the premise of this chapter. First, I want to help you understand how tapes work and help you identify your own tapes. Next, we'll look at the **fixed and limiting beliefs** that form the content of your tapes. Finally, we'll talk about how those tapes yield a **life script** that, like that puppeteer, is probably dictating the outcomes in your life.

TAPES

I call them "tapes" because I grew up in an era when big mainframe computers were run by huge magnetic tapes that "told" the machine what to do. The tape would run and the computer would perform just as the program on the tape directed it to do. It's the same deal here: You, too, can be run by your "tapes," with no independent mind of your own. Once you've finished this section of the book, I think you are very likely to be thinking: Oh, now I get it; now I know why I keep winding up where I don't want to be in my life! I was programmed to behave that way and create those results, because I was being programmed by powerful thoughts I wasn't even aware of.

I want to make sure that you're totally clear about what tapes are. They are as natural, and uncontrollable, as a reflex and work as independently as your organs. Just as your hearts pumps blood and your lungs intake oxygen and release carbon dioxide, tapes run on their own accord and without your conscious awareness. As I suggested earlier, while they have some kinship with internal dialogue, tapes belong to a species all their own. Tapes are long-held, overlearned, lightning-fast, automatic thoughts that: 1. totally ignore current input; and 2. program you for a specific outcome, oftentimes without your even being aware of it.

Suppose, for example, you meet a guy and after talking to him for a while, you say to yourself, This guy is a total mouth breather. He is so boring, I would rather be home in my fuzzy house shoes eating peanut butter out of the jar. What you've just told yourself constitutes internal dialogue. It is a *real-time conversation,* in reaction to *current stimuli.* It all happens in the here and now. You are there, he is there, and you react to him and what is going on, right now. Based on your current reactions, you may decide: Hey, I'm out of here, good-bye.

A tape is different in that it is totally *based on past experience.* It causes you to ignore what is happening in the here and now. In our example, if it was your tape that caused you to bail on the doofus you were contemplating killing some time with, that decision would be based on a prerecorded reflex that occurred independently of anything he did or didn't do. Let's say, for example, that you have dated seven "doofi" in a row. The last one was incredibly insufferable and drank all of your wine, ate all of your groceries, and then bedded down your little sister. You would likely have some powerful baggage, particularly when added on top of the other six bad experiences you had been through. Those experiences and the themes they created at the level of your self-concept would be the building blocks of your tapes. You might have a whole library of tapes, which might include:

Men are selfish when it comes to relationships.
I pick losers every time, so what's the point?
Men always use me, so I must deserve it.
If I don't "nail" them first, they will "nail" me eventually.

Notice that each tape: 1. Includes a judgment of yourself or others: "Men are . . ." or "I pick . . ."; 2. Involves a specific context: "When it comes to relationships . . ." or ". . . Always use me."; 3. Predicts an outcome: "every time," or "will nail me."

In these circumstances, I pity the next poor guy who is standing on your porch all dressed up, car washed, and ready to have a good time. That boy is dead in the water before he ever even opens his mouth. It wouldn't make any difference if he were sweeter than Mr. Rogers or better looking than Tom Cruise. He is toast! Why? Because, at the core of your self-concept, you are playing these tapes, rather than dealing in the here and now. You may not consciously be aware of the existence or content of these tapes, but at the core of your self-concept, you *are* aware and the message is: Danger! Protect yourself, pull back, protect yourself! All of your behavior, and therefore the outcome of this relationship, is being determined historically. You are dealing with the past and ignoring the present. What's more, the determination is happening so fast, thanks to these lightning-quick, overlearned, automatic tapes, that you wouldn't even be able to recognize that you have his poor ass fried up before you ever open the door. You can't even see the guy standing in front of you, because you are so busy looking over your shoulder at what has happened before.

Understand that being controlled by your tapes is different from learning from your mistakes. If you have learned from your mistakes, you will *consciously* make more informed decisions. When a tape is in control, you are not consciously, currently making any decision. When a tape is in control, you are a passenger. That's how tapes work and that's what makes them so dangerous.

Here's another example. Suppose that, while interviewing for a really good job, one you would love to have, you learn that you are one of the final candidates. You've survived a couple of rounds of interviews already and all of the feedback so far has been very positive. It dawns on you that although you never really believed you could get the job, here you are, still in the running. A rational conclusion might be, You know? I think I've got a good shot here; I need to stay focused and make this deal happen.

Here comes that damn tape. It all started when you got fired from your post as deputy assistant dogcatcher forty years ago, when you were in high school. You were really proud of that job and it hurt, and hurt badly, when you got fired. You had been so proud when all of your friends would see you wearing your uniform. And the money was good, for back then. That was the first time you ever truly failed at something you cared about and it changed you in some way. On the basis of that history, your forty-year-old tape may be telling you, You're not bulletproof here; you've been failing since a very young age. Let's face it: Here you are, fifty-five years old and you're having to start a new job. You're the type that gets fired from jobs. They're going to see right through you. Your tape then predicts an outcome: Give it up. You'll never get the job.

If that tape "switches on" just as you go into the next interview, you may find yourself doing and saying the kinds of things that sabotage your efforts to make a positive impression. With your speech, posture, gestures, and demeanor, you may emit a persona that says to that interviewer, in effect, Gosh, I can't believe you're actually considering me for this job. You don't really plan to hire me, right?

And the interviewer may sit there thinking, Well, gee, if *you've* got doubts, then who am I to argue with you?

Again, in contrast to the rest of your internal dialogue, which is reactive to happenings in the here and now, tapes operate in and affect all three tenses of your life: your past, your present, and your future. Here's what I mean:

A tape looks backward, to your past.

A tape is a backward-oriented, thematic reaction to your past, to a particular moment or self-observation in your personal history. It is a prerecorded message with a powerful emotional component. It is an encoded, long-term memory that is highly resistant to change. A painful event happens; you evaluate your reactions in response to that event; and the tape is made. Years later, you don't reevaluate yourself every time you get into a situation that calls for self-evaluation. Your tape is available to tell you, immediately, how to react.

A tape expresses itself as a judgment about who you are in the present.

The tape encodes that past perception, just below the level of your consciousness, where it plays over and over until it is so overlearned as to be automatic. It is spring-loaded to seize control whenever a relevant situation arises. The prerecorded information of a tape addresses every imaginable aspect of your self-concept: your intelligence, your worth, your value, your strengths, and your potential. Since you will tend to treat the tape as gospel truth, whatever the judgment is, that's your reality.

A tape predicts the outcome you will have in the future.

On the basis of that judgment, the tape predicts and therefore controls your thinking and behavior and thus the outcome you will have. You make decisions about the present, and predictions about the future, on the basis of the tapes.

Take, for example, the judgment "I am stupid." As we've seen, tapes are based on history, so somewhere along the way, in reaction to a particular event in your life, you, in your real-time, internal dialogue, started telling yourself that you were stupid. Practice makes perfect and you repeated this judgment so loudly and so long that it got burned into your mind.

Fast forward to the present. In the context of that job interview or an exam, the tape that plays at lightning speed, just below your conscious level, might be, I am stupid; *therefore,* I won't be picked for this job, or, I am stupid; *therefore* there's no way I can pass this exam. The tape anticipates an outcome and the outcome is always negative: I am stupid; therefore this [whatever the event is] will not go well for me. And remember, for every thought, lightning speed or otherwise, there is a corresponding physiological event. Just as soon as you start dogging on yourself mentally, your body and your energy quickly follow suit.

Now you may be thinking, Hey, wait a minute! What about positive tapes? What if my history is positive, so my tapes are programming me to believe I can't miss, that I always come out on top? Sorry, but if you're thinking that that is a good thing, we have two problems: You're wrong, and I haven't done a very good job of teaching you about tapes. There is no such thing as a positive tape. You might think, Well, how can a tape that says positive things be negative? What about the power of positive thinking and all that jazz?

Think about it in a real-world situation. Suppose you are sitting on an airliner at the end of the runway in January in New York City. The weather is windy, icy, and snowy and the pilot has a decision to make: Do we take off or do we not?

Now suppose that instead of evaluating the *current conditions,* your pilot decides to go because he believes in himself and because every other takeoff he has ever made turned out okay. His tape might be: Hey, I always come out okay—I always land on my feet!

Because the tape controls him, the pilot ignores the warning signs of danger and the fact that he has finally met a set of circumstances that his skill cannot overcome. My first flight instructor told me something I have never forgotten. He said, "I've met a lot of bold pilots and I've met a lot of old pilots, but I have never met my old, bold pilots!" If in these circumstances your pilot is emboldened by a historical tape, you could wind up dead. His tape may be "positive," in the sense that it has an affirming message, but it is *not based on the here and now,* and, therefore, can*not* be a plus in any sense of the word. Anytime I'm on an airliner, I want my pilot looking at the current situation and making a real-time, informed decision, not picking his course of action on what happened one, two, or five years ago.

Bottom line: Whatever the situation in which you find yourself, the appropriate questions are, "Can I handle this, or can't I? Is this what I want, or not?" If you're at the mercy of a tape, you simply do not have that dialogue with yourself. Instead, your prerecorded reaction to that situation dictates its outcome. It becomes a knee-jerk reaction.

Thinking about tapes reminds me of a live TV news report years ago, just before a big livestock show and rodeo was set to open in Texas. The reporter had just collared Gus, the foreman of the cattle pens. Wrinkling his nose and grinning, the reporter said, "Golly, Gus, how do you deal with the smell?"

Looking blankly at the reporter, Gus answered, "What smell?" He was so used to his "environmental conditions" that the foul smell did not even register. Although the odor was impinging on Gus, he had become numb to it. He had adapted.

That's the way your tapes work. You may have once listened to them consciously, but across time you've adapted so well that you do not notice them anymore. The bad smell has just become part of the routine. Well, here's a chance to step back and smell the odor. I want you to become aware of your messages now, so that you can begin to make choices in the here and now.

Like any other internal dialogue, your tapes are as unique to you as your DNA. Nevertheless, to stimulate your thoughts about them, you may find it helpful to take a look at a list of common tapes, messages that I'm convinced are playing, in some form or fashion, in lots of people's heads. Do any of the following ten tapes sound familiar to you?

1. I will never have a good experience; my family was so dysfunctional, we never learned how to have fun.
2. I am so ugly; my body and face are so different from those of the popular people that I will have to settle for third class.
3. My future will be like my past: unlucky and nonproductive. I should never expect to be successful, because it is not my destiny.
4. I have done some bad things and I will never be forgiven. Guilt is just my cross to bear. People will always disappoint me and hurt me.
5. I was abused as a child. All men will use me for what they want and be insensitive to how I feel.
6. My family was low class. I will be low class. There is nothing I can do to change that.
7. My father was a loser; I will be a loser, regardless of what happens.
8. I am a leader. People look to me to be strong and set an example. I must never show my weakness. I must be strong, never showing my real self, for the rest of my life.
9. Laziness is a sin, so I should never relax.
10. I am not worthy of people's respect and consideration.

One or more of these tapes, or some version of them, may be at work in your life. I encourage you, as we go forward, to start thinking about what your own tapes include.

FIXED BELIEFS

To learn still more about the content of your tapes, you need to become familiar with what I call **fixed beliefs**. Generally speaking, when a tape plays in your head, automatically speeding you toward a particular conclusion and a particular outcome, that tape is "taking orders" from your highest-level, most powerful, and organizational perceptions about how things are *supposed* to work. These organizing perceptions or worldviews are your fixed beliefs.

Fixed beliefs reflect your overall understanding of your place in the world. They are "fixed" in the sense that you are no longer adding or subtracting new information; they are perceptions that have become rigid and unchanging. Fixed beliefs go with you everywhere you go and are basic to every part of your life. They influence every value you have, your perception of your basic worth as a human being, your core traits and characteristics. They tell you where your boundaries are. They contain your expectations about what ought to happen in your life. Whether the issue is your relationships with the opposite sex, your fulfillment in the working world, or your interactions with your children or spouse, your fixed beliefs exert a powerful influence.

Fixed beliefs express themselves through concepts like "should" and "must." They are, in truth, demands: demands for your compliance with a particular vision of what life is, demands for you not to make waves or disrupt the roles that others play. If your beliefs were not fixed, you might well be asking questions and forming new expectations that would disrupt the assigned order of your life. By contrast, these fixed beliefs are there to keep you "on task." A fixed belief keeps you within your assigned place in this world. It establishes the boundaries of what you are willing to accept from life.

Perhaps the easiest way to get a handle on fixed beliefs is simply to understand that they *define the roles you play in life*. In other words, once you know what your fixed beliefs are, you know something about the **script** that is running your life.

As you know from watching the evening news on TV, the anchorperson typically has an electronic "bug" in his ear, a tiny radio through which he or she takes instructions from the offscreen director. If a particular question needs to be asked, if the show goes off-track, or if a commercial is coming up, the director can bark orders

and nobody but the anchorperson hears. Thanks to that little ear-
piece, the anchorperson stays "on script."

In a similar fashion, you are subject to a life script, a set of instructions that tell you how to run your life.

What is a script? In a game of word association, what would your
responses be to that word? If I said "script," you might reply with
any or all of the following statements:

- A script is the words to a play or movie.
- The script tells everything that happens.
- It contains the beginning, the middle, and the end of the pro-
  duction.
- When you know the script, you know how everything turns
  out.
- The script is like a recipe that tells how all the ingredients come
  together.
- It guides all of the tasks related to the play.
- It's what the actors memorize.
- The script is the overall plan that everyone is supposed to stick
  to.
- When the actors get lost, the script gets them back on track.

We would probably agree that a script is what gives the play its
meaning. We would agree that the script affects the choices made for
the entire production: dialogue, costumes, casting, locations, and
scenery. In addition, after a certain number of rehearsals, the actors
put down their typewritten scripts and simply "become" the charac-
ters. From then on, the script is no longer words on a page; it lives in
the actors' heads. Although they are no longer reading it, it is alive
and active, guiding what the actors do and say. There is no improvi-
sation; there is no creativity, because every player must stick with the
script so that all the other players' lines, actions, attitudes, and positions will work. If one of the actors in our play were to start freelancing, it would be seriously frowned upon, since it would disrupt

the expected flow and that, of course, would be highly inconvenient. So how about you: Are you living your life according to a script? Do you have an assigned role; a role with certain lines to be spoken, certain actions to be carried out? Are the other actors in the play of your life expecting you to be and do certain things, such that you feel as though you, too, can't improvise, can't make up new lines? Do you fear that the inconvenience you would create by freelancing would be unacceptable?

If you are living by a script, maybe written by you years earlier, maybe written by someone else, do you know what it is? Are you living your lines and following your script? Is it what you would write today if you were writing it all over again? Are you spending your days doing what you would write into your script if you could? Are you doing what you're doing, where you would choose to do it, and with whom? Does your script have you spending your life pursuing what you really want or did that get dropped from your script a long time ago? Have you outgrown or just evolved away from the script?

As I suggested earlier, the script of life that you are living builds on and draws its strength from certain cornerstones called **fixed beliefs.** Your fixed beliefs tell you what role you are playing. You have practiced your script so much and for so long that the beliefs you have about you, about your possibilities, about your responsibilities, do in fact become fixed. They become set in stone, but it is a stone that I intend to chip away.

Let's look more at how dependent your script is on fixed beliefs. Fixed beliefs describe the "action." They provide you with a framework for understanding the events in your life and they influence your own reactions to those events.

Fixed beliefs provide you with the words you say. Just as your internal dialogue supplies you with your "lines," the fixed belief is the censor of those lines, making sure you do not get too far afield.

Fixed beliefs tell you how things are going to turn out. They shape your expectations about your outcomes. They anesthetize your fear of the unknown by pushing you in the direction of something knowable and familiar, even if not fulfilling.

When you start to feel offtrack or out of control, your fixed beliefs provide a refuge. Like a panicky actor grabbing for his script, you go back to your fixed belief. It tells you what to say and do and you instantly feel comforted. Equilibrium is restored.

Fixed beliefs influence the "casting" of your life: They determine your choice of who will and will not get a part in your life. They influence setting: the places and situations in which your life will unfold. And they even have a say about costumes and masks: the physical appearance, clothing, and style you choose to present to the world.

Here's the key thing for you to understand about fixed beliefs: When you're at the mercy of a fixed belief—in other words, when you're living from a script—*you will resist any change to that script.* When events go counter to your fixed beliefs, even if you recognize that you've never been happier or more peaceful, a sense of destiny intrudes. You get a queasy feeling, an apprehension that things just aren't right somehow. Your internal dialogue becomes something like, Oh my gosh! I'm going to be struck down any minute. This is not my destiny. This is not my role. What happens is that you cannot be happy being happy. You will be miserable if your script is to be miserable, because that is your self-ordained destiny. You can be miserable even if you start to be happy, because "happiness" was not part of your script. Happiness belongs to some other character in the drama, not you. So instead of enjoying the feelings, you fear that something is wrong or that it is only the calm before the storm, since you know the script and happiness is just not part of it.

I once worked with a patient who was approaching her thirty-fifth birthday. Nancy was married to an abusive husband and was about to mark her tenth year at a job she despised. With a cynical grin, she told me the title she had given to her life script: *Third-Class Drudge.* It was an attitude that pervaded her every move. Early in life, she had adopted the overall tape that she would be third class in every aspect of her life and, because it was a tape so deeply engrained into her self-concept, she was programmed to fight against anything that didn't fit that programming. Being a good "sheep," she acquiesced to a script that called for her to behave in a third-class fashion. The cornerstones of that script, her fixed beliefs, didn't allow for her to entertain any departure from that script. Somewhere along the way, she had adopted the shoulds and musts of those beliefs and learned the lines of her lifelong script: a script based on the fixed beliefs that she was never going to get much better than what she had and that she needed to accept what was offered. The irony was that nothing in this life script accurately reflected who she was: a smart, attractive woman, well educated and highly sophisticated in many fields, who had a passionate appreciation for the arts.

Shortly after college, Nancy had been approached by a man she described to me as very desirable (she described him as being "totally Baldwin"!), who had already established a successful career. But she told herself, He's too good for me. He would lose interest in me soon enough. He'd probably leave me for a prettier woman. Result: She married a "Joe Six-Pack" who she knew would be untruthful and abusive to her, all because her inner script told her she was unworthy of anything else.

Although she had all the makings of a gifted college teacher, when she viewed her career options, she basically told herself, I'm not smart enough to compete in something really good. I'd better take something menial, so I'll be safe. (It boggles the mind to think about all the jobs people do that they're unsuited for: jobs that threaten their mental stability, their emotional well-being, and as a result their physical health—jobs they took in order to be "safe.") Now, even menial work can be done with a sense of passion and purpose, but to settle for a job at the direction of your fictional self is not okay. It is declaring defeat. At some level, Nancy knew that.

Unfortunately, the power of Nancy's life script was such that she could not overcome it. The more we talked, and the more vividly a life of excitement and meaning unfolded before her, the more anxious Nancy became. The possibility of going "off script" in search of the authentic Nancy was more than she could bear. She insisted on remaining with her third-class husband in a third-class neighborhood, doing a third-class job. I, unfortunately, with all of my challenging and probing questions, was not part of her script. Nancy soon made excuses and quit coming to see me. I failed her and she failed herself. Today she is still safe within her own world, limiting and small. Her "job" in life, as she sees it, is to be third class. I suppose that that script is going to limit her for the rest of her life. I do not intend to fail you, nor do I intend for you to fail yourself.

Fear of change, even positive change, is a powerful restraint. The thought of deviating from the narrow path of fixed beliefs and the life script that contains them can be unbearable for some people.

In one of the places where I grew up, there was a large, empty field behind our house. As a kid of ten or eleven, I used to meet my friends back there for bicycle races, dirt-clod wars, and the like. A deep trench ran from one end of the field to the other, about six feet wide and four feet deep.

The typical challenge we set ourselves was to cross this trench, called the "Valley of Death," going full speed on our bicycles over a "bridge" consisting of a single two-by-six. What I learned very early was that if I approached the bridge with the thought of something disastrous, like sliding off the board or missing it, it would happen. If I focused on shooting smoothly to the opposite side, it would happen. It was as if by summoning the right imagery in my mind, I could direct my muscles, and consequently the bicycle, to glide over the Valley of Death. As I approached the board, therefore, I always tried to focus on a single point: the far end of the board. I tried to shut out all other "data," believing that it might cause me to topple headfirst into the ditch.

Now, focusing on a worthy goal is a good thing. But suppose there had been no ditch, just a plank lying on the ground. When people adopt fixed beliefs, when they become fixed at a certain point in life, it's because they think they have no choice. They are fixated on sticking to the dead center of a narrow board, *even when there is no ditch*. They are unwilling to deviate from the fixed belief, because they think that they can't. Even when a smoother, safer, and more enjoyable ride is within easy reach, they will cling to their scripted route through life, simply because it feels safe. Are you walking an "imagined" tightrope, when in truth you could easily step to one side or the other and be just fine? I rode my Valley of Death tightrope as a kid and for fun. If you're doing it in your adult life, I'm betting it isn't much fun at all.

I recall a group of lawyers from Georgia who were scheduled to visit our offices in order to talk strategy for a huge and complex upcoming trial. As is our custom, we put them up in a very nice and convenient luxury hotel with all the comforts and conveniences you could imagine. The rooms were large, with lots of working space for evening sessions, twenty-four-hour room service, and extreme quiet and privacy. When we sent a car to pick them up for the meeting on just the second morning of their stay, the lawyers were nowhere to be found. The front desk reported that they had checked out.

In a little while, the entire group appeared in our conference room, looking like the dogs had had them cornered under the porch all night long! After the hubbub died down, we asked them why they were not at the hotel. It turned out that they had checked out of the luxury hotel in favor of one that I knew would barely pass inspection as an army barracks. It did not have air-conditioning that worked more than half of the time and it sat next to a highway with noise that would deafen a snake. Result: They had had to sleep with their windows open and deal with the racket and wind. Because the rooms were so small, they had left most of their clothes and materials in their rental car outside.

But as they spoke, it became clear that these lawyers actually felt much more comfortable in their Blue Moon sleep haven, with the open-air and free smoke hazards, even though it would not have cost them a penny to stay in the better place. The gist of their explanation was that they could not stay at the luxury hotel because it was just too roomy and too quiet. Bottom line: They felt out of place in any surroundings that were beyond their personal experiences. Their fixed beliefs and life scripts simply did not call for first-class treatment and accommodations and they could not endure being off script for even a short time.

Are you approaching your life in that fashion? Is the steady drumbeat of your internal dialogue something that sounds like:

- This is "less than," and "less than" is good enough for me.
- I can't do this.
- I will never achieve what I think that person has.
- I don't deserve what they have.
- I know I'm getting cheated here, but nice is what I'm supposed to be. I'll be nice, rather than complain.
- I have been the second person in this relationship all the time, I am a supporter; I do better if someone else is making the decisions. I can carry them out, but I just don't have leadership qualities.

The point is that most fixed beliefs are also **limiting beliefs:** The things that we fixedly believe about ourselves are typically negative and so we tell ourselves that "it," whatever "it" is, is something we can't do, don't deserve, and are not qualified for.

As was true for Nancy, limiting beliefs impose upon you such powerful restrictions that the possibility of freedom, of being released from the treadmill of routine unhappiness, seems somehow threatening. Whether your limiting beliefs are like those just listed or something wholly different, anything that casts doubt on your limiting beliefs may seem like a threat. People will limit themselves so dramatically, it is just amazing.

We imagine what our lives will be, regardless of what problems we have or what physical discomfort it affords. We select our environment based on our scripts. People script a life with a certain income, certain relationships, and a certain lifestyle and although we say we want more, we're very uncomfortable about taking any steps toward change. Amazingly, people will often opt for a familiar lifestyle that is admittedly unfulfilling, rather than an unfamiliar alternative, even though that alternative may be clearly superior.

And remember that you are not the only one in your life who may be working from a set of fixed beliefs. Other people may also be working from a script or series of expectations about how you should behave, what you should say and do. When you make the decision to go off script, they may feel highly threatened and anxious.

As an example, I recall an incident that was frequently repeated, in some form, after many of the life skills seminars I conducted years ago. In the course of each seminar, people would go through several exercises targeted directly at their fixed beliefs about themselves. These "stretches" were designed to draw the participants way outside the tight little boundaries of the roles they were living. For example, toward the end of a seminar, we might assign some otherwise grim, anal-retentive accountant the task of role playing, onstage, someone like Tina Turner or Elvis Presley (trust me, you just had to be there!). He would start singing at the top of his lungs. He'd be shaking his wig while the rest of the group danced and screamed, "Wild man!" He would invariably go home really pumped, really seeing things differently. But more than once, wives would call me after their husbands had gone through the seminar, crying, "What did you do to my husband?"

I'd say, "Well, what's wrong?"

"Well, Dave has been home for like two weeks, hugging the children and singing to them and talking to them—what did you do to him?" In other words, the change in Dave was so dramatic that his wife found it uncomfortable. Her position was: "I don't like this. I don't care if it's positive, I don't care if it's constructive—I don't like it."

Whenever I would ask, "What about it do you not like?" the answer was usually something like, "Well, he is just so *different*. Is he crazy or something?"

"Well, is he doing self-destructive things?"

"No."

"Is he hurting you or the kids?"

"No."

"Is he being kind and giving?"

"Yes."

"Does he seem happy and peaceful?"

"Well, yes, I guess so."

"Has he done anything stupid, like run off with the baby-sitter?"

"No."

"Would you like to come to the workshop next month?"

"Yes! I mean no! I mean I don't know, I'll call you back, and thanks, I think."

The problem was that *Dave* had walked away from his fixed beliefs about Dave, but *his wife* had not. In her understanding of "how things are supposed to work," Dave was supposed to keep playing the role of the emotionally absent housemate, not the energized, upbeat husband and dad. This happened a lot. The more free of fixed beliefs the seminar participant became, the more likely we were to get an anxious phone call from his or her spouse. The lesson here is simply this: Your decision to dump your fixed beliefs may not be applauded by the other people in your life, since it will probably affect their own fixed beliefs about you. Change can be painful, even when it is change for the better.

If someone were to ask you today, "What script are you playing in your life?" what would you say? Would you say, "I'm a mom"? "I'm a doting parent"? "A dutiful wife," or "respected husband"? "Successful professional"? "The king of money"?

Or would you identify yourself by your heritage: "I'm the daughter of John and Mary Smith." If so, are you following the family script?

IDENTIFYING YOUR OWN TAPES

At the beginning of this chapter, you learned that your tapes are so overlearned that they play at lightning speed. The good news is that you can slow them down. You can slow them down to a speed that can be heard and analyzed. You do that by listening consciously and by asking yourself key questions about what you believe at various times in your life. What are the tapes in your life?

Be patient with yourself as you stop and listen for your tapes. Stop and take a breath before you make assumptions. Take time to question yourself and write your thoughts down. Doing the following exercises right may require several days of listening, analyzing, and recording. (Use your private journal for each of the following exercises.)

EXERCISE 1

Assume that you are going to meet someone whom you respect tremendously, perhaps a celebrity, a very wealthy and powerful person, or someone whose values and beliefs you hold in high regard. This could be anyone you admire, for whatever reason. Normally you would not interrogate yourself before having this encounter; you would just do it. You might or might not be uncomfortable, but you would do it. This time, as you consider this hypothetical meeting, I want you to question yourself very carefully. It will be important to be totally honest and extremely thorough. If you know you would be intimidated, then acknowledge that. If you would be scared, anxious, or feeling dumb or undeserving, then admit that to yourself.

In anticipating this meeting, what *specifically* are you telling yourself? Take time to think about, and to write down, the words that underlie and describe however you would be feeling as you approached this encounter. What you write down will be very important content from your tapes about you, your adequacy, your value, and your worth.

EXERCISE 2

Every day for the next week, when you awaken in the morning, roll over and write down your attitudes and expectancies for the day. Are you optimistic? Are you fearful or anxious? Are you bitter and resentful?

Would it be something like this? "You're always behind the power curve. You can't get ever get on top of things. Today may very well be the day you get found out." Remember, I'm not talking about your real-time internal dialogue, which might actually include a conscious pep talk, simultaneous with a much-less-optimistic tape. You'll recall that tapes predict a specific outcome. So I'm talking about drilling down and asking yourself how you really expect the day to go.

EXERCISE 3

Assume that your boss sent a message to you that he or she wanted to see you at 4:00 today. (It may be that, rather than a boss, it's more appropriate to your situation to use some other important person in a position of authority over you in some way, like a landlord, minister, or the boss of a spouse.)

Again, do this exercise four times, each time using a different set of circumstances, as follows:

- You know that you have made a mistake.
- You know that a cutback in personnel is imminent or some other bad news is coming.
- You don't have a clue what the meeting might be about.
- You know that you are being evaluated for your performance.

Now I would like for you to try this exercise again, but have the situation involve someone personally related to you; imagine either your spouse, a relative, a friend, or even your child has asked if they can meet with you later to sit down and talk.

Again, do this exercise four times, but use this slightly altered set of circumstances:

- There is a problem in the relationship.
- Something bad, tragic, or wrong has recently occurred.
- Again, you don't have a clue what the meeting is about.
- You have not spoken, or not spoken intimately, with this person in a long time.

Write down all of the thoughts you can identify that are below the level of your conscious self-talk: that is, all the thoughts that only come to mind when you start asking these questions and start trying to identify your predictions.

ASSESSING YOUR TAPES

Looking back over your tapes, do you see any similarities or patterns? Are there particular kinds of scenarios that you associate with this kind of negative self-talk? For example, do your tapes have to do with work-related encounters? Are they about particular family members or acquaintances? It may be that you more readily identified tapes when you were thinking about a particular part of the day, such as your first thoughts in the morning about the rest of the day. Maybe you were more aware of tapes in the context of a particular task, such as preparing to make a speech. Using your journal, identify whatever those common threads or patterns are.

SCRIPT ASSESSMENT

Let's turn now to your assessment of you scripts and fixed beliefs.

EXERCISE 1

Take some time to consider all the scripts that you have played in your life. There have probably been many: They might include friend, worker, loving parent, cheerleader, dancer, professor, athlete, spouse, invalid, the son/daughter of [parents' names], etc.

Remember that a script governs what you say and do; it also imposes expectancies or roles on other people. So in thinking about your script, try first to recall roles you have played that governed your actions and which you felt at the time would directly influence your results. Try to recall those stages and circumstances in which your role influenced or determined how other people responded to or interacted with you. Your script will show evidence of some of the other internal factors we have discussed. For example, you will find a number of labels within your script, a locus of control that colors it, and tapes that provide automatic content. Use those concepts to help identify the script in detail. Once again, use your journal for this work.

First, simply name the script, identifying it by the role you play (mother; wife of alcoholic husband; slut; geek).

Then, in simple terms, list the activities or behaviors that that script calls for. Your purpose here is simply to call to mind what you actually *did* as a result of playing the role that was scripted.

Next, in a paragraph or two, describe how people respond or react toward you as a consequence of your role. What did this role elicit from the other players in the script?

Having done this first exercise for one script, turn to any other scripts that you play and, one by one, write about them, using the same instructions.

EXERCISE 2

Now that you have identified some of the scripts you have played, go back and do the following:

1. Circle those roles you felt to be most congruent with what you want your life to be. If you were describing yourself to another person, what scripts would you be most proud to share and

want that person to know about you? Which roles did you enjoy playing? Circle them.

2. Similarly, if you were describing yourself to someone else, which roles would you be most ashamed of? Put checks next to those roles you absolutely hated having to play.

3. For every script you've identified, positive or negative, write two paragraphs about whoever it was in your life that had the biggest role in imposing that particular script. Then write two paragraphs about why you think that person cast you in that role and what they got out of it.

CONNECTING THE DOTS

Just as we discussed in the previous chapter, the job is to now evaluate this group of roles and scripts and decide what the meaningful connection is between them. You'll want to figure out how they've come together to define who you have become and whether or not each one contributes to or detracts from your being who you authentically are. It is extremely important that you learn which ones are consistent with your authentic self and which ones are not. Your emotional responses to those scripts will give you some vital clues in this regard.

I have a friend who had a major life role and script of being an athlete. He particularly loved football. He played in junior high, high school, college, and the pros. But, as is inevitable, he was all too soon past his prime and was forced to give it up. One day when he was whining to me about being tired and old and hurting, I had him do the imagery of calling his playing days back to mind. I told him to play out his script to the point that he was back in his uniform in his mind. It was almost scary, even to me who expected the result, to see him physically change before my eyes. The energy came back, his eyes sparkled, he sat up straighter. His voice became vibrant and energetic. In his mind and heart, he was experiencing the feelings and muscle memories of that role he had loved so dearly. In a span of a few moments, the emotions of that role transformed him.

The point is that the emotions associated with the roles we play are powerful. That will be true whether they are positive, as with my friend, or negative, such as when the role is one that has generated pain. It is important that you identify which roles create which emotions in your life. Here's how:

Using the list of scripts you have made, I now want you to "project" yourself into each and every script, one at a time, by speaking in character for a few minutes. Speak the words that you would typically say when you are in that particular role, and **speak them out loud.** For example, if you have chosen the script of "mother," pretend that you are mothering someone, and say what you might say aloud. For example, you might find yourself saying something like: "Now be sure and bundle up, because I don't want you to get a cold. Remember Mother loves you and she doesn't want to worry about you. Here, wrap up tight and go out and play. Be careful now. Here, you're not doing that right; let me fix it. Check in with me every hour or so."

Understand that I'm not saying that this first script you're examining, or any other script, is inherently bad or good. But every script has feelings attached and I want you to pay attention to how you feel when you are in that role. So talk long enough that you can identify those feelings and emotions that come to you. The feelings may be positive and calming or they may be anxiety- and anger-provoking. That is what I want you to note. Whichever is your experience, the feelings are likely to be significant and I want you to identify them.

Lastly, *write in as much detail as possible that life script which you would write for yourself,* given an unfettered choice. Do not try to please anyone or even to think about whether it is appropriate or not. Let yourself dream a bit here. What script would you choose if you could do anything you wanted? What emotion would you feel and with whom would you share it? This is, again, work that deserves your undivided attention and a willing spirit. Give this "dream script" enough of your time and energy and creativity for it to have some real meaning. (By the way: If this exercise isn't fun to write, you're doing it wrong. Start over.)

By now I hope that you are exploring, in earnest, what story you want to write for yourself and what role you want to play in it. I also hope that you know how it feels inside when you have the right script in your heart. It may not be a popular script, since it may be at odds with the expectations of those around you. But it will be yours, no one else's.

What you will do with this script you have written is up to you. Read on.

INTRODUCTION TO THE

FIVE-STEP ACTION PLAN

*"In flying, I have learned that carelessness
and over confidence are usually far more
dangerous than deliberately accepted
risks."*

— WILBUR WRIGHT, IN A
LETTER TO HIS FATHER
DATED SEPTEMBER 1950.

EARLIER I suggested that your life could be thought of as a chain, which is, of course, a series of connected links. You have been working very hard to identify many of those important links. It's now time to bring all of your hard work together, assess what it means to you, and make a plan to do something about it.

Having grown up around my dad, who worked in the "oil patch" of Texas, Oklahoma, and Colorado, I vividly remember that the first chains I ever saw were those used around drilling rigs. Bulky, greasy, and dark, some of them had individual links you could barely pick up. Working around those chains was a hard, dangerous, and dirty way to make a living. As a kid, whenever I heard stories about prisoners being chained in a dungeon, I always thought of those huge, hideous chains, wrapping some poor soul around his neck and his ankles. They represented to me a very confining force. Chains controlled you, they held you back and took away your freedom. I guess that gives you a clue as to how I see your personal life chain. Not a pretty mental image, but a representative one nonetheless. I believe that way too often what we find ourselves doing in our lives is the product of negative momentum, the product of our life chain linking our past into our present and our future.

Your self-concept, whether fictional or authentic, is a product of this linking. That continuity may be positive or it may be negative, but either way the connection is undeniable. How that chain gets made and evolves into who you become has been the subject of this book. Creating, or re-creating exactly the chain and self-concept you want, is the subject of this chapter and the next.

I started this process by getting you to look at your past life, because I believe that the best predictor of future behavior is past behavior. That being true, the links in the chain of your history predict your future. For most people, that means that if life has been a mess in the past, it will most likely be a mess in the future. That does not have to be true for you. You now have the wherewithal to change your momentum by breaking your chain and starting a new one. Once you have identified which links from your past control which experiences in your current life, you know where you need to focus your energy. If your history predicts your future and you want a new future, then you begin by creating a new history.

At first, perhaps, it's just one day of new history, then one week, then one month, and then one year. Soon you have a whole new history, predicting a whole new future. If you have been a drunk or an overeater every day for years and years, then the best prediction is that you will be a drunk or overeater this year. But as soon as you behave differently for even one day, your life goes on alert: "Hey what's this, a new deal?" A new prediction is made. As each day of new behavior is stacked up, that new prediction gets stronger and stronger and stronger and more and more accurate. The challenge then is to break from the old and come in with the new. The reason we have spent so much time on the old was to ensure that you had the blinders off and knew exactly what specific parts of your past were tied to what specific parts of your present. Now you know.

Your own external experiences in life, and your internal reactions to them, have hammered out a self-concept that has defined you throughout your life. Just as surely as a blacksmith hammers out and forges hot metal on an anvil, the shaping of your self-concept has been no different. You have pounded on yourself with your internal perceptions and self-talk and you have been pounded on and been shaped by the behavior and messages of those you have encountered in your life. Your defining moments, critical choices, and pivotal people have been among the hammers that have pounded on the metal of your self-concept.

It may very well be that much, if not all, of that hammering and shaping took place without your being consciously aware that it was going on. Looking back, you may feel as if your "chain of life" has been wrapped around your neck from before the time you could even speak. It may be that yours has you bound up, feeling suffocated and "stuck." As I have said, you can't change what you don't acknowledge. But the flip side is just as true: You *can* change what you *do* acknowledge. Get real about the links in your life chain and those that need to be broken and discarded can and will give way to the will of your authentic self.

Toward that end, I have a new and bold plan. It's time for you to become the blacksmith of your own life. It's time for you to stop being passively shaped by the internal and external forces in your life. It's time to start consciously and actively challenging and directing those very same forces. Doing so will move your self-concept away from the world-defined, fictional end of the continuum toward the self-defined, authentic end of the continuum. It's time to start moving in a new direction that is grounded in the vibrant here and now, instead of continuing in the old direction that is grounded in a tired, outdated, and irrelevant history. You can create a momentum that will allow you to be and do what *you* truly value and care about.

To redefine your life and your self-concept, you must do two things. First, you must acquire some very specific tools. Second, you must commit to being totally and courageously honest in evaluating and using all of the information you have amassed thus far. Some of that which you have identified has been ugly and unpleasant to acknowledge and now is the time to do something about it. Insight without action is worse than being totally asleep at the switch. At least when asleep, you can cling to the old "ignorance is bliss" argument. To do the hard work necessary to figure out your life, with all of the whys and why nots, and then just stagnate and go right back to the same old grind is not okay; it's just a bunch of mental masturbation. You must be accountable and action-oriented to effectively deal with the unvarnished truth and make important changes. To do any less is a waste of your time. What I'm saying is that if you want to maximize your quality of life and escape from the traps that have contained you thus far, you're going to have to find the courage to continue to be real, and you are going to have to get active in changing your life pattern both internally and externally. No con, no excuses, no blaming others for the choices you've made. You must decide which elements of your self-concept you value, and therefore want to keep, and which you do not. It is time to sort the fictional crap from the authentic truth, so that you can reject it and finally uncover and live consistently with who you truly are. As I have said, this has taken great courage in the identification phase and will for sure require that same courage in the implementation phase.

Remember that not everyone will be excited about you rejecting some of the roles that you have passively been accepting, in favor of those you truly and actively choose.

To speed the process along, let's quickly review what you have learned about how you have formed your self-concept so you are organized in your approach:

Point One

You began this life with a constellation of gifts, skills, abilities, traits, and characteristics that uniquely define you. You have within you every skill, capacity, insight, and wisdom necessary to your mission in life. If your journey through this life has been such that it has developed and nurtured that uniqueness, and you have stayed focused, then you have lived a life consistent with your **authentic self**. If not, a world-defined, fictional self has dominated you.

Point Two

Your journey through life, whether twenty years or sixty years, is in part characterized by a **learning history** that tremendously impacts that uniqueness with which you were born. You have learned from and been changed by your experiences: experiences that led to peace and joy, turmoil and sorrow, or some combination of the two.

Point Three

Although your history comprises literally millions of both internal and external experiences, an amazingly small number of these events have come together to shape your self-concept. As we've seen, three basic types of **external factors** have shaped what you believe about yourself: your ten defining moments, seven critical choices, and the five pivotal people you have encountered. The ten defining moments were those experiences so powerful that they marked you, either positively or negatively, in some lasting way. Some defining moments may have affirmed your authenticity and some may have distorted your self-concept by pulling you away from your authentic self toward some fictional expectancy of who you were "supposed" to be.

Your seven critical choices were those important decisions you have made that either maintained your authentic self by generating results that affirmed your uniqueness or instead caused you to question who you were, leading you into mythical fabrications that contaminated your self-concept. These outcomes—either affirming or denying your authentic self—were also impacted by your interactions with your five pivotal people. Your interactions with these people, again, either supported the authenticity within you or gave you false information that became a central part of your self-concept.

Point Four

As a thinking and feeling individual, you have interpreted and reacted to every event, large or small, that has ever happened in your life. Specifically, as you learned in the latter half of this book, five internal factors have influenced how you internalized these external events. These five factors are your **locus of control, labeling, internal dialogue, tapes,** and **fixed beliefs.**

Just to review, your **locus of control** identifies how you perceive and assign responsibility for the causes of what happens to you. **Labeling** is the assignment of lasting judgments, incorporated into your self-concept, that classify what you are to yourself. **Internal dialogue** is the perceptual window through which you see and understand the world and you. It is the self-talk that goes on within you, in real time, as your life unfolds around you. **Tapes** are those judgments and self-fulfilling prophecies that are so overlearned as to become automatic messages that play in your head at the speed of light: messages that predict outcomes in your life and your struggle for success. **Fixed beliefs** are long-held and change-resistant positions that you use to organize your world and predict what you think you and others are prone to do. They are the cornerstones of your script of life, creating boundaries and barriers to who you can become and what you do.

With this five-part "internal processing center," you have messaged your self-concept in ways that have either affirmed your authentic self or buried it, in favor of a fictional self. One of these two has been in charge of running your life.

Point Five

Failing to live congruently with your authentic self robs you mentally, emotionally, physically, and spiritually. It allows your life chain to suffocate and strangle you, draining and diverting critical life energy. Suppressing your authentic self and denying its need for expression, and living a life for which you have no passion, wastes tremendous amounts of life energy that could be spent on creating what you want.

There's a prayer that asks for the wisdom to understand the difference between things that can be changed and things that cannot. I can tell you that, as we develop your action plan—the plan to create more of who and what you authentically are—your internal factors will become the central elements of that plan. Here's why: *If you know the events that have driven your self-concept, and you can identify the reactions that you've had to those events, then you know what the levers are that you can pull to change it.* Those levers are your internal factors.

External events are important because they can be the first links in your life chain. But the internal factors that we have discussed are where the real power is. Changing your life direction, and getting back in touch with your authentic self, will be a function of changing your internal actions and reactions. The reason is simply this: While you may not be able to change your ten defining moments, seven critical choices, or five pivotal people, you can dramatically alter the manner in which you perceive those external events of life. You can use the power of the internal factors that have been controlling your life to reinterpret and reanalyze those events and to set up new reactions that are consistent with your authentic self. So long as you have the power to choose, you have the power to change. I predict that, with the knowledge and tools you have acquired in these pages, a new view of your life, history, and potential will flourish.

That is not to say that we're going to disregard your outward behavior. There's a raging controversy in psychology about how "best" to bring about positive changes in people. The controversy boils down to this: Do we change feelings and emotions first and let behavioral change follow? Or do we change behaviors first, hoping that when people *do* different, they will *feel* different? I've listened to "brainiac" academicians go on, ad nauseam, about who in this debate was right and who was wrong; meanwhile, the people in need of the change sit there thinking, Hell, I don't care—just give me a plan!

As many a politician has often said, "I feel strongly *both* ways." In short, who cares how the debate comes out? Why not do both at once: work on changing how you think and feel, while at the same time behaving your way to success?

The plan you're about to learn is designed to help you do just that. It will help you make changes **internally,** focusing on all five factors that we've discussed, *and* change the way you engage the world **externally** at one and the same time. As you think, feel, and behave differently, you will be observing yourself and creating new, accurate data for your concept of self. You learn about yourself by observing yourself, just as you would observe another person. As you see yourself "behave" differently, behave more authentically, behave with more loyalty to yourself, both internally and externally, you will be creating a new history that will predict a new future.

In its simplest terms, the plan works like this: I will ask you to revisit the external and internal "life audits" that you performed and recorded while working through previous chapters. You'll identify which of the external events in your life have contaminated, rather than contributed to, your living consistently with your authentic self. You'll examine the internal factors and how you have continued to engage these "toxic" events. You will then know which areas must be "cleaned up" in order for you to maximize your life. Finally, you will take up some very specific tools for doing that cleaning, which, in turn, will set you on the path back to your authentic self.

As I said earlier, we may not be able to change what has happened in your life, but we can certainly change the messages that have emanated from those events. We can change how you now respond and, therefore, change what power those events have in your current daily life. What this plan challenges you to do is pick up a particular "link" in your life chain, examine it, test your responses to it, then and now, then question the conclusions you have drawn and the behaviors you've engaged in as a result. I intend to challenge thoughts, feelings, and reactions that you may have been passively accepting for years and years. You may not have known better then, but you will know better now. You will be amazed at the power you have. You do not have to be a prisoner of your past. You do not have to walk this world with open wounds. You can heal, but that healing will occur from the inside out. It will be a product of what you do for yourself, not what someone does for you.

THE PLAN

Let's turn to the specifics of the plan. In this chapter, I will introduce each step to you with a short discussion of the concept. Once we've talked briefly about all five steps of the plan, I will then share with you, in the next chapter, the history and life chain of a former patient of mine. We'll consider how she might put each of these steps to work in her own life. Then it will be your turn.

Step 1: Isolate a Target Event

To put the plan into action, it's important that you understand the first and most powerful links in the causal chains that ultimately created your self-concept as it is today. The first links in those chains are the external factors we have worked with: **defining moments, critical choices,** or **pivotal people.**

As I have said, you can't change these external events, because they have already happened. Whether they happened yesterday or thirty years ago, they are history. You can't alter the moments, un-choose the choices, or change the pivotal people. Even so, it is still a crucial first step to identify these external events that have had such a profound impact on your current self-concept. Don't despair that you cannot change what has already happened, because your **real power lies in your internal factors.** It is in the five areas of internal response that you will find the tools and opportunities to redefine your self-concept and your life in a way that is congruent with who and what you truly are when all the distortion is stripped away.

Step 2: Audit Your Internal Responses to That Triggering Event

Once you select a triggering event, you'll need to give it your complete attention and focus to determine how you responded to and internalized that event. It can be really overwhelming to try and think about your whole life at one time. It can even be overwhelming trying to think just about your personal list of defining moments, critical choices, or pivotal people all at once. But we are going to take this personal audit and analysis one step at a time. It's like the old analogy: "How do you eat an elephant?" The answer is: "One bite at a time." Forget that you have an entire elephant to chow down on; that would intimidate anyone. What you do is just grab an ear and start chewing. Before you know it you've made some real progress. Same deal here: One event at a time, we are going to deconstruct your history and demystify how you have become who you are. Having isolated one event, we are going to look really closely at what happened inside you once the event occurred. How did it change your self-concept? Did it shake your faith; did it steal your confidence; was it the death of your innocence?

This is where your five internal factors come into play. I'll challenge you to assess how that defining moment, for example, impacts your internal dialogue to this very day. If it was truly a defining moment, you will still be talking to yourself about it now, even as we do this work. Your internal dialogue may be influenced indirectly, even when you are not thinking about the specific defining moment.

Similarly, is your locus of control dictating where you place responsibility or blame for that event? What labels have you generated as a function of that defining moment? What tapes has this event generated or contributed to? What are the fixed beliefs that you have constructed as a result of this defining moment and how have they played into a life script that you have been living since the precise moment of the triggering event? You will be writing down or reviewing what you have written down about each of these internal processes, so that you can see what the impact has been and exactly where you must make adjustments.

Step 3: Test Your Internal Responses for Authenticity

Once you have identified your target event and learned what your responses to it were and are, now what do you do? You need a litmus test, a standard against which you can test those perceptions to see if they are worth keeping or if you've just been jerking yourself around all this time. You need to measure them against a standard of rationality and truth and authenticity. Knowing and applying that standard, so as to challenge the acceptability of your internal reactions, will be the focus of this third step. Soon I will give you that litmus test in very clear and usable terms.

Step 4: Come Up with an "Authentically Accurate Alternative" Response

Any internal response that fails Step 3—in other words, it fails the "jerking around" test—needs to be thrown out. When you examine your own perceptions, self-talk, fixed beliefs, and so on, and you find that they are irrational, untruthful, and anything but authentic, then you need to get rid of them; you need to break that bad internal habit. "Break" is actually a misnomer, because we don't actually "break" habits. In order to eliminate one habitual behavior, you must *replace it* with a new behavior that is incompatible with the one you want to eliminate. Generating that new internal response pattern is what this step is all about. Step 4 challenges you to engage in what I call "Triple-A thinking": that is, to generate an Authentically Accurate Alternative response, one that *does* pass the test for authenticity. Replace any response that does not support your authentic self with one that does. Replace any response that causes you trouble and pain with one that moves you toward what you want, need, and deserve.

Step 5: Identify and Execute Your Minimal Effective Response (MER)

This last step acknowledges that *action*—an external behavior—is often needed if you're going to get emotional closure. The question then becomes, Okay, what will it take? What behavior will be most effective in getting you that emotional closure, *with the least cost to you* in terms of energy, risk, and so on? The fact that we are looking for the least demanding, yet effective response is why I call it your MER. What real-world steps can you take that will resolve the pain, free you up, and allow you to create more of what you want instead of what you don't want, without putting you in further jeopardy?

Those are the broad outlines of your action plan. Now it's time to get specific and to put the plan to work for you.

11 PUTTING THE PLAN

TO WORK

> *"We either make ourselves miserable, or we make ourselves strong. The amount of work is the same."*
>
> —CARLOS CASTANEDA

AS you take up this five-step plan, let me encourage you to look back at the work you've already done. It's perfectly acceptable, and, in fact, a good idea, to use your journal as a stimulus or "prompt" for the upcoming exercises. Maybe it helps to reexamine the internal dialogue you recorded or to take another look at the tests you completed with respect to your locus of control. The point is that this five-step plan is designed to build on and incorporate the foundation you have already laid. You don't need to feel as if you've got to build from scratch.

If you have faithfully worked through the exercises in earlier chapters, some of the mechanics of this plan should already look somewhat familiar to you. For example, the internal factors chapters asked you to do some self-auditing of how you've responded to certain external events. As a result—again, if you have honestly completed the exercises—it would be fair to say that you are a different person now from the one who started this book: Your self-knowledge has advanced from Point A to Point B. I hope and trust that the work you've done so far has brought you some much-needed clarity and that you already feel some lightening of your load. What the five-step plan can do is get you much, much farther down that road.

Since I believe it's always helpful to have a model or example to refer to, as you apply any plan to your own life, allow me to share with you the story of a former patient of mine. I will tell you up front that today Rhonda is a happy and productive mother of two college-age sons. She is happily married and stays busy with a variety of things she enjoys doing. I'm confident she would tell you that she is, today, living consistently with her authentic self. However, this was far from true just a few years ago. Please understand that in telling you about Rhonda's history, my intention is not to shock you. In fact, your own history may contain elements that are even more tragic than hers. My purpose in sketching in the general outline of Rhonda's story is simply to show you how one person might put the five-step plan to work in her own life.

When she first came to my office, Rhonda was in her early thirties. As soon as she started talking, it was clear to me that her authentic self had been all but destroyed. She clearly despised herself and had absolutely no self-confidence or sense of worth. She felt that she had nothing to offer people and as a result deserved nothing in return. She even apologized for "wasting my time," which could "surely be better spent on someone who deserved it." Rhonda was living a horrible life, dominated by a fictional self-concept that in no way reflected who she really, authentically was. She was lost, and lost big time. It did not take long to find the first link in this horrible chain of life. Starting at the tender age of twelve, she had been beaten, raped, and sexually exploited by her biological father. The horrors of that treatment unfolded over several sessions that we spent together, with Rhonda initially actually making excuses for her tormentor.

Rhonda eventually told me that her father, a regional marketing rep for a major manufacturer, had often required her to go on sales trips with him during her summer vacations, trips that involved driving several hundred miles in order to call on customers in several states. It soon became apparent that her father was a sick drunk with a terrible psychopathic mean streak. Late at night, staggering drunk, after an evening of drinking and partying with customers he was "entertaining," he would frequently bring them back to his hotel room, where they would gamble, yell and scream, fight, and have sex with the prostitutes or women they had picked up in the bars. On a number of occasions, these drunken slobs would force themselves upon Rhonda while her father sat by watching as he drank himself into a mindless stupor. He would zone out, but his anger was never far below the surface: The slightest resistance on her part would provoke both his words and his fists. If she cried out or tried to get away, he would beat her brutally and guilt-induce her by saying: "You selfish little bitch, why are you trying to ruin my business? These men feed you; they keep a roof over our heads. Do you want your mother and your brothers and sisters to starve? You're nothing but a little whore, anyway. You crawl in the backseat with your worthless boyfriends while they feel you up; you can damn sure do it with those that put food on our table." (Boy, oh boy, did I ever want to meet this mouth breather!) Of course, none of what he told her was true and Rhonda had certainly never crawled anywhere with anyone before her father stole her dignity. This precious child was a virgin before her initial trip with her father that first dark summer. Once this heinous behavior had begun, Rhonda's sense of self-worth—all of her hope, optimism, and esteem—was shattered. Through her father's actions, she had been assigned and browbeaten into a role, and with a broken spirit she accepted that fictional self-concept and the painful life script that came with it.

As if to add insult to injury, her father had recently passed away. As a result, Rhonda was a caldron of emotions. On the one hand, she was relieved that this evil man no longer walked this earth; on the other, she felt guilty that she wasn't sorry. Also bubbling around in her emotional pot was a sense of rage and frustration that he had died without ever having been held accountable for his actions. It would be an understatement of unbelievable proportions to say that when she came to me for help, Rhonda had a seriously damaged and distorted concept of self and some major, unfinished emotional business.

The sick indoctrination from her father, which she had internalized and was pounding herself with each day, was false and perverted information. At her young and vulnerable age, her authentic self-concept had been easily banished and replaced by a total fiction. Clearly, our challenge was to wash away the confusion and the contamination of pain, doubt, self-condemnation, anger, hatred, and bitterness. The goal was to get Rhonda back in touch with an authentic self she hadn't experienced since she was a child. I wanted to get her to the point where she could regard herself with respect, dignity, value, and optimism. All of her internal factors, where her real power resided, were offtrack. Her internal factors were horribly distorted and working in the service of a fictional self as she lived with this psychic disfigurement. Her internal dialogue now, some twenty years after her first trip and exploitation, still sabotaged her. The tapes that raged in her head spoke of worthlessness and hopelessness. Her labels were "dirty," "whore," and "slut." Her locus of control was irrationally internal and the fixed beliefs that defined her life script offered her no way out. These horrible things had happened and she was "scarred for life."

Having learned something about Rhonda's situation, you understand the challenges and concerns that were facing her as she sat down to apply this five-step plan to her life. Now let's put the plan to work in your life, using Rhonda's tragic and toxic life chain as an example.

Not surprisingly, since these will be the exercises that gather together and give particular meaning to all the work you've done in previous chapters, I cannot overstate the importance to you of doing the job right. I have found that the best approach, by far, is to take one triggering event, that first link that you identify in Step 1, and to follow it through the entire series of five steps. Bring every step of the plan to bear on that event before you take up another, separate event and start working on it.

Don't rush the process. I make no apology for the fact that this work is time and labor intensive. The rule of "garbage in, garbage out" applies with particular power to the exercises you're about to do: If you rush the work, if you "skim" the information, rather than committing yourself to an honest and thorough self-appraisal, then a superficial result is all you'll get. I trust that the following is obvious to you, but I'll say it anyway: There could be no more appropriate moment in your life than this one for deciding you're going to give 100 percent of your energy, attention, and effort to a task.

As before, get your journal and find the quietest, most private place and time you can. Ideally, you will be able to set aside a solid hour or more to take one event through the entire five-step process. Depending on your particular target event, you may find that the process takes several sessions, scattered across several days. Understand that I want you to dig until you find the absolute bottom in terms of your internal reactions. Be careful that you do not deal with only part of that which is crippling you or haunting you. You must be willing and able to face everything, to go below your emotive responses, and work through each factor affecting your life. Once you've subjected one event to the process, the next event deserves its minimum of one hour, and so on.

For each step, consider Rhonda's situation and possible responses as examples only. Your answers should be the result of quiet reflection on and honest appraisal of your own life. If your events are less dramatic than Rhonda's (thank God), don't be deterred. If an event is important to you, then that is enough for it to qualify for your full attention and effort.

Let's begin.

Step 1: Target the Event

With a quiet attention to your own breathing, and a relaxed mind and body, consider your life chain: the series of events, circumstances, and responses that have made you who you are at this moment.

Begin by deciding which, among those key external events that you identified earlier, has been *the single most toxic factor in your life*. It will be one of the following:

A defining moment
A critical choice, or
A pivotal person

Looking back at some of the material you wrote earlier about each of these external factors may be very helpful at this point.

Now write a short description of that target event. This description need not be more than a few sentences and may already be captured in what you wrote earlier. However, you may have changed since that first writing and if you need to edit or add to that response, do so now.

By way of example, here is what Rhonda wrote in her step 1: "On that first Tuesday morning in June, as he began loading up the car, he told me to pack my things and get ready to go. I knew him, I hated him, and I knew that I shouldn't get in the car with him; I had no idea what was going to happen, but I knew that I'd regret it. I could have run to the kitchen and begged my mom to let me stay with her. I could have run away. Or maybe, if I'd said it right, I could have persuaded my mother to come with us and protect me. Instead, I did just what he told me. That was, at one and the same time, my number one, most toxic defining moment and my most devastating critical choice. That was the most horrible choice I've ever made." Now, I know that as you read this, you're probably thinking: That's crazy! How could she have any responsibility or accountability for what this sick bastard did? You're exactly right, but remember, this is Rhonda's confused, guilt-induced, internal reaction and it reflects the fiction that she has been living with ever since. Obviously it is not rational, but try telling that to a scared and guilt-ridden twelve-year-old girl.

Now, having read this brief excerpt, look back at your answer for your own life. Have you found that most toxic moment and are you being honest in describing it? Remember: We are going to clean this mess up and remove it as a distorting force in your life. Don't miss the mark even a little bit. You don't want to kill just half of the "snakes" in your life.

Step 2: Audit Your Internal Response to That Event

Remember that your answer to this step will address any or all of the five internal factors, each of which has been defined and discussed in its own chapter. Use the following questions to stimulate your thoughts:

Looking at the event you described for Step 1,

1. **Where do you place a responsibility or blame for that event, your locus of control?**

    For example, the first series of questions I addressed to Rhonda were: To whom do you attribute the responsibility for this event? Did you really have a choice at twelve years old to refuse to get into the car? Did you, could you, know what was going to happen? Did you make the rapes happen? Do you "own" the sickness of your father and the other perverts that he hung out with? Clearly, she assigns herself the blame, judging from her answer in Step 1.

    I have never seen anyone make anyone else sexually assault him or her, so I am quite sure that both you and I can see that the answer for Rhonda should be a resounding, "No!" But again, we have a different perspective than that of a twelve-year-old girl under the control of her father.

    Next question, still related to this issue of placing responsibility: Who decided how you were going to respond to this event, such as by saying horrible things to yourself?

Since no one can insert this reaction from the outside, Rhonda's answer had to be, "I did."

Next question: Were you in control of the situation?

This question focuses directly on responsibility and shame. You would be astonished by the number of people who shame themselves for events for which they were only the victim, not the perpetrator. In addition, many families desperately want such events swept away and so they deem the victim guilty for being so selfish as to want to make it public, or in any way force it to be dealt with.

Apply these questions about locus of control to your own event and write your answers down. Caution: Do not write what you intellectually think you should say. It is easy to guess at what the "correct" or socially desirable answer is. That's not what I want you to write down and see. Write what you really think when you are alone and living with the most toxic event in your life. You cannot change what you don't acknowledge, so be brutally honest here. What do you really believe about responsibility for your event, whether you intellectually know better or not?

2. **What has been the tone and content of your internal dialogue since that event? Do you find your real-time, "normal speed" conversations in your daily life reflecting the changes that occurred within you and are associated with that event?**

On those occasions when you reflect on the event, what do you say to yourself? On those occasions when you're not reflecting directly on the event, but it causes you to experience guilt and shame, what is it that you say to yourself then, even if it does not specifically reference the event?

As Rhonda's responses might suggest, many victims of sexual abuse report that at first they did not perceive or would not allow themselves to perceive what was going on. Many victims of molestation, for example, report that they first thought that they were getting special attention and that only as the events continued did they discover more destructive intentions. Some feel fooled and stupid for their naïveté. Others purposefully design different perceptions in order to protect their assailant, especially if it is a family member. For example, a girl who has been molested by a male family member can cause herself to perceive that it was an accident or that it was about a special friendship. Whether your event was similar to Rhonda's or completely, totally different, relevant questions might be: What was your perception of your behavior? What was your perception of the intentions or behaviors of the others involved in the situation? What are you telling yourself about those things today? How does the way in which you have labeled and reacted to this event affect your confidence and style of engaging the world? For example, if you are having a disagreement with your current mate or life partner, do you say derogatory things to yourself because you feel "damaged"?

In any case, if a negative internal dialogue appears to be a result of this event, describe that dialogue, in writing. Understand that the internal dialogue may not be specifically about the event. It may be an internal dialogue that is laced with messages of doubt and incompetence or some other residual of your most toxic event. If some event shook your faith in you, even though the current-day manifestation does not involve specific references to the origin, it is still highly relevant.

3. **What labels have you generated for yourself as a result of your event?**

As a consequence of your event, what have you told yourself about you? Rhonda discovered that she used labels for herself such as "dirty" or "damaged goods," "nothing to offer," "ashamed," and "a thing to be used for someone else's pleasure."

Consider whether you, too, have come up with labels for

yourself, labels that you use as a result of this specific event. Review the labels you wrote down in the labels chapter and add to or take away from that list. You may discover more labels, now that you have been working on all of this so much more—write those labels down.

4. **What tapes has this event generated or contributed to?**

As a result of what you have "learned" in the wake of this event, have you developed an automatic, unthinking response, one that judges you and predicts what your outcome will be in a given situation? If you suspect that in your most stressful situations a particular tape is screaming messages of failure, is that tape a consequence of the event that you're addressing here?

For example, Rhonda recognized that she expected a similar outcome from every relationship she attempted to have. She identified a number of tapes about men, relationships, being used, and shame with intimacy. She fully expected to be tossed aside when she had any intimate relationship with someone. An example of one of Rhonda's tapes was: "Men are pigs, and they're only interested in me if I 'put out,' and then they dump me when I do. I am trapped for life." Explore the expected outcomes or predictions that linger in your mind as a result of your external event. Identify your specific tapes in as much detail as possible.

5. **What are the fixed beliefs and resulting life script that you have constructed as a result of your event?**

Do you suspect that you live to a "script" derived from this event, a set of words, thoughts, and behaviors that you blindly obey, time after time? How have you limited yourself as a result of this event? Have you simply given up on expecting the world to treat you differently? Have you limited yourself to what you are as of this very moment? Rhonda, for example, lived a life script in which she resisted any opportunity to socialize with men, even in a safe and relaxed environment, fearing that that might upset a predictable—although painful—way of life. She lived to her beliefs, alternating between blatant promiscuity and complete shameful, withdrawal.

How do these beliefs relate to your early experience? Identify any connection you see between the event you are considering and the fixed beliefs that you're living with.

Again, don't hesitate to look back at the individual chapters on internal factors, and to the material you wrote for each, to stimulate the most thorough responses you can provide to each of the five questions under Step 2.

Let's pause for a moment to consider where Rhonda might be at this point. By the time she had completed Step 2 in her plan, she might have identified a number of internal behaviors that were quite telling.

Rhonda, just like you, cannot change the external events in her life, including some of the choices she made after her tragic mistreatment. What she can change is what she says and does about them now. While that may seem like a hollow victory, I can assure you that as it unfolds in your life you will come to see that it is not.

I trust that you are already changing your internal dialogue. I trust that you are learning as we go. For example, you might have discovered that you could not possibly have been responsible for the event you are reviewing. Many, many people, in doing this work, for the first time see the event with mature eyes. They discover for the first time that they have been remembering it, for years, with the eyes they had when they were children. These new perspectives allow them to make new judgments about themselves.

I recall a man who constantly judged himself as irresponsible, never trusting himself for any event or cause, all as the result of the accidental drowning of his little brother. Although he had been in school at the time of the accident, one day he overheard his mother say that if he had been home, the tragedy would not have happened.

The result was that, throughout his life, at some level he had been carrying the guilt for his brother's death. However, once he objectively audited the event, he discovered that his mother actually was complimenting his high responsibility: Her point was that it was such a tragedy that he could not be there to save his brother. When he visited his mother shortly afterward, she corroborated this new, more mature interpretation as the accurate one; she was horrified to learn how profoundly he had misunderstood her. You can hardly imagine the relief and delight that he felt.

Once we begin to listen to our internal dialogue, the audit can have amazing results. We can learn astounding things about ourselves. His little brother is still lost forever, but his interpretation and perception of it is dramatically changed, and so is his life.

Step 3: Test Your Internal Responses for Authenticity

As we've just seen, insight into what we tell ourselves can be therapeutic. But the return to authenticity requires more than that. *This is the stage when you equip yourself with some clear-cut criteria for authenticity, the standard by which you can test your internal responses.*

For all of her progress, in other words, it's not hard to imagine someone like Rhonda saying, "Okay, I can see that the sexual abuse psychically disfigured me. And I see that my reaction to it was highly counterproductive: I've done an audit of my internal factors and I can see how I reacted to what happened. It's no wonder I feel so bad about myself. I feel bad because that happened and because I reacted to it in that way. I get that. *Now what am I going to do?*"

Well, what you're going to do now is learn the four criteria for an authentic self-appraisal. You will then evaluate each one of your internal responses—beliefs, dialogues, labels, and so on—against these criteria.

These authentic criteria will help you determine whether your responses and reactions contribute to your authentic self or pull you instead toward the fictional end of the self-concept continuum.

These four rules give you the yardstick you'll use to evaluate each attribution, label, internal conversation, tape, and fixed belief. *And all of those responses either pass or fail.* When they fail, you'll know you need to open your mind to new options. In other words, I am now ready to teach you how to test everything you are saying to yourself so you can sort out what's fictional and what's authentic. I want to get you to the point that trying to slip a lie past you will be like trying to smuggle sunrise past a rooster!

Think of the four test criteria as questions or challenges. When you use these questions to evaluate your every thought and perception, you will see clearly how authentic or fictional your internal thoughts are. The four questions are:

1. **Is it a true fact?**

   Is what you are thinking, feeling, perceiving, or assigning something that is objectively, verifiably true? If your internal dialogue, for example, was reviewed by independent observers, if people with absolutely no dog in the fight listened in, would they agree with you or not? Is this just something that you believe now, because it is something you believed then? Much of the time, we act on beliefs that are totally wrong and we have never even evaluated them. It may be that you are holding on to beliefs that were true when you were three years old, or seven, or maybe they were never true. Maybe you really do not know. If you don't, don't act on something that you simply, perhaps mindlessly, accept as true, with no consideration for testing it.

2. **Does holding on to the thought or attitude serve your best interests?**

   At times, you may hold beliefs because you're afraid to let them go, yet holding on to them causes you pain and suffering, frustration and loss. This criteria is simple: If what you're thinking, feeling, or doing is not working for you, if it is not helping you be and do what you authentically want, then it fails this test criteria. Does it make you happy, calm, peaceful, and fulfilled? This is a *huge* deal. Apply this standard and your life quality will change, and I mean right now. In applying this standard, be very unyielding. Don't listen to your own justifications for why you are tolerating thoughts and beliefs, actions and inactions that are not working for you. If it's not working, STOP DOING IT!

3. **Are your thoughts and attitudes advancing and protecting your health?**

   Do your thoughts about yourself push you into situations that put you at risk? For example, does your false pride about driving a car when you are not safe cause you to come closer to injury? Does your insistence on being right put you in harm's way? Does the pain and stress of how you think, feel, and believe about yourself take a physical toll that you can ill afford? We have selfish beliefs that make us defend ourselves when we don't have to. Are the thoughts that you cling to generating a physical harmony within your body? Or are you constantly aroused and agitated, wearing down your body and subjecting you to disease? It may be that now is the time to understand that holding such beliefs is not helping you; that in fact, it's hurting you.

4. **Does this attitude or belief get me more of what I want, need, and deserve?**

   This question is as straightforward as it sounds. What's your goal? What is the target that you're trying to hit? Perhaps you say, "My goal is to have a sense of peace within myself, an unshakable tranquility that flows from a rock-solid awareness of my own value." Maybe the goal is "a stronger, more loving relationship with my kids." Maybe it's a better marriage or a promotion at work. Whatever the goal is, test your internal response against it: Is the attitude, belief, or thought getting you closer to what you want? Or is it leading you toward or keeping you in circumstances that you *don't* want?

Let's put these criteria into action, using the event that Rhonda is considering. Let's say that Rhonda has adopted the fixed belief that she is dirty, disgusting, and despicable to other people. She feels ashamed about what has happened to her and what she has been a participant in, however involuntarily. She is ready to pass this belief through the authentic criteria to determine whether it is authentic or fictional.

Question 1: Is it a true fact? Is it something whose truth everyone would agree upon?

No! No! No! Rhonda would probably answer, "It is not true. I now know, as a mature and objective adult, that I was used and abused. I am not disgusting and damaged and despicable. I was victimized by people who are, but that is not me. People don't even know the events of my life, much less know which ones are affecting my life . . ."

Question 2: Does holding on to the thought or attitude serve your best interest? A possible answer: "It is not only worthless, it is limiting my life. Why would I want to hold on to it? Does it give me courage? Or does it give me weakness? Does it make me happy or sad? Unless I just want to have something that reminds me to feel sorry for myself, I'd better let it go—now."

Question 3: Do your thoughts and attitudes advance and protect your health? A possible answer: "My insisting that I am a disgusting human being may not cause acute death; it certainly does not promote my health. It could certainly cause me to make judgments contrary to my happiness and often times my health."

The lesson of step 3 should be clear. If you answered no to either one of the first two questions, or yes to the third, you are holding that belief as a fictional concept. That belief is poisonous. You cannot move into the realms of peace and joy as long as this poison resides in your mind. Let it go immediately.

Question 4: Do your thoughts and attitudes get you what you want? Rhonda might answer: "No, it does not. I want to feel clean and healthy and happy. I want to feel worthy of dignity and respect and not one of my reactions, perceptions, or beliefs leads me to getting what I really want."

Looking back over your responses to Step 2, take up each response that applies and test it, using the four criteria we've just talked about. It may be useful to look at your written description of the response and to write a short explanation of how it fails this test of authenticity. Be thorough. Your application of these four questions, both now and in the future, must be ruthless. Bottom line, don't listen to your own crap anymore. If it doesn't pass the test for authenticity, then dump it, and dump it now.

Here again are the four criteria:

1. Is it a true fact?
2. Does holding on to the thought or attitude serve your best interest?
3. Are your thoughts and attitudes advancing and protecting your health?
4. Do your thoughts and beliefs get you what you want?

Step 4: Come Up with an Authentically Accurate Alternative Response

Having committed yourself to finding a way back to your authenticity, you might be saying to yourself: What do I have to do to get past this toxic event? First off, I have to quit taking responsibility for things I didn't control. I need to change my internal dialogue, which is what I'm saying to myself each and every day when I am out in the world. I need to understand what my labels are and challenge those to see if they're authentic. I need to identify what tapes I have that hold me back and what beliefs and judgments I have about myself that cripple me. I've got to identify all of those before I can move on.

Having done all that, you say, "Okay, I realize what I'm saying to myself, and I have challenged each one of those responses. *Now what happens?*"

When you test your fictional internal dialogue and when it fails (and it will: It is not true; it doesn't serve your best interest; it doesn't advance and protect your life; it doesn't get you what you want), then it's time for you to do what we'll call Triple-A thinking. To replace the fictional responses, you've got to generate Authentically Accurate Alternative patterns of behavior (AAA). And for them to be AAA, those responses have to meet the four authenticity standards. You must generate these new AAA options, and then use them to replace the ones that do not work.

Suppose that Rhonda's internal dialogue sounds like this: I am dirty and depraved. I'm a no-good piece of garbage that no man would want for any reason other than for sex.

Once she tests that internal dialogue against our four rational authentic criteria, and they fail (which we've seen they do), Rhonda has to step up and do some AAA thinking; she has to generate authentically accurate alternatives.

Instead of holding the belief that she is "damaged goods," Rhonda will have to adopt the new view that she should be looking at herself as important and respected. She might need to consider the alternative belief that she is not guilty of one single thing and that no one is entitled to judge her. She must also generate an AAA that says: "I have to stop judging myself. I did nothing wrong. I must be there for myself now and accept the qualities that make me unique and special."

A second alternative that could be tested might be for her to consider herself as someone who has let her past dissolve or at least that she has let go of the importance of this event. She has made a positive decision to live in the present, not in the past.

Here's a simple technique that will help you engage in AAA thinking. You're going to make a chart, as follows. First, divide your page vertically. On the left side of the page, list your present fictional beliefs. You now know what to put on that list: You know what is fictional, because you have applied the four-pronged test and know which of your thoughts, feelings, and beliefs have failed the test. On the right side, do some brainstorming: For each of your present be-liefs, list as many alternative beliefs as you can. Then you'll take each alternative belief and (remember Step 3?) test it for authenticity. Those beliefs that pass the test are the truly authentic ones.

Here's a sample of what Rhonda's chart might look like:

Present Belief	Alternative Beliefs
I am damaged goods	1. I am a quality human being who has suffered but can now be healed.
	2. I am a worthy human being who can live with dignity and respect.
	3. I am living in the present, where I can decide for myself, instead of being a prisoner of the past and its memories and pain.

Let's challenge these sample alternatives now:

1. Is the alternative true? Yes.
2. Is it in Rhonda's best interest to hold these beliefs? Yes.
3. Do the alternatives advance and protect her health? Yes.
4. Do the alternatives get Rhonda what she truly wants? Yes.

Conclusion: All three alternatives seem to be authentic, so Rhonda has a pleasant choice to make: She can adopt one, two, or all three of her alternatives.

Now work through your own AAA chart. Give this Step 4 the time that it deserves. For every AAA thought, remember to test it against the four authenticity criteria.

As the last part of Step 4, and so that there is no mistake about what your options are, put a circle around every AAA thought that passes the test. You are beginning to forge the links of the life chain of your choosing.

Step 5: Identify and Execute Your Minimal Effective Response (MER)

Remember that this step, which we'll call your MER, asks, If you need to take action, what will it be?

The goal of Step 5 is emotional closure, meaning that you can "close the book" on your situation and its associated pain. You can put that Book of Pain on the shelf and you will no longer have to take it down and read from it on a daily basis.

Notice that MER includes the word "minimal." Your MER is the *least* thing that you can do that allows you to get emotional closure. As an example of what MER is *not,* I sometimes hear people who are in pain plotting major events to embarrass someone, when all it would take for them to feel some emotional resolve was an explanation and apology. The concept of MER seeks to satisfy your need for resolution, without creating a whole new set of problems. It aims to conserve your resources. It may help you to consider those ancient warriors who took long deliberations, discussing the most effective actions they might take, for the lowest cost in suffering and blood. They were not out to scorch the earth, but to get maximum results for minimal expense. When it comes to your MER, you are your own counsel.

Analyze your alternatives for action. In thinking about your MER, use this four-part test:

1. What action can you take to resolve this pain?
2. If you were successful and achieved this action, how would you feel?
3. Does the feeling you will have match the feeling you *want* to have?
4. Remember the word "minimal": Could there be some other, more emotionally or behaviorally economical action that would give you the emotional resolve you want to feel?

Turning again to Rhonda, she would consider possible MERs by asking herself, What is the least thing I can do in order to feel vindicated, to feel justice, feel liberated from this emotional prison that I'm living in?

Her father has died, but maybe she knows the whereabouts of one of his "buddies." Maybe Rhonda's MER is to go see that person and look him in the eye and say, "Don't you think for a minute I don't know what you did to me and I want to be heard. You need to know the pain you caused me. You need to know the crippling effect what you did had on me. You need to know what it's done to my life and my marriage and my relationship with my children, you no-good, rat-bastard son of a bitch."

Maybe that's her MER. Maybe she needs the cathartic effect of getting that said. On the other hand, maybe that won't do it for her. Maybe Rhonda needs to take advantage of the fact that there is no statute of limitations on molestation and go to the authorities, file a complaint, and have this SOB arrested and put in jail.

As you consider your own triggering event, and the nature and degree of the suffering you've endured, what is your MER? Maybe you don't feel the need or have the courage right now to do either one of the kinds of things that were contemplated for Rhonda. Maybe what you need to do is write a letter and write down all your thoughts and all your feelings. Maybe that does it for you. Maybe you even need to mail the letter, if your event involves another person. Perhaps, like Rhonda, if you can't mail the letter, then you might need to go to the offender's grave and read it to him or her in the graveyard.

I will share with you that that is exactly what the real-life Rhonda did. Initially, she thought that her MER might involve reading the letter to her mother, as another way of venting her feelings. However, she soon discarded that option, feeling that it was more of a "maximal effective response": While it might get the job done, it had unnecessary side effects, including possible guilt, grief, rage, and denial on the part of her seriously ill mother.

Ultimately, she decided that she must travel to the cemetery where her father was buried, visit his grave, and read him the letter. While others might feel that it was a futile behavior, it absolutely worked for Rhonda. When she read that letter to her deceased father, she permitted herself to scream, cry, and voice her most extreme outrage. When it was over, she reported that it felt as though a thousand-pound weight had been taken off of her chest.

If in that situation that response would not have been your MER, then maybe you need to dump trash on his grave. But whatever your MER is, you need to identify it and you need to do it: You need to emit that response until such time as you can say, "Okay, that's it. That's enough. My lens is clean. My emotional business is finished and I am free to go back to being that person that I now know that I am."

FORGIVENESS

Part of what makes an MER effective is the action taken; part of it is the AAA thinking that goes with it; part of it is forgiveness; and part of it is rescripting your life so as to behave your way to success. Let's talk for a moment about one of those, forgiveness.

Although every situation is different, I can tell you that forgiveness is the common element I have observed as being at least a part of every successful MER. Forgiveness can be a very difficult step, but one that may be essential to your getting emotional closure. Understand that when I use the word "forgiveness," I'm talking about something that happens entirely within you. You should also know that when I use the word "forgiveness," I in no way mean that I am asking you to take the position that whatever may have happened to you in your life is now "okay."

The reason I believe forgiveness is such an important element is that, without it, you are almost inevitably destined to a life marred by anger, bitterness, and hatred. Those emotions only compound the tragedy. You are the one who pays the price by carrying the negative emotions with you, allowing them to contaminate every element of your current life. Forgiveness is not a feeling that you must passively wait to wash over you. Forgiveness is a choice, a choice that you can make to free yourself from the emotional prison of anger, hatred, and bitterness. I am not saying that the "choice" is an easy one, only that it is a necessary one.

Should Rhonda forgive her father for the molestation, rape, and inconceivable exploitation? The answer is an unequivocal yes. She should not do it because he deserves forgiveness, rather she should do it because *she* deserves to be free. Many people are reluctant ever to forgive, because they believe that it dishonors them and trivializes what they have been through. Nothing could be further from the truth. But people who carry around the burden of anger invariably say they do so because they could never get emotional closure on the treatment they got at the hands of another person. The feelings we are talking about here are the open wounds of unfinished emotional business with somebody, somewhere: whoever is the target of all that negative emotion. And there comes a time when you have to say: "The hurting stops here, the hurting stops now. I have to heal and I cannot do it with these open wounds of anger, hatred, and bitterness. I give myself permission to move on. If this sick predator is released from my negative emotions at the same time, so be it. People who do those heinous things will face a much more grievous judgment day than I could ever visit upon them myself. I leave that to a higher power and choose to heal my wounds." How you find the strength and courage to forgive, in your unique circumstances, is specific to you. Maybe you find the strength to do so by giving the matter up to God. Maybe the five-step process outlined above helps you to find the strength.

Apply the criteria of authenticity to these responses, your anger, and your perception. For example, suppose you believe that your parent harmed you by failing to praise you enough, that life was never a joy as you grew up. *Is that thought true?* It may very well be. They in fact may have cheated you of praise and, therefore, your critical thinking meets the first criteria. But remember that forgiveness of those who have transgressed against you, or those you love, is not about them, it is about you. It may be true that they hurt you in some way. There is certainly nothing nonauthentic about acknowledging that you were hurt. I am not asking you in any way to try and sweep that under the rug or pretend that it didn't happen. I'm not even asking you to trivialize it and tell yourself it wasn't that big a deal. On the other hand, you must also ask: How much have you hurt yourself by maintaining your anger? *Do these thoughts serve your best interests?* They are useless for any satisfaction against your parent and definitely a negative burden for you. As a result, your perceptions and reactions fail the second standard of authenticity and, therefore, should be rejected. *Does your unforgiveness advance and protect your health?* Clearly, no. Anger and vengeance eat away at the body, as they do the soul. Once again, the thoughts fail a test of authenticity. So in other words, what you're telling yourself is true, but it is not in your best interest and does not advance and protect your health. As to the fourth prong of the authenticity test, it should be clear that continuing to haul around a heart full of bitterness *will not get you what you want.* Therein lies the power of forgiveness. Something did in fact happen to you, but you still, in the interest of yourself, must lay it down and move on.

By contrast, a belief that can survive and pass authenticity testing would be the belief that you are in control of the quality of your emotional life and that no one can lock you into a destructive bond where they control you. You can make a choice, consistent with your authenticity, to *block* any attachment to these people through hatred, fear, or resentment. You can resist giving any energy to them through your self-talk. Consider the technique used by Native American tribes to punish abusive behavior: The whole tribe simply disconnected from the offender, refusing to acknowledge his or her presence. He or she was made "invisible." Of all possible responses, this response was the worst punishment imaginable. Instead of responding to him or her with the rage of unforgiveness, thereby giving the offender more power, there was a total detachment. They reserved their energy for more important things. That's the freedom and release I'm talking about when I talk about forgiveness. Withdraw your investment of energy from the perpetrators in your life and they will wither and disappear from your radar screen.

The objective of the MER, then, is to clean up your self-concept. If your internal responses are cleaned up and your lenses of perception are clear, instead of causing you to react impulsively with angry, exaggerated, and inappropriate reactions, your self-concept will move you toward constructive behaviors that get you more of what you want and less of what you don't want.

Remember what has led you down the path of pain and distraction: It is the various negative external events, and your internal reactions to those events, that have pulled you away from your authentic self. These events are the door dings; these are the potholes; these are the collisions of life that have created damage to the "vehicle of you" and buried your authentic self below a rotting heap of life-experience garbage. In order to get back to your authentic self, you must make sure you clean up *all* of the unfinished emotional business that is contaminating your current life and view of yourself. Clean the lens on that projector that we talked about. Hit the focus button and get the image of yourself back to clear and sharp once again.

When you actively apply the principles set out in this book and start scripting your language for your own needs, you will find yourself focusing on the path of success. Committing to test all of your life struggles using AAA testing and thinking, you'll feel the sense of heaviness and restriction abate. You'll find more energy for your purposes and discover that the promise of joy and peace is indeed true.

At first, the process may feel clumsy. Testing each negative belief of your self-talk takes practice. You will catch yourself sliding into fictional labeling and tapes. You have a long history of learned habits—habits called internal responses—and they will not go away quickly. But you *can* change your internal dialogue. You *can* change how you label yourself. You *can* hit the eject button on the tapes that you have generated and can overcome the fixed beliefs that have held you back. You *can* audit all of these internal responses for authenticity and generate AAA alternatives to those that don't pass muster.

Choosing the authentically accurate alternative means that you'll acquire genuine habits, the agendas of who you really are, so that your life can be carried out in the truth of who you are, rather than in the service of a false identity.

Your authentic self is characterized by confidence, hope, optimism, joy, and purpose. It's time to start behaving that way.

Starting today, it is you who must step up and accept the responsibility of the authentic life. It is you who must create the life chain that you want. You have the tools, now use them.

12 SABOTAGE

"To speak ill of others is a dishonest way of praising ourselves."

— WILL DURANT

JOAN was ecstatic. She had worked so hard for so long. After her marriage failed, she had decided it was time to be there for herself. It was time to quit trying to make the whole world happy while she got pushed to the bottom of the priority list. She had spend so much time and energy sucking up to his overbearing, know-it-all mother that once she got the divorce, it was like someone lifted a huge weight off her chest. At first she had been furious with herself for all the stuff she had put up with from mother-in-law *and* "sonny boy." She felt so violated and stupid for having gone along to get along. Now, after what seemed like ages, things were beginning to change. She had stopped beating herself up. She had decided that the only time was now and she had to get back to her life. Really, it was more "get to" her life than "get back" to her life, because she had bailed out on Joan a long, long time ago.

She had pushed herself into the shadows from as far back as she could remember. A big "sell-out moment" had come when she let her father, a CPA, insist that she major in accounting in college, instead of getting a teaching certificate in the arts, a field for which she once had an unbridled passion. "Get serious," he had said. "You have to make a living in this world. You'll never be a success teaching brats how to play with clay!" She had "sold out" so many times before that it had really been almost automatic for her to accept his telling her what to do. It had gotten easier each successive time. Decisions large and small had been made to please others: whom to marry, where to live, what to drive, where to go on vacation, agreeing not to have children. Her life plan had become simply: Don't make waves.

But that was all behind her now. She had found her strength and her self. She had read endlessly, gone to therapy, and challenged herself in every way she could imagine. She had written hundreds of pages in her journal and was sometimes shocked at what she put on the page. Shocked or not, she just kept on digging and getting real with herself. Finally, after months and months of hard work, she had rewarded herself with the culminating trip of a lifetime: She had spent four wonderful weeks at a spa in Arizona, where she had lost all of those last twenty pounds that seemed absolutely glued to her hips. She felt great. Returning to her cottage one night, she had picked up a voice mail from home and learned she'd been accepted into a graduate program in the arts, one that put her squarely on the career track she had longed for. And not only had she shed those last stubborn pounds; not only did she look and feel stronger than ever—she had fallen in love! It was as if she were discovering a whole other person inside herself, a long-lost Joan who, she realized, might be amazing. It was all coming together. She had found her authentic self.

Reliving memories of the past year on the plane trip home, Joan could hardly contain her giggles. She thought about exactly how she'd tell her friends her good news. She knew that Alice and Becky would be dying to hear all about her life and her changes, especially because she had sort of "gone underground" the last few months while she worked so hard on getting her life in order. In phone calls to them from Arizona, she had tried to describe for them the magic of the spa, but she had not yet said a word about Mark. That was to be a surprise.

Alice would be thrilled. It was Alice, after all, who had recommended the spa to her in the first place. She was the one who, knowing how painful the divorce had been, insisted that Joan start a new life. Like an enthusiastic coach, Alice had kept reminding Joan that this was the time in her life to reflect and pull it all together, a chance to put those "crappy days" behind her and start all over. Yes, Alice would be as excited as anyone could be and Joan couldn't wait to tell her the news.

Becky would be excited, too, but Joan knew Becky and knew that she was a pessimist. No doubt at first, Becky would question whether this was all for real. Witty and fun as Becky was, there was always a kind of grim certainty in her voice, a tone that said she recognized how life "should be." When people tried yet failed to change their lives, Becky never seemed surprised. No matter how much people might struggle for happiness, she seemed to take it as a given that they would ultimately fall short, for one reason or another. But this time, it would be different. Surely Becky would come around. Soon enough, she would see the difference in Joan and she'd have to acknowledge that the changes were genuine. This time, even Becky would understand and appreciate how wonderfully transformed Joan was. Joan hoped that was true, yet in a way that felt really strange it didn't seem to matter nearly as much as it used to. If Becky was happy for her: great. If she wasn't, that would be okay, as well.

Through all of their experiences—some good, others not so good—Joan, Alice, and Becky had been soul mates, their three-sided friendship growing sturdier and more certain than when it was forged fifteen years ago, in the eighth grade. All three had seen their marriages wax and wane through these times, Joan's being the one that cratered first. While Joan and Becky had office jobs, Alice stayed home with her kids. The three made a point of having lunch every Saturday; they considered it a not-to-be-missed chance to share their lives. Sometimes they'd gossip, taking note of who in town was cheating on a spouse or who'd been seen wearing what and where. Their Saturday chats were invariably sprinkled with grim jokes about how miserable they were in this little town, about the fact that no one seemed to be happy in what they were doing. But this Saturday would be different: Joan was breaking out. She was about to soar above it all, into a new life.

Nothing could have prepared Joan for the shock she got on Saturday. True, her friends expressed interest in her adventures, but their interest seemed forced. They were anything but enthusiastic. After she talked about her weight loss, there were some lukewarm congratulations—then an awkward silence. Finally, Becky spoke. With a knowing smile and the slightest, most subtle raising of an eyebrow, she agreed that, yes, the weight loss was definitely an achievement. But wasn't it a shame, she sighed, that Joan would likely regain that weight in less time than it had taken her to lose it. Becky even quoted some statistic from a magazine to support her prediction. When the talk turned to Joan's love life, and to details about Mark, Becky became even more doubtful. With concern in her voice, she murmured that, while of course she had never met Mark, how could Joan know he was "legit"? He sounded to her like the typical hustler at any tourist resort. Good for Joan to allow herself a fling; but it was just a fling, nothing more. She gently suggested that Joan might never see him again. Becky might as well have shouted her unspoken message to Joan, it was so clear: "Get over it. Fantasy time is over. Have some dessert and jump back into the ditch with the rest of us."

Knowing Becky as she did, Joan at least had had some experience of this cynicism. But Alice's reaction left her speechless. It was as if Becky's comments uncorked feelings that Alice had been holding in for weeks. Now that she had "permission," Alice let loose a stream of bitter criticism, comments that burned Joan like acid. She said that Joan had starting dressing "like a hussy" and was acting "high and mighty." Who did she think she was? Even if Mark could be trusted, what could he possibly see in some small-town girl like her? Alice was beside herself, calling Joan everything short of a prostitute and a fraud, a traitor who thought nothing of turning her back on her friends. And this stupid idea of going back to school at her age: I mean, come on, get a life! All so Joan could work for peanuts as a teacher—right! If Joan wanted to set herself up as better than her friends, she should just go do it, go run after what she wanted, and deal with the consequences.

Trembling as she made her way through the parking lot after lunch, Joan could barely find her car keys through the stream of tears. She had not felt so wounded since college and one of those bitter confrontations with her father. It was as if she had stepped out of a movie theater and discovered, suddenly, that things were the way they always had been. She was utterly mystified. She thought that she had found her self, had made dreams about her future start to come true, and had even found someone who loved her for who she truly was. Didn't they see all that? Didn't they see that she was happy? Here she had finally found a path toward what she wanted, instead of what other people told her to be—yet her best friends were telling her that she had it all wrong, that her perceptions were fake, that the whole wonderful adventure was some childhood fairy tale. Together, Alice and Becky had always been her wise counsel, her sounding board. Could they be wrong? Or was she? Was she still the ugly duckling that she had always felt she was? Was it all a dream? Should she give up her true passions and return to her life as she had always known it? After all, it was pretty hard to imagine "good old Joan" being the star of anything, even her own life. She was at a critical crossroads: Would she stay the course or get sabotaged and sucked back into playing the roles that were expected?

What happened to Joan was not new. Too often, as we get a glimpse of our authentic self we hear a whisper of what our potentials are and then threats arise. We can get pulled back to our life script. We can be persuaded that it was all a dream. We can be convinced that our passions, the convictions we have felt with such intensity and clarity, are silly. We start to fear that we look strange to the people whose opinions we respect, that we are somehow screwing up. We become embarrassed at our audacity in believing that we are different. It often happens that, just as we are about to escape our fictional self, our "friends" hold us to the way we were and, in their view, always will be.

Please understand, first of all, that this reaction is not always intentional. Friends and family do not always plan to hold you to a fictional self. Some do it out of a desire to protect you. Others are trying to protect *themselves* from change. Still others may be trying to protect the predictable world that the two of you share.

What I have found is that most people really do not know how to promote the welfare of someone else's authentic self. Doing so takes both wisdom and a great big dose of trust. Trusting your choices, deciding to step back and allow you to live in your authentic self, requires that the other people in your life trust the process perhaps even more than you do. It is easy for them to feel threatened: They may fear losing you, because you appear to be outgrowing them. As a result, they may try—consciously or otherwise—to maintain the status quo. In essence, it takes an authentic person to know and understand what your quest for getting back to your authentic self is all about.

Getting support and empathy from the people in your life is tough, because to them your situation looks so unstable. You are questioning every value and belief you have had about yourself, you are questioning your relationships, and it may not appear to them that you have clear ideas yet. You start experimenting with new concepts and these new ideas may appear ridiculous to someone else. To complicate things, the process is often one of refining: You moderate and change your initial experimenting; you are testing and fine-tuning your changes until they reach a much deeper level of conviction. In this way, they become much more meaningful and long lasting than changes you adopt overnight. Seeing these "tweaks," your moderations and changes to your first experimenting, the naysayers may leap to the conclusion that you've failed; they might say, "See, I told you so!" The point is that your life is a process and you are going to kiss a few frogs along the way. Don't be deterred from your quest for your authentic self just because somebody notices that the journey has a lot of twists and turns. Often those same people are the ones who are too afraid to confront their own twists and turns. They are only challenging your new script because it challenges their old one.

For example, it may happen that you question your relationship with God. Doing so is not "selling out" to the devil. You are certainly entitled to question whether your understanding of God is one you have accepted wholesale from somebody else. You might be asking whether it is true, whether it resonates at the deepest levels of your faith, or whether it just "is," because somebody said so. This kind of questioning, honestly pursued, can bring you to a stronger, more relevant, and more personal relationship with God. But you need to recognize that there may be people in your life who will not encourage you in that process.

It's similar to what happens when people decide to take charge of their physical health. Experience teaches that the most effective therapies tend to be those that take into account the patient's own preferences—but that doesn't mean the patient's family will like it. This point was made convincingly a few years ago in a TV docudrama about a woman named Deborah Frankie Ogg. Having been diagnosed with cancer, Debbie Ogg soon decided that traditional medicine had nothing to offer her. Instead, she chose to experiment with some alternative therapies, including some highly focused guided imagery, as well as the use of medicinal herbs.

When it became clear to her family that she was committed to this alternative approach, they responded by belittling it. There were expressions of concern, wisecracks about "witch doctors" and those "kooky" herbs, and a whole range of tactics designed to get her back into conventional cancer treatment. Finally, in a memorable scene at the dinner table, Debbie asked her family to leave and not come back until she had completed her journey into her methods. As she put it: "I cannot find and fight my cancer if I have to fight you at the same time. I need someone to believe in me and if you cannot do that, then you will have to leave until this is over."

The point of her ultimatum was that she would decide who would be on her team and who would not. She would decide who would be her doctor, who would be part of her support system, and who she needed to be with her. She was going to make her own judgments as to what treatments had the most benefit for her. As it turned out, some of her choices were of great benefit; others were not. But she made it clear that she was paddling her own canoe and was prepared to live with the result, even when her outcome was either life or death. Happily, the therapies she chose eventually worked and she is alive today to tell her story. She would tell you that her approach might not work for you, but that you have the responsibility to search for the approach that does.

You must be no less committed to finding your own path back to your authentic self and your authentic life. Just like Debbie, you must learn to paddle your own canoe and the fewer passengers you invite onboard, the easier it will be for you to reach your goal. You have the right to choose those people who will be around you while you do your work and to choose when and where you will do it. You have that right and you must claim it unapologetically. Don't continue to pretend that you don't know who has your best interests at heart and who does not. You know it as surely as you're sitting there. It's time to give your self permission to act on that knowledge. You have the right to choose your team and, if you want to succeed, you will do it with your eyes wide open.

I have discovered some of the dynamics of how people react toxically to your becoming consistent with your authentic self. You need to know these dynamics so that you won't be sabotaged along your path of healing.

There are four basic destructive patterns that others can introduce into your quest for authenticity. Go on the alert for these patterns. Be cautious when you are most vulnerable and always plan a way out in case you get trapped into a conversation, as Joan did. Remember that the people who respond to you with one of these pattern behaviors are "carriers of toxicity" to the self, whether they intend to be or not. And as I said before, they are normally not trying to do you harm, but rather they are trying to protect their own lives, their own fears, and their own fictional selves.

Understand that I am not concerned here with intentions. Whether these people mean to hurt you or not is not the issue. I'm being selfish on your behalf here, which means I am looking only at results. If someone "accidentally" runs over my foot with their car, they may not have intended to hurt me, but my foot is crushed just the same. Right now, you haven't got the luxury of being magnanimous about intentions. You cannot afford to say, "Well, gee, I'm screwed here and am right back where I started, but I know you didn't mean it."

The four categories that I typically see among the "carrier" population can be identified as:

1. Overprotection
2. Power manipulation
3. Leveling, and
4. Safety in the status quo

OVERPROTECTION

This type of sabotage has a basic message of fear: "I really don't think you are capable of being more than what you are. You're just setting yourself up for failure. Just calm down or you'll get hurt. If you reach too high, you can fall and destroy yourself and everything you have. You mustn't get too lofty in your thinking. Just stay here with me and I will take care of you. It's a tough world out there and, really now, what have you ever done?"

I once worked with the family of a high school track star, a boy who was a remarkably gifted pole-vaulter. He was a talented, committed, and passionate athlete, but he had a mother who wanted to shelter him from potential disappointment. She kept telling David that he shouldn't put so much into his sport. She reasoned that if he worked so hard, expecting to be the best and even to win the state championship, he would surely be disappointed and she just couldn't bear to see his "little heart" broken that way. She feared that failure would crush his sense of pride; therefore, her attitude was, Don't try, don't fail; don't fail, don't hurt. Truth be known, I just don't think she could take the pressure. We all know how hard it is to watch our children compete.

The good news is that while David couldn't "take her off his team," he could and did tune her out. David did compete in the state championship and his mother was there every step of the way, telling him, "Don't care so much, get some rest, quit working so hard." I'd love to tell you that David won, but he didn't; he came in third. He was disappointed with his result, but justifiably proud of himself and his work ethic. After winning an athletic scholarship to a small but excellent college, he enjoyed many first-place finishes as a pole-vaulter and a sprinter. He is now a track coach and he absolutely loves it. Sometime soon, I know he'll get that state championship, and boy, oh boy, is he enjoying chasing it!

Although he was young, David was strong enough in his convictions not to allow his mother to sabotage his vision for himself. He knew in his heart what he wanted and he also knew that he would be tested and have consequences. I have seen too many other people who did not challenge themselves and their parents, because the ones who should have been cheering them on were trying to "protect" them from the pain of failure. Those are the people you never read about, because they did not believe in themselves enough to win or lose; they never even got in the game.

Overprotectors like David's mother are extremely dangerous because their methods are virtually invisible. They seem so loving, so well intended. Their influence can be especially powerful because it usually comes from someone you trust. The "wisdom" that they want to share is given in the name of love and concern, making it very hard to fight, particularly if you are a little unsure of yourself.

Yes, it may be painful to try and fail, but it is the attempt that should be honored, not the fear of failure. Put simply, your journey back to your authentic self is not going to be a success-only journey. Steel yourself against the naysayers and do what you have to do.

POWER MANIPULATION

Power manipulation is the sabotage of your personal power in order to maintain a relationship. Joan's scenario from the beginning of the chapter is typical. She had found a new base of power in herself. She had found that she could lose weight and find a lover based on her own talents and efforts. Joan started believing in herself enough to pursue a new career. Unfortunately, all of this success threatened her lifelong friends, even to a breaking point. Their power to control and have access to her was threatened and they feared they would lose her. Instead of putting her interests ahead of their own, or choosing to be inspired alongside her, they tried to drag her back down into the relationship they had known before. Whether they did this consciously or otherwise was of little consequence to Joan and so it will be in your life, as well.

Learn to evaluate the messages you receive from those closest to you. I don't want you to become paranoid, but I do want you to listen and think for yourself. Is your mate telling you you "can't" because they will be threatened if you do? People who genuinely care will tell you the truth, even if you don't want to hear it, but they will also try to find a way to help you get what you want, even if it scares them for you to change. Don't assume you are being sabotaged if someone disagrees with your plan, because they may be genuinely trying to give you valuable feedback. But *do examine their motives,* with your eyes wide open. They may be threatened by your personal empowerment, so that, consciously or otherwise, they'll try to keep you in their safe little cocoon. The specific mechanism of this sabotage is to infantilize you: to treat you as a child, so that you will yield in a childlike fashion to the authority of their power.

It makes no difference at what age this exchange takes place.

Power struggles can last a lifetime. You may hear phrases like: "Who in the hell do you think you are?" "What do you think you are doing, acting like you're holier than thou?" "What fool have you been listening to now?" Power is addictive and if anyone has had that authority over you for any length of time, it will be difficult to change him or her. After all, if they have the power, why should they change? Why should they give it up to you?

And remember: As you scan your landscape, looking for the source of these messages, be listening for your own voice, too, because it may be the culprit. Your fictional self, with all of its momentum, may be speaking the loudest about what you can't or shouldn't do. Either way, whether it is your voice or someone else's, be very careful about what messages you are willing to internalize.

LEVELING

Think about the person who feels deficient, inadequate. Something is missing, something necessary to being all that they want to be. If someone else arrives on the scene, apparently possessing that something, a sense of injustice rages.

Resentment, anger, and fear emerge.

You show up at lunch and announce to your friends, "Guess what! I just won the lottery *and* I'm getting married! Look at my new ring!"

Now, as we've seen, they might all wiggle and giggle, but there's a good chance that at least of few of them are thinking: Bitch! People just aren't always really happy for your successes. If you let them control you with that jealousy, if you let them drag you down and define who you are, they will define you in a way that is convenient and nonthreatening for them. That's what I mean by leveling: the attempt that others make to compromise you, to bring you to a level lower than the one they see themselves occupying. Subtly, so subtly, and consciously or not, jealous people are going to sabotage you for reaching a higher level than they have. This can be major league confusing, because jealous people flip-flop on you: They work *for* you when you are failing and *against* you when you are succeeding.

SAFETY IN THE STATUS QUO

Even when their life circumstances have never been sorrier, many people still crave the status quo: They do not want change, even change for the better. That's because there's safety in the status quo. They are living in their own fictional script and who are you to try to mess up their performance. In showing your success, they may not be ready to look at their own weaknesses because even if the life they are living is inauthentic, it appears to be easy. At least everyone knows the rules and everyone knows what to expect—even if it's destruction.

I vividly recall a family I worked with for almost a year, the Lincolns. I still think of them as "the fightin' Lincolns," because they were the wildest, most contentious bunch of people I ever encountered. In their frustration with one another, they tore up more stuff than most people ever own. They would throw lamps, put holes in the walls, and wreck cars and anything else you could tear up. They came to see me, presumably to change these patterns. After many sessions, it became obvious that although everyone clearly reported being miserable, no one really wanted to change the system. The father was frustrated because the wife undermined him. Mama was constantly upset because the kids were abusive to her, showing total disrespect. The kids were exasperated because their parents had no idea what was going on. All of this constant frustration led to out-of-control tempers and spectacular brawls.

Now, things in the Lincoln household were obviously in the toilet, but when I had the nerve to suggest that anyone of them actually change, you would have thought that I had accused them of murder. It was like they had made a pact to fight to the death and that any change would be a betrayal. It was just too scary to try some new way of handling things. To maturely concentrate on their personal needs would have meant that each one would have to become honest and open with the family and themselves. Way too scary. Instead, they had adopted the unspoken understanding that they'd stick with the status quo.

In one of our last few sessions, Susan, the mother of this bunch of knotheads, announced that she had decided to go to night school to become a nurse. She wanted everyone to know that she was tired of the constant fighting every night and was just going to take herself out of it all. You should have seen the revulsion from the rest of the group; it was unbelievable. Said one of the kids: "What are you talking about? How could you leave us every night? Why would you want to do something like that anyway? You're too old and dumb. And what about us? You don't really care about us. How selfish."

Remarkably, it took the rest of the family less than an hour to convince Susan that she was incapable of doing anything other than carry on the fight in the family. I confronted them about what they were doing, but Susan herself soon joined ranks. In a matter of minutes, they all turned on me like a pack of wild dogs for threatening the status quo. (Gee, I wonder why I don't do therapy anymore?)

The point is that the status quo offers a refuge from the fear of change. A shift of position by anyone is seen as a major threat to all. That means that any move you make toward reconnecting with your authentic self may trigger resistance: The group or partner that you're dealing with may rise up against the perceived threat.

Don't let this mind-numbing commitment to the status quo dampen your spirit or your passion for authenticity. You are alive for a special reason and that reason is to be the best that you can be. Do not allow anyone or any group to take that responsibility from you, especially not for the sake of their own comfort.

TRY THIS EXERCISE

You'll need to be particularly guarded and discreet in approaching the following exercise, since it may involve people who have great meaning to you. The goal is simply to help you focus on how other people might sabotage your efforts to reconnect with your authentic self.

Remember that these people may not be *consciously* robbing you of your authenticity. In fact, they may be telling themselves that they are protecting you, that they want only the best for you. Their reasoning may be lofty and gracious, but the result is the same.

Step 1

In your journal, write down the names of the people you feel—intentions aside—might sabotage you in your quest for your authentic life. Next to each name, and looking back at the descriptions I've given you, write down the category of their likely sabotage, the particular way they may sabotage you. Please understand that this is not a blaming exercise. It is merely a way of alerting yourself to those people who could undermine your pilgrimage in even the kindest of well-intended ways.

Step 2

As to each person in the list you've created, decide what response you are going to give. Are you going to smile and express appreciation, courteously deflecting his or her interference, even as you know within yourself that you are going to pursue your own path? Or will you need to be more direct, telling that person to get out of your face and let you run your own life? Let the chart below guide your thinking as to both steps in this exercise.

Possible Saboteur	Probable Method of Sabotage	My Response
_____	_____	_____
_____	_____	_____
_____	_____	_____
_____	_____	_____
_____	_____	_____

There's a moral to this story and you already know what it is: The world is not devoted to your nurturance. It is devoted to your *conformity* and *compliance,* independent of how that dovetails with your gifts, skills, abilities, wants, and visions. If you leave it to the world in general, if you leave it to others to determine who you are, you will not be living your authentic self as it was originally composed. Instead, you'll be living a fictional self, which is nothing more than a structure of convenience for the world at large and for all of the people you encounter within it.

To deny your authentic self is to sell yourself down the river. It is to betray yourself in all that you truly are. That is why I have sought to inoculate you against manipulation by the people in your life and by a society that is running its own agenda. That is why I close this book as I began it: by blowing the whistle on the con job.

The marketing machines, your parents, employers, friends, all have needs for you to be a certain way. And in all likelihood, you have complied with and conformed to those expectancies, at the expense of your own gifts, abilities, and dreams. When those needs are at odds with your being your authentic self, *you must prevail.*

Statesmen who sign important treaties know how important it is to "trust, but verify." The two parties can commit their promises to paper; they can shake hands and say to each other, "You have my word on it," but that doesn't relieve either of them of the duty to keep watch on the other. You may tell me that you've drastically reduced your supply of nuclear missiles, but hey, how about letting me be the one to count them? In the same way, when it comes to reconnecting with your authentic self, you need to take the attitude of "trust, but verify." Trust that this is work worth doing. Trust that you have within you everything you need in order to be, have, and do everything you want from life. Trust that you are the best judge, by far, of what is best for you. At the same time, be ruthless about testing your thoughts. Verify that your own internal responses and interpretations will stand up to the test of authenticity.

When it comes to verifying, make use of the tools that you've been given. Remember the "litmus test" for authenticity, the four-part test that we talked about in Chapter 11. Whenever you feel yourself to be at a crossroads, as Joan was in that parking lot after lunch, take command of the situation by putting that test to work. I submit to you that if Joan simply sat in her car for a few minutes, applying each of the four criteria to her thoughts, she would quickly detect the sabotage going on. She would soon see that the option of reverting to her old self, the fictional self that Alice and Becky seemed to prefer, would flunk the rationality test in a big way. She could regain much-needed optimism and balance simply by discovering the defects in her own thoughts. The same is true for you: When you suspect sabotage, don't hesitate to apply the test. Be ruthless about discarding any thought that fails.

Likewise, you'll need to develop authentically accurate alternative thinking. Having discovered that your initial response fails the test of authenticity, what other options can you come up with? Throw yourself as many lifelines as you can. Give yourself permission to generate as many alternative responses as possible—then test each one of them for authenticity. Pursue only those that are truly Triple A.

I'm not saying this two-step process will come naturally, certainly not at first. But neither does learning an instrument, or being an effective parent, or anything else that is worth doing. You already know that doing something well takes time and effort. Likewise, if you will only commit to doing it, day after day, you *can* become an expert in Triple-A thinking and Triple-A living.

You couldn't stand up for your authenticity when you were a child, but you can stand up for it now. The first person that you need to assert yourself with is you.

EPILOGUE

*"If your ship doesn't come in, swim out
to it."*

— JONATHAN WINTERS

YOU and I started this journey together with me confessing my own personal "sellout" of self. I told you that I caved to expectancies, life-chain momentum, and money. I was trapped for ten years and had neither the courage nor the focus to do anything about it. I completely ignored my own voice, needs, and passions, and fulfilled what I perceived to be the expectancies of others. Looking back, that story probably did not inspire your confidence in me! You were probably asking yourself: "What the hell was *he* thinking?" (There's a switch: You dogging on me, instead of the other way around!) Uninspiring as it may have been, it was the truth, and one that I had the power to control if I had just claimed it. Fortunately, I eventually exercised that control, or I wouldn't be here writing this book.

In a strange way, even though I was caving to the expectancies of others, they were my expectancies as well. Clearly, I was not doing what I consciously wanted to do, but I felt a vague yet strong pull to conform and comply. The tug of that life chain was amazingly powerful. I mean, you hang with family, right? You go where your people are, do what they do, and live in their world. My personal truth was terribly limiting as I felt the need to stay in the flow of my family and their patterns. It seemed selfish to think of doing anything different just because I wanted something else. It was familiar, it was safe, and at one level it did feel right. Or so it seemed at the time.

In those ten years, which felt like forty, I cheated myself and my wife and children. I know what I now know not because I'm smart but because I did it all wrong for so long it finally sank in. You either get it or you don't. I didn't get it then, but I sure get it now. Here's the rest of that story.

After my conversation with Robin that fall afternoon, we jointly decided that regardless of expectancies, possible consequences, or the ever-present fear of change, we would stop "burning daylight" in our lives. We decided that the life we were living was the real thing, not some dress rehearsal that we would get right the next time. Time is the one resource you cannot regenerate, and we were blowing it big time. We decided, for openers, that I would stop whining about what I did and didn't have in both my personal and professional life and would do something about it. I will give us—me—credit in that we didn't waste any more time. We made a decision, pulled the trigger, and in less than ninety days that long and heavy life chain was broken and a new one was begun. At first we talked about a lot of different options, most of which kept one foot on safe ground while one foot was reaching for the new ground. Reaching, but just sort of reaching. Fortunately, we came to our senses and quickly concluded: "Hey, don't halfway fix this deal. Don't be mealymouthed around here because we don't have the guts to go for it. If we are going to do it, we need to do it right, do it all the way."

Robin was also kind enough to point out that I must have had my already-bald head stuck where I could look out my belly button, because I had so totally missed the fact that she loved change. She added that her passion was her husband and boys and that she would absolutely and without missing a single beat bloom wherever she was planted, so long as it was with all of us together. (I hate it when she is so much smarter than me, particularly when it's in my supposed area of expertise!)

Because my "data window" had been closed by fixed beliefs and a life script that were set in the "you're trapped" mode, I had completely missed the resource that lay in my wife. She wasn't nearly as trapped as I was, and was way more flexible than I gave her credit for. I had failed to see her willing spirit about change. Live and learn!

To make a long story longer, we decided that what I really wanted was to be somewhere different, doing something different, in a whole different world of people. With that overt acknowledgment of what I really wanted, with the event of saying it out loud, a course was charted.

I told my dad first. I said: "Love you, love the family, hate my life, my career, and this town. I'm gone." He said, "Son, you haven't got a brain in your head. You worked ten years to build all of this, and you're going to just walk off and pursue some harebrained deal? We must have dropped you on your head when you were a baby." Being ever the smart-ass, I responded that I wished that they had dropped me harder, because then maybe I would have left sooner. I then pointed out that he, in fact, had done exactly the same thing in his life, or he never would have gone to college, never become a psychologist, and never left the his family's small town of five thousand people. That gave him pause, but then he said that was different because he, unlike me, had enough sense to come in out of the rain, while I, on the other hand, obviously "didn't know come here from go sic 'em!" (I've cleaned all that conversation up quite a bit for those of you with tender sensibilities, but suffice it to say he thought I had gone way crazy!)

Notwithstanding that counsel, leave we did. We went to a new town that *we* chose, started a new profession that I was wildly passionate about, and embedded our lives in a world of new people who shared our visions and passions, both personally and professionally. There were some difficult times and some scary moments, but I can honestly tell you that I never had one second of doubt that I had done the right thing for me and my family. I had no doubt because, for the first time in years, it felt so right. Once I plugged into and listened to my authentic self, "beach balls" were popping up everywhere, and "boulders" were rolling downhill. I immediately felt vibrant and alive, as though I had gained back those ten years. My life energy surged without limit. I couldn't wait to get up in the morning and hated going to sleep at night. I couldn't wait to get up and at 'em. Whether I was working, hanging our with the family, coaching the boys' basketball teams, or just being with me, I felt totally alive.

Everything that had been good during those ten years was better. Everything that had been a chore was now so very much easier. I never had doubts about succeeding careerwise. Because of the passion I felt, and because my new life fit me so naturally and authentically, I knew I couldn't miss. I was so passionate that there was absolutely no way that anyone—my partner, clients, co-workers, or staff—could keep from being caught up in the energy. At last, I had that feeling at the end of the day that I had done a good job, a job I was proud of. And guess what? When my "data window" reopened for business, the possibilities I saw personally, spiritually, and professionally were everywhere. The company my partner and I started became the industry leader worldwide. I started writing books and doing television. I found new ways to make a difference with an education and profession I had lost energy for. I am thriving, my wife and boys are thriving, and all those family members who thought I was nuts when I broke the life chain (including my dad) saw what happened with the changes we made and followed us to our new life within the year. I guess I should have changed my name and identity along with everything else! (Just kidding there, sisters, just kidding.)

For me, geography, career, and lifestyle were important components of effective change. For you it may be all or none of those things. What matters is that you commit to finding and reconnecting with your authentic self, whatever that may call for. What matters is that you challenge and rewrite your personal truth and live a life that lets you be who you really are. All that's left to do is to create for your self a chance. Every one is uniquely different, and only you know what that means for you. If you don't fight for the chance to live that uniqueness, no one will. A racehorse has to run, a bird has to fly, an artist has to paint, a teacher has to teach. There is something in you that you have to do. If you've done all the considerable work in this book, then all that's left to do is to do it.

See you in the sunlight.

APPENDIX A

HEALTH CONTROL ATTRIBUTION QUESTIONNAIRE

For each statement below, decide how much you agree or disagree with it. Of the four answer choices, select the one that expresses how you feel about the statement: If you agree totally, with no reservations, then circle (A); agree mostly, but with some reservations, (AS); disagree mostly, but with some reservations, (DS); or disagree completely, (D).

Agree: 8 points	*Disagree Slightly: 2 points*
Agree Slightly: 4 points	*Disagree: 1 point*

	Agree	Agree Slightly	Disagree Slightly	Disagree

Section I

1. If I get sick, it is usually because I have not followed sound nutritional diets.   (A)   (AS)   (DS)   (D)

2. In order for me to get well from a disease, I will have to change my life habits and try hard.   (A)   (AS)   (DS)   (D)

3. I believe that good health is related to good life habits, such as exercise and stress management.   (A)   (AS)   (DS)   (D)

4. I believe that if I need to get well, I need to take responsibility for getting well.   (A)   (AS)   (DS)   (D)

	Agree	Agree Slightly	Disagree Slightly	Disagree

5. Whether or not I get well is based on my efforts, not on those of doctors or hospitals.   (A)   (AS)   (DS)   (D)

Section II

6. The most important thing in getting well is having a smart doctor.   (A)   (AS)   (DS)   (D)

7. I depend on my health providers to be experts, and to take care of me so I will not get sick.   (A)   (AS)   (DS)   (D)

8. Either our or some other government agency is using some weapons that make us sick.   (A)   (AS)   (DS)   (D)

9. The real reason I get well is because I take the right medicine.   (A)   (AS)   (DS)   (D)

10. I have to depend on doctors for my health status. What they say is right.   (A)   (AS)   (DS)   (D)

Section III

11. If I get sick, it is the luck of the draw that day.   (A)   (AS)   (DS)   (D)

12. I am very lucky if I do not get sick.   (A)   (AS)   (DS)   (D)

13. It is an accident if a person dies, because no one really knows when you are going to get sick.   (A)   (AS)   (DS)   (D)

14. If I get a cold, it is because I happen to run into some cold germs that day.   (A)   (AS)   (DS)   (D)

15. Life is based on chance and luck.   (A)   (AS)   (DS)   (D)

APPENDIX B

CONTROL FOR SELF QUESTIONNAIRE

Same deal here as for the Health Control Attribution Questionnaire (Appendix A): For each statement below, decide how much you agree or disagree with it. Of the four answer choices, select the one that expresses how you feel about the statement: If you agree totally, with no reservations, then circle (A); agree mostly, but with some reservations, (AS); disagree mostly, but with some reservations, (DS); or disagree completely, (D).

Agree: 8 points	*Disagree Slightly: 2 points*		
Agree Slightly: 4 points	*Disagree: 1 point*		
	Agree	Agree Slightly	Disagree Slightly	Disagree

Section I

1. If I do not know myself, it is because I have not taken the time to assess who I really am.   (A) (AS) (DS) (D)

2. In order for me to understand myself, I will have to look at my life perceptions.   (A) (AS) (DS) (D)

3. I believe that I have the power and talents to be the person I want to be.   (A) (AS) (DS) (D)

4. I believe that if I want to become who I am, I have to answer these hard questions about myself.   (A) (AS) (DS) (D)

	Agree	Agree Slightly	Disagree Slightly	Disagree
5. Whether or not I can be my authentic self will depend on my honesty with myself.	(A)	(AS)	(DS)	(D)

Section II

	Agree	Agree Slightly	Disagree Slightly	Disagree
6. The most important thing in getting to who I am is to ask my friends.	(A)	(AS)	(DS)	(D)
7. I depend on my friends to be experts of who I am.	(A)	(AS)	(DS)	(D)
8. There are experts who will tell me what my authentic self is.	(A)	(AS)	(DS)	(D)
9. The real me is what others think I am.	(A)	(AS)	(DS)	(D)
10. I have to depend on others for my self-esteem and status. What they say is right.	(A)	(AS)	(DS)	(D)

Section III

	Agree	Agree Slightly	Disagree Slightly	Disagree
11. If I get depressed, it is the luck of the draw.	(A)	(AS)	(DS)	(D)
12. I am very lucky if I get what I want.	(A)	(AS)	(DS)	(D)
13. It is an accident if I win or lose.	(A)	(AS)	(DS)	(D)
14. If I get to be myself one day, it will be because somebody happened to feel sorry for me.	(A)	(AS)	(DS)	(D)
15. Life is based on chance and luck.	(A)	(AS)	(DS)	(D)